HOVV
TO
FIND
ZODIAC

HOW TO FIND ZODIAC

(or: *MANAC ES CEM, J.K.*)

Jarett Kobek

we heard you like books • los angeles california
2022

PUBLISHED BY WE HEARD YOU LIKE BOOKS
A Division of U2603 LLC
5419 Hollywood Blvd, Ste C-231 Los Angeles CA 90027

http://weheardyoulikebooks.com/

for: *Tom Voigt, Mike Morford, Richard Grinell, Mike Butterfield, Mike Rodelli,*
Dave Oranchak, Jarl Van Eycke, and Sam Blake & Tahoe27,
and everyone else who did the hard work

ISBN: 978-1-7378428-0-4

February 2022

First Edition

This book assumes that the reader
possesses fluency with the
long story of Zodiac.

If the reader does not, it is
recommended that they find
Motor Spirit by the same author.

chapter one

how to be useful
during a pandemic

THE BALD-HEADED WRITER JARETT KOBEK, the American, the Turk, tried to write a book called *A Year of Death*. He wanted to catalog every San Francisco murder in the year 1974. But he couldn't make it work. Some killings had so little information, some offered more than anyone could want, and there was no way to achieve symmetry. Then he attempted a biography of the Swiss banker and terrorist François Genoud. 35,000 words into the project, COVID-19 shut down the Swiss Archives. It interrupted Kobek's maniacal translations of German and French documents. When the Archives re-opened, the writer could not get back into the rhythm. Then he attempted a book called *15 YouTube Suicides*. It would be 15 chapters long, each detailing a YouTube content creator who'd committed suicide.

Kobek's books traded in misery. Terrorism, Bay Area micropolitics, genocide, murdered SoundCloud rappers. In his arrogance, he thought that he could stomach anything. Then he examined fifteen average lives filtered through social media and corporate rapacity, their spirits conquered by cartoons and screen ghosts. Halfway through the fourth chapter, the writer realized that he was too weak. He gave up.

Kobek returned to an old idea. He'd had it years before. *Why not do a book about Zodiac? Why not write about Richard Gaikowski?* The Internet said that Gaikowski was Zodiac. A deceased San Francisco resident, a former reporter and filmmaker. Kobek'd looked at the theory and thought that the idea was suspect. Everything about Gaikowski screamed gay. Everything about Zodiac screamed straight.

Gaikowski fell into a pattern of potential Zodiac suspects, one enacted by both law enforcement and amateur sleuths. A disproportionate number of homosexuals had been fingered as the killer. If someone was looking for mid-century individuals with a hidden life, homosexuals were obvious targets. They'd concealed their lusts and loves. But they weren't Zodiac. They were just dudes who dug the pleasure of fucking other men.

And had a secret.

Kobek saw Gaikowski as another weirdo who'd outlived his era and lingered while Internet money transformed San Francisco. In the first decade of the Twenty-First Century, people like Gaikowski were as common as hydrogen. They wandered the city's streets with the dazed quality of someone punched in the face by a stranger. Some of these people were friends with Gaikowski. And some of Gaikowski's friends were friends with Kobek. The writer had never met the suspect. But he knew one thing. The mutual friends were appalled by the accusations.

The writer assumed that the accusers meant it, that it wasn't a cynical exercise, that it was a genuine expression of suspicion. But to turn Gaikowski into a credible Zodiac, information had to be bent.

The accusers were looking for The Zodiac. Who was different than Zodiac. The Zodiac was myth. Zodiac was the killer. Murder myths require the highest possible body count. Enter Cheri Jo Bates, a teenager murdered in 1966 in Riverside, California. Four years after her death, she was connected to The Zodiac. Letters had been written to the police, theories floated. The idea was nonsense. But it stuck.

The Zodiac was accused of killing Cheri Jo. And so was Gaikowski. Despite published articles proving that Gaikowski was not in Riverside at the time of her death. He was in New York State. On the other side of the country, writing for Albany's *Knickerbocker News,* attending a meeting of that city's African-American power brokers.

Gaikowski's presence in Europe in December 1968 and January 1969 was documented by another article about the troubles in Derry, Northern Ireland. Written after September 1968, when Gaikowski resigned as a staff reporter at the *Knickerbocker News*. And then disappeared into Europe. He'd sent the piece back to his former employers. Freelance.

The first Zodiac attack occurred on 20 December 1968. It happened on Lake Herman Road in Benicia, California. Lake Herman Road wasn't much more than a back pathway between the cities of Vallejo and Benicia, small cities on the outskirts of San Francisco. Zodiac shot two teenagers. David Faraday and Betty Lou Jensen. They'd gone into the darkness. To make out. And been killed.

For Gaikowski's accusers, the only answer was to impugn the article. It was a fraud, Gaikowski establishing an alibi. He hadn't left America. Gaikowski flew to California, stayed with his friend Bob, drove out one night and shot two teenagers. Then flew to Europe the next day. The article, as printed, lent itself to this theory. It contained distortions and material copied from another text on the same subject. Thus Gaikowski never went to Ireland. He was too busy killing teenagers in California. And then pretended he was in Derry. Wrote an article. To establish an alibi. Somehow he'd known that, decades in the future, the yet-to-be-invented Internet would cotton on to his bloodlust.

To the professional writer, the claims made no sense. What text, especially in the 1960s, appeared untouched by the editors? Gaikowski had written something, yes, and he'd sent it to his former employers. And, yes, the article contained inaccuracies and plagiarism. But where was the evidence that the text, as printed, was written by Gaikowski? He'd left his job, now worked freelance, wasn't in the office, lost in another country, hanging out on the Portobello Road. He could not babysit his creation. The editors could do whatever they wanted. They could incorporate other people's material, introduce inconsistencies, rewrite the entire piece. No one would stop them. The edited result—and almost every newspaper article is edited—went out under Gaikowski's name. Newsroom practices became evidence of Gaikowski's murderous rampage.

If Kobek were amongst those accusing Gaikowski, he knew how he would solve this problem. On 31 July 1969, Zodiac mailed three near identical letters to three different newspapers. This was roughly four weeks after his second attack. 4 July 1969. It happened in Vallejo, in the parking lot of Blue Rock Springs Park, about two miles from Lake Herman Road. A young woman named Darlene Ferrin died. A young man named Michael Mageau survived. They'd both been shot. The three letters claimed 4 July 1969 and 20 December 1968, offered information about the crime scenes.

The 20 December details were barebones, could have been picked up through the Bay Area grapevine. The 4 July details were specific, contained an error that only the shooter could have made.

When the letters were published, the Vallejo police asked the killer to provide more information. He'd responded, apparently hand-delivering a letter to the *San Francisco Examiner*. Published on 4 August 1969.

This letter was the first time that the killer called himself Zodiac. Which suggested that, four days earlier, he'd yet to coin the tradename. The text offered new details about both crime scenes. Again, the details of 4 July were hyperspecific, could only come from someone who'd been there.

Describing the 20 December 1968 attack, Zodiac wrote:

> Last Christmass
>
> In that epasode the police were wondering as to how I could shoot & hit my victoms in the dark. They did not openly state this, but implied this by saying it was a well lit night & I could see the silowets on the horizon. Bull Shit that area is srounded by high hills & trees. What I did was tape a small pencel flash light to the barrel of my gun. If you notice, in the center of the beam of light if you aim it at a wall or celling you will see a black or darck spot in the center of the circle of light about 3 to 6 inches across. When taped to a gun barrel, the bullet will strike exactly in the center of the black dot in the light. All I had to do was spray them as if it was a water hose; there was no need to use the gun sights. I was not happy to see that I did not get front page coverage.

The story made no sense. Betty Lou Jensen was shot multiple times across a distance of 27 feet. A pencil flashlight's beam was too weak to traverse this distance. And, if it somehow had managed, the black dot at the beam's center would have been huge. Useless for aiming.

Kobek did a little digging. He discovered that Zodiac copied this story from the December 1967 *Popular Science*. Written by Erle Stanley Gardner, creator of Perry Mason. The article was about the development of anti-riot technology. The relevant section went like this:

> **Flashlight aiming beam.** Still another development in the works is a flashlight-revolver that will throw a concentrated beam of light with a small black dot in the exact center. When a button is pressed, the revolver fires a projectile at the exact point covered by the black spot.
>
> As matters now stand, an officer making an arrest at night has to hold a flashlight in one hand and, if needed, his gun in the other. If the person arrested has a firearm and tries to use it, the officer must try, simply by the feel of the weapon, to put a bullet within the circle of light thrown by his flashlight.
>
> With the new weapon, a projectile will speed unerringly to the exact point necessary to subdue the prisoner.

Gaikowski was in the Bay Area on 4 July 1969. That was definitive. And he was there for the next two Zodiac attacks.

27 September 1969 at Lake Berryessa, a manmade lake in Napa County, north of Vallejo and Benicia. This attack was unique. Zodiac wore a kitschy medieval executioner's hood. He tied-up and stabbed two college students. Bryan Hartnell and Cecelia Ann Shepard. Hartnell survived, she didn't.

Less than 24 hours later, Hartnell gave an interview to the cops. A transcript has come down through the ages. The primary document of Zodiac studies.

The next attack was on 11 October 1969. Zodiac went to San Francisco and shot a cab driver in the head. The victim was named Paul Stine. Zodiac cut off some of the driver's bloody shirt, pieces of which he included in the envelopes of his next few correspondences. The bluntest authentication.

Minutes after Zodiac left the Stine crime scene, he encountered two cops. They let him go. Because he wasn't Black. And then he disappeared into myth.

If Kobek were accusing Gaikowski, the writer would discount Zodiac's responsibility for the 20 December 1968 attack. The only evidence was the killer's words. Half a year after the attack. When asked for more evidence about the crime, he copied out of a magazine. Later, after the San Francisco cab killing, the moment when Zodiac appeared to stop murdering, the killer would claim other deaths. Ones that he did not commit. So it was plausible.

But Kobek wasn't accusing Gaikowski.

Throughout most of the Zodiac era of 1967 to 1970, Gaikowski wrote for the *San Francisco Good Times*. An underground newspaper that catered to hippies and freaks. Gaikowski's accusers discovered *Good Times*. They scoured its contents, found secret messages in its articles, buried confessions. A body of knowledge was formed. It was self-reflexive and solid and impenetrable, and its internal consistency was absolute. Maybe it was right.

But Kobek doubted it.

The problem with the American Twenty-First Century wasn't the Internet. The Internet was a symptom. Americans had come to believe that if they accumulated enough raw information, enough disparate facts, enough stuff, then this accumulation could be a functional substitute for an existence based in skepticism and understanding. Add up trivia about Gaikowski and it equals Zodiac. But Kobek could not make the equation resolve. Its two sides were not equally true. The trivia was factoids, pointless relics of history, and their collection was the byproduct of a culture so failed in its present that it could no longer believe in the future. It could only obsess over a past which it did not understand.

Kobek reasoned that if he wrote about Gaikowski, he could write about his own era. Without buzzwords or contemporary proper nouns.

†

Kobek wrote what became the book *Motor Spirit*. He started with the first year of Zodiac. 20 December 1968 to 31 December 1969. The writer ignored other books, tertiary works. He went to original sources. It meant police files and newspapers. The more he read, the more he realized that the received story was invented. The accumulated cruft of decades. Or contemporary misapprehensions. There was The Zodiac, the myth, and then there was Zodiac. Who killed five people and mailed about fifteen correspondences. The letters were the thing, they said less than people thought but more than anyone could imagine. Reading the letters in their original context, the writer could see hints and inferences.

Popular Science was not an isolated instance. Zodiac's letters were rife with cultural references and quotations from a wide array of source materials. The method was there in the first communications, the three letters of 31 July 1969. Each included part of a cipher, an encrypted message. Pieced together and decoded, it read like this:

> I LIKE KILLING PEOPLE BECAUSE IT IS SO MUCH FUN IT IS MORE FUN THAN KILLING WILD GAME IN THE FORREST BECAUSE MAN IS THE MOST DANGEROUE ANAMAL OF ALL TO KILL SOMETHING GIVES ME THE MOST THRILLING EXPERENCE IT IS EVEN BETTER THAN GETTING YOUR ROCKS OFF WITH A GIRL THE BEST PART OF IT IS THAE WHEN I DIE I WILL BE REBORN IN PARADICE AND THE [missing text] I HAVE KILLED WILL BECOME MY SLAVES I WILL NOT GIVE YOU MY NAME BECAUSE YOU WILL TRY TO SLOI DOWN OR ATOP MY COLLECTIOG OF SLAVES FOR MY AFTERLIFE EBEORIETEMETHHPITI

From the moment that this message was decrypted, its initial lines were taken as a reference to the short story entitled "The Most Dangerous Game." Published in 1924, it's about a Russian count who gets so bored with normal kinks that he invents a new one. He traps people on an island and hunts them like animals. The blinding heights of aristo decadence.

On 26 July 1970, the killer mailed what's known as the Little List letter. In its first two pages, Zodiac listed six methods of torture that he planned to inflict upon his afterlife slaves. The remaining three pages were a phonetic transcription of "And Some Day It May Happen." A song from Gilbert & Sullivan's *The Mikado*.

The lyrics are a little list of society offenders. Who will all be executed. The transcription was recognized, immediately, for its content.

One of Zodiac's six tortures also derived from *The Mikado*. What no one had picked up on, then or since, was the source material for another of these methods.

Zodiac wrote:

> **Others shall be placed in cages & fed salt beef untill they are gorged then I shall listen to their pleass for water and I shall laugh at them.**

Kobek traced this to two possible sources. The first was William Black's Nineteenth Century novel *MacLeod of Dare,* which contained this:

> He put his nephew into a deep and foul dungeon—so the story says—and left him without food or water for a whole day. Then there was salt beef lowered into the dungeon; and Macdonald he devoured the salt beef; for he was starving with hunger. Then they left him alone. But you can imagine the thirst of a man who has been eating salt beef, and who has had no water for a day or two. He was mad with thirst. Then they lowered a cup into the dungeon—you may imagine the eagerness with which the poor fellow saw it coming down to him—and how he caught it with both his hands. But it was empty! And so, having made a fool of him in that way, they left him to die of thirst.

The second possible source was Sir Walter Scott's *Tales of a Grandfather,* which contained this:

But the vengeance of his uncle was of a more refined character. The stone which covered the aperture in the roof was lifted, and a quantity of salt beef let down to the prisoner, who devoured it eagerly. When he glutted himself with this food, and expected to be supplied with liquor, to quench the raging thirst which the diet had excited, a cup was slowly lowered down, which, when he eagerly grasped it, he found to be empty! Then they rolled the stone on the opening to the vault, and left the captive to perish by thirst, the most dreadful of all deaths.

From what Kobek could tell, no American publisher had issued either book in the Twentieth Century. Which meant that Zodiac was copying from very obscure sources.

Another example was the so-called Halloween Card of 27 October 1970. Zodiac mailed this to Paul Avery, a reporter at the *San Francisco Chronicle*. On the card's rear, Zodiac had drawn the following:

In December 2013, Zodiac researcher Tahoe27 discovered that much of this was copied from the cover of an old Western comic book.

Tim Holt #30. Published in June 1952.

The cover looked like this:

The quoted material was in the details.

Which looked like this:

In the previously quoted cipher, Zodiac claimed that his victims would become slaves in the afterlife. The phrase reappeared in subsequent correspondences. It was referenced on the back of the Halloween Card.

The words never changed, remained consistent across so many different letters. They ruptured the texts that preceded and followed. Kobek was responsible for enough bad writing that he knew how to spot the pointless reference, the knowing wink telling the reader that the writer had read far and wide. Slaves in the afterlife had to be like salt beef torture. Lifted from a previous source.

The real coup would be identifying the source material, proving that Zodiac copied the phrase from another text. The world had taken the phrase as the expression of a religious ethos. But maybe Zodiac was just someone with access to a public library.

Tim Holt #30 gave Kobek an idea. What if the source material could be found in comic books or pulp fiction? "I WILL COLLECT THEIR SOULS

FOR SLAVES IN MY AFTERLIFE!" sounded like a villain in an issue of *Captain Future* or *Ghost Comics.*

Kobek spent days hunting the reference. The best that he came up with was the original Black Widow, a comic book character from the early 1940s. Black Widow's real name was Claire Voyant. She worked for Satan. The devil dispatched his employee to the collect the souls of evil men. Clair Voyant sent these souls to Hell.

But the necessary phrase, slaves in the afterlife, never appeared.

†

Kobek had another impression. Zodiac was not from San Francisco. Zodiac was from the Vallejo area.

The first two attacks happened around Vallejo. On Friday nights. One in December 1968, another on 4 July 1969. If you kill late on a Friday night, there's not going to be a great deal of travel. You murder after work or the holiday party. The next attack happened on a Saturday at Lake Berryessa. Zodiac dressed up for that one, put on a hood. The next was the killing of a cab driver in San Francisco. Paul Stine. Another Saturday. Lake Berryessa requires a drive, travel. As does a visit to San Francisco where you figure out how to stage a murder. For both incidents, you need a weekend, a day without work.

†

Thousands and thousands of comic books had been published. Even with obsessive Internet nerd culture, there was no full index of the contents. It was like looking for a needle in a haystack that was several storeys high, a haystack that defied elementary physics.

The writer knew an expert on Golden Age comics. An old friend, someone whom Kobek had met in the writer's wasted teenaged years. A man named Dave, who was extraordinarily well-read and capable of keen insight that seemed to elude everyone else. In the writer's senior year of high school, Kobek came up with a harebrained scheme. He wanted to go to Lawrence, Kansas and meet the ancient William S. Burroughs. Kobek asked all of his friends if they would come along. They laughed at him. But Dave said yes, had himself thought of the idea but couldn't find anyone to make the trip. The two took the train—36 dull and slow hours across America—and ended up in Lawrence, and then, a few days later, through dumb luck, were invited to meet the old junky. They visited Burroughs at home. They stayed for about an hour and a half. Kobek only asked one stupid question. In those days, this was a major triumph.

By 2017, Kobek and Dave hadn't seen each for over a decade. And then Kobek did an event at The Strand bookstore in New York City. It was a dismal affair in support of a work destined for failure. Somehow the event earned a mentioned in *The New Yorker.* The only highlight was when Kobek entered the rare books room and saw his old friend sitting in the back row. The two talked, promised to stay in touch.

Both parties kept their word. In their renewed correspondence, Dave mentioned an expertise in Golden Age comics.

Which Kobek now remembered.

He e-mailed Dave:

> You might be the person to ask this question—I don't know how familiar you are with the epic tedium that is the ZODIAC KILLER but a few years ago someone realized that text in one of his communications was lifted from the cover of *Tim Holt* #30.
>
> It's occurred to me that this is probably also true of the first decoded message:
>
> "I like killing people because it is so much fun - it is more fun than killing wild game in the forest because man is the most dangerous animal of all - to kill something gives me the most thrilling experience - it is even better than getting your rocks off with a girl - the best part of it is that when I die I will be reborn in paradise and all the I have killed will become my

slaves - I will not give you my name because you will try to slow down or stop my collecting of slaves for my afterlife."

Specifically all the shit about the people he's killed becoming his slaves when he's reborn in paradise. This motif reoccurs through several letters but the language never really changes. It sounds to me like an old golden age comic thing. As you are a demi-urge of the golden age, I was wondering, does this by any chance sound familiar?

Hearing nothing, Kobek sent the following text message to Dave on 7 March 2021:

Did you get my email about Zodiac? Does that shit ring any bells?

Dave responded:

Yeah, I had been thinking about a reply. I read that Tim Holt book a while back. The quote doesn't sound overly familiar (except for the book/movie reference), but I was going to look thru some golden age books to see if there's something familiar. Honestly, it reminds me of Fletcher Hanks.

Kobek responded:

I'm 100% convinced it's either golden age comics or pulp fiction

At 10:32 AM PST, 7 March 2021, Dave responded:

I'd think so too. His flower language pings my nerd genre alarm. Like that dude wrote a fanzine.

chapter two

sen ve ben, bebek

EARLY ON, KOBEK ABANDONED the classification of Zodiac as a lust killer, a serial killer with no control over his own impulses. Zodiac was not Ted Bundy. Kobek thought that a better, if inadequate, classification was Zodiac as a mass shooter working in slow time, someone who existed in a historical moment before the creation of his natural genre.

The writer couldn't speak to mass shootings before Columbine. But he saw a common denominator in the massacres that came after. It was not the killing. That was there, always. As was the underlying suicidal impulse. But death was a means to an end. The goal was media coverage. Blaring headlines and a dynamite Wikipedia entry. A way of making the world notice.

The school shooter lived on the other side of a spiritual divide. The divide had no name but was visible on social media. Every second of every day. How many people in Iowa were tweeting about individuals whom they did not know, dissecting human lives in New York City, in Los Angeles, in San Francisco, and Washington DC? And how many people from those four cities tweeted about people in Iowa? The gap couldn't be quantified. But didn't need to be measured. Some knowledge requires no study. Some answers are obvious. The Sun always sets in the West.

To be an American was to believe that you deserved happiness. That you would get what you wanted. In the five decades since Zodiac stopped writing, happiness had been redefined, broadly, as fame. To be happy, you had to be known by millions. But fame was cruel. It was a byproduct of genetics. To become famous, you had to be born with a natural gift. Beauty, brains, athletic ability. Or be raised in an environment that endowed you with the social fluidity to make up the difference.

Most of the country's citizens did not fall into these categories. If you lacked natural gifts and didn't come from a class background that brought you into proximity with the naturally gifted, then attacking a school was a rational choice. The decision asked that you die or spend the rest of your life in prison. It asked that you murder your fellow human beings. But this was an ask only for people with skin in the game. For someone desperate enough to take up an AR-15, the status quo was misery. A working definition of Hell is the unemployed male living in a single parent's basement, skin blued with Vitamin D deficiency and light from an LCD display, surrounded by the detritus of a culture in which they are a consumer and not a creator, the scent of masturbatory semen wafting up from unwashed laundry.

The obsession with fame was built on a foundation of lies. These were so embedded within the national character that they could not be questioned without the questioner becoming a heretic. From the minute of their birth, every American child learned that, if only one worked hard enough, they could get every thing that they wanted. Every day on social media, miserable people reiterated these lies. Of which their very lives were the repudiation. *Every cloud has a silver lining. There is no I in teamwork. Not every new beginning is meant to last forever. These mountains that you are carrying, you were only supposed to climb. Live your best life. Don't wish for it, work for it.*

The mass shooter had a special knowledge. They knew that America was not going to give them what they wanted. If they could not be rich and famous, they could be dead and famous. Or imprisoned and famous, free from the concerns of money. When life is intolerable, the differences between fame and infamy are mute. The crimes were a byproduct of media, acted out by people anointed with understanding, individuals who saw that the quickest route was murder. Kill enough people, kill them in the right way, and you get what everyone wants. America will know your name and your face. The incandescent heat might only last a week, maybe even a day. You might be too dead to enjoy it. But its afterburn is forever.

Zodiac was like a school shooter. He did not kill for the sake of killing. Zodiac killed to be published. To be famous. The murders were a necessary spark. The evidence was in Bryan Hartnell's police interview, conducted a day after he was stabbed at Lake Berryessa. The victim reiterates a point. The killer was nervous. Really, really nervous. As if he didn't want to be there. It wasn't what he wanted to do. It was what he had to do. To get the attention that he wanted. Zodiac split his first cipher into three. And mailed each part to a different newspaper. Maximizing the likelihood of publication. It suggested someone who understood something about how to achieve the goal.

Murder works on two levels. There is the cessation of life. And then there are the circumstances. Choice of weapons, choice of victims. The circumstances are the expression of the murder's personality, reflections of everything that comes before. The hobbies, the obsessions, the pathologies.

Which is why, reading the correspondences, Kobek asked himself a question. *Why do we assume that Zodiac's letters of 31 July were his first? Isn't it likely that someone who writes letters to the editor during a murder spree has spent some time, prior to the killing, writing letters to the editor?*

†

After every broken adolescent shot up a school, as the bodies were cataloged and numbered, the world descended upon that adolescent's Internet presence. Digital relics exhumed. Their tweets examined. Their Instagram posts. Their Facebook updates. Their YouTube videos. From these droppings, a fragmentary portrait emerged. The warning signs were there all along. As ever. As always. And ignored. As ever. As always.

Some killers left manifestos.

Kobek's to-die-for favorite was by Brenton Tarrant, who'd livestreamed two mosque shootings in New Zealand. 51 dead Muslims, 40 wounded. Tarrant's manifesto, entitled *The Great Replacement,* expressed how very bothersome the shooter found it when Turkish people came west of the Bosphorus River and polluted the European blood line. It was, literally, a White Supremacist manifesto about Kobek, confirming all of the writer's suspicions. Kobek himself was the problem.

Which he'd assumed all along.

†

In 2014, a young man named Elliot Rodger went on a kill rampage at UC Santa Barbara in Isla Vista, California. He'd murdered his room-mates, murdered sorority girls, driven his BMW through town, shooting and crashing. The story was a shock. Then people found his manifesto. *My Twisted World.* It was the ugliest of texts, unexpurgated misogyny from the depths of Hell, pathological resentment filtered through two decades of Internet English. And it made Rodger famous, coverage everywhere, set a template for all who came after. Within a week, the shootings had faded. But the manifesto lived on. The killing wasn't the important thing. The killing was the necessary spark. The writing was the important thing.

Zodiac was different from the other famous killers in his era. For those tiny sad men, killing was the thing. Zodiac was the letters. What they delivered. The fundamental point.

What was Zodiac if not someone who'd done a mass shooting in slow time, gotten away with it, and incorporated the manifesto into the crimes?

What if someone shot up a school and escaped? Could that same process, the exhumation of digital relics, establish a killer's identity? As far as Kobek knew, it had yet to happen. This didn't mean that people hadn't tried. During the manhunt for the Boston Marathon bombers, the Internet decided that an individual named Sunil Tripathi was responsible. He wasn't. Tripathi was dead, a suicide, body in the Seekonk River. But his life and his family's lives were uprooted and destroyed. And then forgotten.

Assuming that Zodiac's letters of 31 July 1969 were not his first, might it not be possible to go through the published material around the Bay Area and find Zodiac? But this would not be easy. And Kobek had no interest. He didn't care about finding Zodiac. He couldn't think of anything more boring than finding Zodiac, of having the magic word appear in the first clause of one's obituary. His book wasn't about Zodiac. The killer was, there, yes, but the book was about phenomenology of The Zodiac and the chaos of California, about an entire society copping a habit and experiencing a shame so great that America now pretended methamphetamine psychosis was the same thing as politics.

Kobek had the idea.

But let it die.

Then Dave texted him a magic word.

Dave texted: "fanzines."

†

To understand the fanzine, one must comprehend a different time. It's an era when Science Fiction is not popular, not yet international lingua franca.

The genre emerged in newsstand pulps, low-cost periodicals issued on the very cheapest paper. These magazines, with titles like *Amazing Stories* and *Miracle Science and Fantasy Stories,* published fiction about the future.

In theory, the stories rested on a writer examining contemporary developments in engineering and extrapolating a vision of What Might Be.

In practice, the pulps were heavy on fiction and light on the science. The genre was ill-defined. What makes something Fantasy? What makes it Science Fiction? How to differentiate between Hard SF and a space opera about lurid intergalactic sex?

Most attempts at classification rested on an assumption that the genre was defined by its content. This was wrong.

Science Fiction was defined by its means of production, crap magazines printed on wood pulp. Science Fiction was toilet literature consumed by the working classes. This freed the genre from the pretensions of Literature. Which, it turns out, were class affectations of the bourgeoisie. Get past the minimum threshold of sentence construction and all writing is good. After that, it's just a matter of taste, the writer's intelligence, and a reader's socio-economic background.

Pulp magazines printed letters from the readers, allowed customers to become part of the text. The pulps would often publish those writers' postal addresses. Some printed lists of readers and their addresses. It created a culture of correspondence.

People might never meet in the flesh. But they could exchange complicated thoughts about the nature of reality and philosophy and what to expect from the future. Many of these people were very bright but lacked any formal education. They were self-taught, autodidacts.

Science Fiction was born in a moment when reproduction technology had gotten cheaper and easier. There were spirit duplicators—also known as ditto machines—that used wax paper and rolling drums and alcohol to produce copies. And there were mimeograph machines, which used stencils upon which one typed or drew. The machine pushed ink through the stencil and created copies. These technologies were not perfect, and their results were often unattractive, but they allowed people to present their own writing in the formalized context of a print run.

This was perfect for the early days of Science Fiction. If someone printed 300 copies of their amateur publication, it was enough to reach most hardcore fans. And that culture of correspondence made it possible to get everyone's postal addresses. This milieu gave itself a name. It was called *fandom*.

These small run periodicals also earned a name. They were called fanzines. Dave's magic word. They began appearing in 1930. By 1950, one could no longer mail a copy to every dedicated fan. There were too many adherents. But the number of fanzines had expanded. If someone was on two-or-three mailing lists, they'd get the news.

The editors of fanzines needed content, couldn't be responsible for eight or more pages every other month, so they solicited letters from subscribers. Which were reproduced in the fanzines.

As Science Fiction expanded, its disparate groups became factions. These factions each had their own fanzines. On occasion, warfare broke out.

By the 1970s, the fanzine ecosystem was a cacophony of voices. Mostly peaceful. Some disquieting. It was impossible to read every fanzine. The rarefied elite who'd come up with the idea were displaced by a spectacle of unwashed hoi polloi offering every possible opinion.

Fanzines required a dedication that might elude most people. They weren't easy to produce. And the machines were expensive. Which is why some people wrote the editors and were published on other people's platforms. Everyone could be included, really, as long as they could hunt-and-peck on a QWERTY keyboard. Or handwrite a letter.

Fanzines were the Internet before the Internet.

†

Debased as his currency might be, Kobek had forgotten about fanzines. He was blessed in ignorance. Now Dave texted the magic word. Kobek thought back to his other conclusion. Zodiac lived in Vallejo. And while the writer had no interest in finding Zodiac, he figured, well, *What the hell? What's the worst that could happen?*

He stood in his kitchen and used his smartphone to Google two words:

FANZINES VALLEJO

The second result was a PDF scan of Science Fiction fanzine entitled *Tightbeam*. Dated Jan-March 1970. On its twelfth page, there was a letter from a man named Paul Doerr. A return address was included.

Box 1444, Vallejo, California, 94590.

The letter's first paragraph was about proposed raises in the postal rates. Doerr was upset that, quote, the anti-poverty people, unquote, had forced the post office to hire unqualified workers. These new workers had caused delays in service, particularly around Christmas. Doerr suggested a series of civil disobedience tactics. Like only using 1¢ stamps on letters and packages. The other paragraphs were about smoking cigarettes, Doerr's discontent with conventions in the Sword & Sorcery sub-genre, and whether or not writers should be forced to write in the English language. The letter ended with a question: "Is anyone around the Bay interested in skin diving or sailing?"

From the reference to Christmas mailing delays and the fanzine's date, Doerr's letter must have been mailed after 20 December 1969, the anniversary of the first attack at Lake Herman Road. Zodiac had marked the occasion by sending a letter to a local celebrity, the lawyer Melvin Belli.

The envelope looked like this:

1¢ stamps.

And then there was Doerr's question about sailing. On 26 June 1970, Zodiac mailed a letter that contained a cipher. And a map of the Bay Area, a Zodiac symbol transformed into a compass. Superimposed atop Mt. Diablo. The map included the following instructions: "O is to be set to Mag N." A month later, when Zodiac mailed the Little List, he'd included the following: "PS. The Mt. Diablo Code concerns Radians & #inches along the radians."

Magnetic north. Radians.

It suggested an individual with some knowledge of navigation.

Kobek didn't think Doerr was Zodiac. But it was a parallel. The writer went to his computer and investigated. He was able to piece together a fragmentary biography.

Doerr was born in 1927 in Sharon, Pennsylvania, apparently abandoned in early life by his father, served in the Navy as a medic during World War Two and the Korean War, and, in 1963, had moved to California. For decades, he'd worked at the Mare Island Naval Base. Doerr hadn't lived in Vallejo. He'd lived about twenty miles northeast in Fairfield, a twenty-minute drive on the I-80. He'd kept the Vallejo post office box from 1964 to 1976.

Much of this information was established through genealogical records and old newspapers. The rest came from Doerr's writing. Which seemed endless. The man spent his whole life sending letters to the editor. The earliest available missive appeared in the June 1945 issue of *The Acolyte,* an early fanzine. When he wrote the letter, Doerr would have been 17 or 18-years old. The final letters dated to a few years before Doerr's death in 2007. The man spent seven decades writing letters to the editor.

One such letter appeared in the 10 April 1972 *San Francisco Examiner,* sent in response to a column by Guy Wright. On 27 March 1972, Wright described Native Americans, as encountered by the original English colonists, as savages. In response, Doerr wrote the following:

> **MR. WRIGHT:** Who are the savages? The people "without writing, metal tools or even the wheel," as you say? Or the people with those things, plus the rack, the stake, the gun, rampant disease and ideology that lets them treat less "civilized" people as animals and slaves?

In the early 1960s, Doerr placed classifieds looking to buy or trade guns. In the early 1980s, Doerr advertised in *Soldier of Fortune.*

This was a magazine that, putatively, targeted military mercenaries, soldiers for hire. In reality, it was war porn for the powerless. One of Doerr's advertisements, appearing in the September 1980 issue, read like this:

WANT 308 ASSAULT RIFLE & 03A3. Prefer M14 or Garand. Trade new Ruger Mini-14. Doerr, 225E, Utah Fairfield, CA 94533

Doerr was a gun nut. He'd been one in the early 1960s. And was one in the early 1980s. But here he was, in the middle, in the 1970s, writing that the gun was a sign of higher barbarism. Kobek re-read the letter and realized that, in its final line, it contained two major words from Zodiac's first decoded cipher. Animals. Slaves.

Kobek didn't believe in handwriting analysis. It was a pseudoscience that put poor people in prison on the words of experts employed by the state. But he did believe in writing's capacity to reveal the writer. Particularly the untrained writer. He thought again of the first letter, the one in *Tightbeam,* the one about postage and 1¢ stamps. It didn't suggest that Doerr was Zodiac. Lots of people were interested in the mail. But it did suggest a commonality of interest.

†

Doerr's major Internet relics, the ones that could be found without much effort, were things that Kobek could not understand or explain. They were echoes of a lifetime of belief.

Doerr believed that subterranean races of pre-human creatures lived beneath the Earth's surface. In caves and caverns. And were accompanied by prehistoric survivals. For a while, this had been a common belief in Science Fiction circles. In 1932, a man named Richard Shaver heard voices coming up through the ground. He found a willing partner in Ray Palmer, the editor of *Amazing Stories,* who transformed Shaver's letters into rollicking works of fiction and published the results. Many readers believed these stories to be true, to be accurate representations of life beneath the planet's surface. It boosted circulation and set off a frenzy. Like all fads, the mania died out. But some people still believed. Paul Doerr was one. He seemed to think that a conduit to this hidden world was California's Mt. Shasta, up near the Oregon border. And he believed in other fantastic things. He was fixated on Bigfoot, on Yeti, on Abominable Snowmen. His first available letters were on this topic. There was evidence that Doerr kept these interests into the late 1980s. If not later.

This sounded like a garden variety maniac, a person with the capacity to believe anything. Kobek knew the type. His own late father was a man who saw ghosts in every shadow, who found no conspiracy too implausible. If you asked Kobek's father about Bigfoot, he would attest, with great ferocity, to the monster's existence. And Kobek's father never killed anyone.

(The writer assumed.)

The writer's father had been exactly the type of man that Kobek presumed of Zodiac: an autodidact. He'd been raised in stinking poverty on the outskirts of Izmir, Turkey. In the writer's father's childhood neighborhood, the kids called themselves *çiyan*. It meant centipede. Kobek wasn't sure if his father had graduated high school. But he'd been just about the most brilliant person whom Kobek ever met. He lacked the sophistication of a trained intellect, of the person who picks up the *au courant* dialect of higher education, the *lisan* of the *asil adamlar*, and thus had no hope of his brilliance being acknowledged by the wider world. But the writer's father was smart enough to see the future, way back in 1983, before anyone other than a handful of people in the corridors of tech. This vision, this insight, shaped every aspect of Kobek's life. The writer's father grew up in a place where the sole expectation was that he become another Turkish Baba, the small decent men who lead quiet lives, the ones who fondle their worry beads and never leave the place of their births. Drive through any Turkish town and you'll spot them. With nothing more than raw intelligence, the writer's father ended up with an astonishing existence, a five times polyglot who'd gone everywhere and done everything and become an American and then returned home and lived most of his remaining years in splendor. He hung around long enough to read Turkish-language news coverage about his son's ephemeral literary success. One piece quoted a character from the son's novel, a character based on the father. Kobek had transcribed his father's conversations and used the words, almost verbatim, as the character's dialogue. Consider this as the marker of a successful life: a man born to be nobody somehow reading himself quoted, in the language of his birth, by a newspaper with a circulation in the millions. Because he'd pulled some shit in America.

Other than bank accounts stuffed with 000,000s and shares in mutual funds tracking the S&P 500, the writer's father acquired everything that anyone could ask of life. He might not have died rich. But he didn't need money. The man had won. He died in total and absolute triumph.

If there was any real sadness, it was that the writer's father couldn't see how much he had achieved. And that there was no acknowledgment, no *New York Times* obituary to inform the *bien pensant* that one of the world's most unique and brilliant men was gone.

Yet Kobek had been there. He'd witnessed. His father was difficult enough that the writer had every reason to pretend otherwise. But it couldn't be denied. Old Mr. Kobek man was often blindingly terrible at human interaction, but the guy was a stone fucking genius.

†

Old Mr. Kobek was the best case scenario, the autodidact whose intellect matched his ambition. And self-image.

The old man gave the writer sensitivity to the contours of these men, of their disappointments at not being understood or recognized, of their capacity for intellectual drift. Of how, by missing the virtues of formal education, they could believe nonsense alongside empirical truth. And experience no contradiction. Of how they could destroy themselves and others in the frustration at not being seen.

And Paul Doerr, like Zodiac before him, was lighting up some very well-established synapses.

†

Traces of Doerr went beyond letters.

Doerr published his own fanzines.

These were not available on the Internet. But were referenced. Kobek couldn't get a sense of when Doerr began issuing his own publications, wouldn't realize the dates until much later, but the writer could tell that some publications ran contemporary with the Zodiac moment. One was called *Hobbitalia.* It was, apparently, about J.R.R. Tolkien. Another publication was called *Pioneer.* The only descriptions referred to it as a "survivalist" magazine.

Kobek thought, well, *What the hell? Is it possible to find copies of these things? What's the worst that can happen?* At the very least, they would disqualify Doerr as Zodiac. And provide another reference point for the moment, one beyond the headlines.

chapter three

a constitutional replay
of mass production

KOBEK DISCOVERED three issues of *Hobbitalia* at Marquette University in Milwaukee, Wisconsin. *Pioneer*s #13 and #14 were in the Hargrett Library at the University of Georgia in Athens. Issue #9 of *Pioneer* was held by Murdoch University in Perth, Australia.

The writer came up with a ruse. If any librarian asked why he wanted these ancient relics, Kobek would say that he was engaged in genealogical research and discovered that Doerr was a distant relative.

Genealogical research was the domain of the desperate and the insane. Kobek believed that the world's librarians knew this, understood the lunacy of people attempting to discern meaning through pointless heritage. And thus would not ask too many questions of an amateur genealogist.

Anything was less embarrassing than saying ZODIAC.

†

Marquette University sent PDF scans of all three issues of *Hobbitalia*. Free of charge. Kobek had one goal.

To exclude Doerr as a candidate for Zodiac.

Internal references dated *Hobbitalia* #1 to early 1970. The first pages contained very little of note. There were introductory remarks about the publication's purpose, which was celebration of J.R.R. Tolkien and his works. Followed by reprints of external material. A review of *The Lord of the Rings* from *Seattle Magazine,* and an article by Lin Carter about the formation of the Tolkien Society of America.

Then came a long article, by Doerr, about jewelry and beryl and other gemstones. It was boring beyond belief. But it proved something.

Doerr was not stupid. He was exceptionally smart. Just rough and untouched by formal education. He was not a good writer. But he had command of his subject.

On the penultimate page of *Hobbitalia* #1, Doerr wrote about his attempts to establish a grammar and dictionary of Cirth, a runic alphabet used by Tolkien's fictional characters. Describing how most people in fandom used the alphabet, Doerr wrote:

> As we are using Cirth now (substituting a symbol *[sic]* for a letter, one for one) this is not a language. It is just a cypher, a code, and a rather simple one. We are insulting the brilliance of Mr Tolkien by perverting his language to such a simple use.

Doerr used the words "cypher" and "code."

In each of the three 31 July 1969 letters, Zodiac wrote some variation of the following: "I want you to print this cipher on the front page of your paper." In the 4 August 1969 letter, Zodiac wrote: "By the way, are the police haveing a good time with the code?"

Across all Zodiac letters, the word cipher was spelled "cipher."

With one exception. The 31 July 1969 letter to the *Vallejo Times-Herald.* The first instance of the word was spelled "cyipher." This was the first composed of Zodiac letters. This was early days, when Zodiac was working out his character, deciding how he would misspell certain words.

Zodiac had written: "Here is a cyipher or that is part of one." And then never used the 'y' again.

Doerr had spelled it "cypher."

Kobek turned to the final page of *Hobbitalia* #1 and saw this:

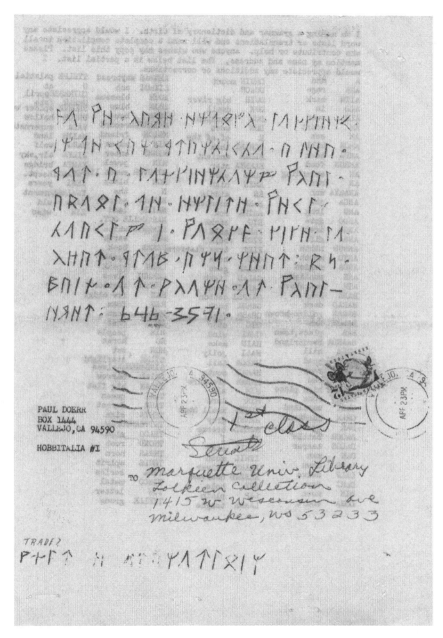

(Courtesy of Marquette University)

It was a cypher, a code, and it used Tolkien's Cirth alphabet. It was messier than Zodiac's first and second ciphers, both designed on a rigorous grid. But.

Here was something that could not be ignored. Kobek believed that Zodiac lived in or around Vallejo. And here was a mailing from Vallejo that referenced ciphers and codes and included one of its own. And then there was the postmark and the stamp. A 12¢ stamp from the Prominent American line. Most of the stamps on Zodiac correspondences came from this series.

Color inverted for clarity, the *Hobbitalia* #1 postmark looked like this:

APR 23 1970.

Smack dab between two Zodiac correspondences mailed on 20 April 1970 and 28 April 1970.

Kobek decoded Doerr's cipher. It read:

DO WE HAVE ENOUGH TOKKIENS*[sic]*
IN THE SAN FRANCISCO AREA
FOR A TOLKIENCON? WHAT
ABOUT THE ENTIRE WEST
COAST? I WOULD LIKE TO
HEAR FROM ANY NEAR. BY
MAIL OR PHONE OR WHAT
EVER. 646-3591.[1]

At the bottom of the page, there was another line in Cirth. Transliterated into English alphabet characters, it read: PLDR E ORANORTUIN. Most of this was in Quenya, an invented language used by Tolkien's Elves. It translated, roughly, as: PLDR OF SUN RIVER.

Or: PAUL DOERR OF SUN RIVER.

†

Hobbitalia #2 contained more content than the first issue, its pages spaced out with drawings of supernatural creatures. Doerr wrote about how he'd made huge maps of Tolkien's Middle Earth and included a small map that he'd drawn of The Shire.

Then Kobek read the following:

Many hobbits are members of the Society for Creative Anachronism (2815 Forest ave berkeley ca 94705). This a group, organized in kingdoms, who practice the chivalries and wear the clothes of old, from 1650 to as far back as you

---

1 Contemporary classifieds establish that this number was in the 707 area code. It wasn't located at Doerr's home, which had the same number for decades: 707-425-1869. In 707, the 646 prefix was reserved for the Naval Base on Mare Island. Presumably this was Doerr's office phone. No working theories as to the omitted area code.

care to go. One very pretty slave (female, of course) wears only two pieces of dearskin and a slave bracelet on her ankle. The owner wouldn'd *[sic]* sell......Most waer *[sic]* the clothing of the Medieval Ages. The men of course wear, and use on the field of battle, armor, chain mail, helmets, swords, maces, spears, knives, morningstars, etc. The names chosen by the nobility (everybody is nobility if he wants to be... its *[sic]* easier to rise in the world now than it was in the dark ages) are from Tolkien, as Shire, Moria, Dunharrow, Rivendell, etc.

Kobek thought of a lingering Zodiac mystery. Why had the killer dressed like a medieval executioner at Lake Berryessa? What if there were a practical reason for the hood, rather than generally accepted idea that the garment expressed a religious ethos?

Kobek decided to see if there were any Renaissance Faires around the 27 September 1969 attack.

And there was.

The Third Annual Renaissance Pleasure Faire & Ha'penny Market. It was open every single weekend day of September 1969, including the 27th. It was happening in San Rafael, in Marin County, across the Golden Gate Bridge from San Francisco. About an hour and a half drive from Lake Berryessa.

The Third Annual Renaissance Pleasure Faire & Ha'penny Market. Where people who wanted to dress in medieval garb went for fun on the weekend. Other than events hosted by the Society for Creative Anachronism, this was the one place in the Bay Area where an individual could dress in an executioner's hood and not be taken for an LSD casualty. Is it possible that Zodiac attended this Faire? And if he did, was he in the hood?

There's an obvious objection. If Zodiac was at the Faire, then other attendees would have recognized the costume. It's the smart idea. But, in the moment, no image of the hood was released to the public. The costume's appearance was unknown. The first printed description suggested a Spanish *capirote*. Conical in shape. But this was wrong. Bryan Hartnell's interview makes it clear that Zodiac's hood was square on top.

In 1969, the Pleasure Faire had a daily capacity of 10,000. By 2PM each day, attendees were turned away in the hundreds. A day after Zodiac stabbed Hartnell and Shepard, KPIX-TV ran a story about the traffic caused by the Faire. The footage demonstrates that many people, organizers and attendees, arrive in costume. Most of these outfits look homemade. Amongst the 10,000, how would anyone notice one more?

As far as Kobek knew, no Zodiac researcher had noticed that this event took place in the same month, let alone on the same day, as the Lake Berryessa attack. A connection between the Renaissance Faire and the hood seemed a much better explanation than assumptions of Satanic ritual. Particularly if one remembered Bryan Hartnell's description. The victim said nothing about magic. The killer was a nervous low class guy who said that he'd escaped from prison.

Kobek was convinced that Zodiac had not lived alone. The evidence was there in the letters. The baseline of Zodiac's writing was a desire to be understood, to make sure that the language conveyed the message.

Son of Sam's letters were the obvious counterpoint. Barely coherent, written for the killer's amusement. Their language was often a direct rip of Zodiac. Zodiac wrote to Melvin Belli wishing him a Happy Christmass. Son of Sam wished a Happy Easter to the people of Queens, New York. Zodiac like hunting. So did Son of Sam.

The Son of Sam correspondences were filled with meaningless phrases. "I miss my pretty princess most of all. She's resting in our ladies house. But I'll see her soon." "Papa Sam is old now. He needs some blood to preserve his youth. He has had too many heart attacks. Too many heart attacks. 'Ugh me hoot it urts sonny boy.'" "Because Craig is Craig / So must the streets / be filled with Craig (death)."

Zodiac never did that shit. Zodiac always wrote to be understood. It made Kobek think that Zodiac wasn't like Son of Sam, a chubby behemoth living alone with no one to help develop communication skills.

If Zodiac didn't live alone, the hood posed a problem. How does someone keep an executioner's hood in the house and not raise questions? The answer was now, theoretically, clear. The hood is for a Renaissance Faire.

It's the perfect cover.

†

Several pages in *Hobbitalia #2* were instructions for building a "smial." In Tolkien's fictional universe, these were the homes that Hobbits burrowed into the Earth. Doerr presented these dwellings as a serious alternative to standard housing. He'd devised his own method of building smials and included an illustration:

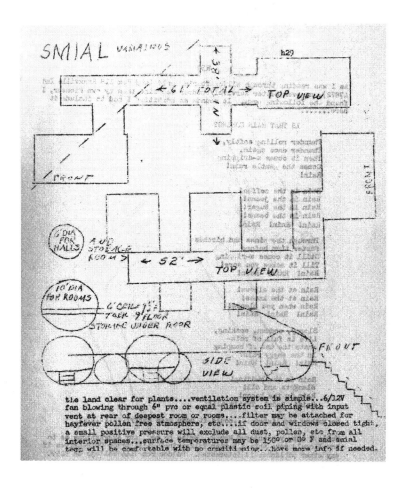

Hobbitalia #3 was the shortest of the three issues. Its main contents were more information about building smials and Doerr attempting to establish a universal language that used Cirth as its alphabet. The smials were accompanied by another small illustration. It looked like this:

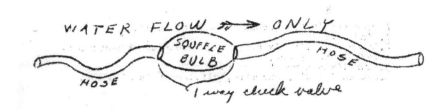

On 9 November 1969, Zodiac had sent in a long letter that included a diagram of a bomb. It looked like this:

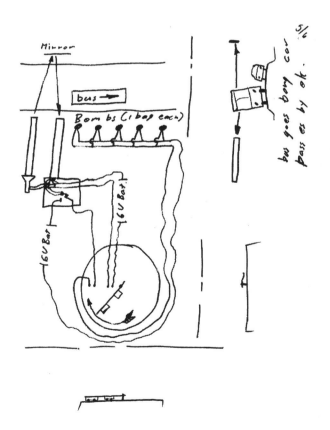

Zodiac used two types of arrows. There were standard diagrammatic arrows, indicating distance and the spacial relationship to components by placing a directional indicator on either side of text or an object. And a single instance of a second kind of arrow. A fully drawn feathered arrow. Both types were present in Doerr's illustrations.

It didn't prove anything. But the three issues of *Hobbitalia* had not done what Kobek wanted. Nothing disproved Doerr's candidacy for Zodiac.

†

That night, Kobek searched the Internet for Doerr's Vallejo post box. Without either his given or surname. He came up with several classifieds. A few appeared in the *San Francisco Examiner* and *Chronicle*. The ones that interested Kobek had appeared in underground newspapers. Paul Doerr was many things. But he was not a hippie. He was not a wild child. He was a middle aged eccentric who worked on Mare Island. He was a strange man, but he was a square. That much was obvious. And here he was advertising in the *Berkeley Barb* and publications like *The Seed* and *it ain't me babe,* a short-lived San Francisco feminist underground newspaper. Kobek now suffered from confirmation bias. Based on the content of the letters, he'd theorized that Zodiac was not part of the counterculture but rather someone who beheld the counterculture with a gaze of envy and malice. Zodiac used an ersatz version of counterculture dialect—he was always threatening to do his thing—and had written four letters about people wearing buttons, a slightly dated affectation of the youth. And called himself Zodiac.

The classifieds placed Doerr in the Bay Area near dates associated with Zodiac. This was no remarkable thing. Doerr lived in the Bay Area. He worked a job in Vallejo. He was going to be present.

In the 1-7 November 1968 issue of the *Barb*, Doerr ran this classified:

In the 23-29 January 1970 *Barb,* Doerr ran the following:

> WANTED - CHEAP - BOOKS -
> Botony, Anthropology, Archaeolo-
> gy, Old Greek and Medit Civili-
> zation. Lowrainfall Flora Fauua
> Living Methods. SHELL ZEN
> YOGA OCCULT HEALTH. List,
> title, date, price, cond. Doerr.
> Box 1444 Vallejo.

In issues of the *Chronicle* dating between 6 August and 10 August 1970, Doerr ran the following:

> 10 Ac. north Calif. coast. $2500.
> Doerr. Box 1444. Vallejo 94590.
> (707) 646-3591.

In the 5 October 1970 issue of *The Seed,* Doerr ran the following:

> Anyone interested in working communal farm in
> Oregon, please write P. Doerr, Box 1444, Vallejo,
> Cal. 94590.

In the 30 October 1970 issue of *it ain't me babe,* Doerr ran the following:

> Anyone interested in a working
> communal farm in Oregon, please
> write P.Doerr, Box 1444, Vallejo,
> Calif. 94590.

The November 1968 advert was about a month before the killings on Lake Herman Road. 23-29 January 1970 was a month after the letter to Melvin Belli. The advertisements about communal farming were on either side of the 27 October 1970 card to Paul Avery. *The Seed* advertisement appeared on 5 October 1970, the same day that Zodiac mailed an index card on which he'd cut-and-pasted material from several local newspapers.

The most interesting classified appeared in the 8-14 August 1969 issue of the *Berkeley Barb*. It looked like this:

> **.WANTED – Girl for sailboat trips Some to Mex. Cair, Europe, etc. Send Picture, etc. Paul, Box 1444 Vallejo, Cal., 94590**

In 1969, Doerr lived in Fairfield with his wife and a teenaged daughter. On each Monday or Tuesday before publication, the *Barb* telephoned people who'd placed personals classifieds and verified that they were a real individual. In this case, it meant a call on either 4 or 5 August 1969.

On 4 August, the *Examiner* ran the letter debuting the Zodiac tradename. This was the classified of a man who wanted to get out of town.

†

The next day, Kobek received *Pioneer* #13 and #14. Doerr's "survivalist" publication. The writer started with #13. Postmarked 6 January 1975.

It took an hour before Kobek could make faint sense of the thing. Although Doerr had labeled the front page as *Pioneer* #13, the publication was issue #2 of another Doerr fanzine called *Livaboard*, a forum for readers to send in letters about their experiences and questions regarding life on boats. The layout was so amateur that it was almost impossible to tell who was writing, when the letters stopped and Doerr's responses began. One of the letters was from Richard Shaver, the man who heard people talking from beneath the earth. But otherwise the issue was a wash. Maybe this was was the disqualifier, maybe this level of disorganized thinking was not what one associated with Zodiac. But the postmark was 1975.

A lot of things can happen in six years.

Kobek opened *Pioneer* #14. It was postmarked 23 January 1975. It was as if another person were writing. There was organizational incoherence, but it wasn't anything as bad as *Livaboard*. The thing could be followed from the first page. Doerr wrote about coming to California in an 18' sloop that he'd sailed from Lake Erie. Kobek had seen references to this before, in letters to the editors of multiple publications. Doerr was building a new 28' custom ship. Doerr planned to live aboard. Kobek had read about this, too, in letters, including one from a much later date in which Doerr admitted that he had never used this ship. Doerr called his new boat NOMAD. Doerr wrote about the perils of water fluoridation.

There was a comment that read as either serious or sarcastic: "Read the papers, particularly one like the San Francisco Examiner that carries more than controlled political news." There were random quotations from H.P. Lovecraft and his acolyte August Derleth. And a quote from A. Merritt, a long forgotten writer of pulp fantasy. There was a panoply of random factoids, divorced from anything. And Doerr had written an extended section about how treasure hunts were a lifelong hobby.

The passage that stood out, the surprising thing, was this:

> If anyone wants phono records (hundreds), 7" reels of sound tape, muzzle-loading pistol, $165 bow, knives, swords, guns, books, record player, 4 band portable and about ten tons of other stuff just write and tell me your wants and what youll *[sic]* give.

In October 1968, the United States Congress passed a ban on unlicensed mail order guns, the consequence of the assassinations of John F. Kennedy, Robert F. Kennedy, and Martin Luther King Jr. And here was Doerr, seven years later, offering to sell unlicensed mail order guns. It was reminiscent of what Zodiac had written in his letter of 9 November 1969: "my killing tools have been boughten through the mail order outfits before the ban went into efect. Except one & it was bought out of the state."

Kobek found two classifieds placed by Doerr in the 1960s. Before the ban went into effect. One appeared in a 1962 issue of the *Aquarium Journal*. It looked like this:

> **Sell or Trade for Guns—About 200 aquarium hobby magazines, 8 years bound, 1941-1955; write Paul Doerr, Box #62, Wheatland, Penna.**

Another appeared in a 1966 issue of *Gems and Minerals*:

> **BRAZILIAN OPTICAL QUARTZ** crystals. Trade for Greek coins, artifacts, stamps or guns. Doerr, Box 1444, Vallejo, Calif. 94591.

In *Pioneer* #14, Doerr advertised his willingness to sell guns through the mail. He put it into print. And distributed it to the world. Doerr's other writing felt crazy. But it was a safe crazy. The village eccentric. This was reckless crazy. It was *evidence of my willingness to commit a felony* crazy.

Pioneer #14 also contained a long section in which Doerr complained about gun control. And the mail order ban. Like Zodiac in the letter of 9 November 1969, Doerr understood that it was illegal to sell guns through the mail.

Kobek took stock of what he knew. It wasn't much. But there were some things that were difficult to explain away. And there was a bigger problem. The writer had now read about ten thousand words of Doerr's writing. Many of these words existed in the Zodiac moment. And there hadn't been a single thing excluding Doerr. If anything, the new information did the opposite.

†

Murdoch University sent Kobek *Pioneer* #9. This issue was long, 18 pages, made longer by the fact that it was a single-spaced collection of random factoids. From internal references, Kobek dated the fanzine's composition to 1972. The 3 December 1972 issue of *Son of the WSFA Journal,* a fanzine that Kobek found on the Internet, stated that *Pioneer* #9 had circulated in November 1972.

Doerr described *Pioneer* #9 on its first page: "This issue will be somewhat different. I have dozens of short bits of info here goes."

There were cooking tips. There were discussions of Roman numerals. There were farming tips. There were recapitulations of contemporary news articles. There were survivalist tips. Doerr achieved the dream of a character in a Borgess story: an infinite library of pointless information contained within a definitive space.

Kobek's eyes glazed over. He didn't care about chicken feed or bone meal. But he kept reading.

And then he found it. Two things on page 10, one paragraph apart. One read like this: "pop. sci article 1959 do extinct animals still survive by e h ortner"

In his letter of 4 August 1969, Zodiac offered evidence about the murders of David Faraday and Betty Lou Jensen. He wrote that he'd taped a pencil light to his gun. The evidence was bogus. The language copied from the December 1967 *Popular Science*. Written by Erle Stanley Gardner, creator of Perry Mason.

Did *Pioneer* #9 indicate that Doerr was reading *Popular Science*?

There was an ambiguity. In Doerr's contemporary moment, the only other person who'd paid attention to "Do Extinct Animals Still Survive?" was John A. Keel, a writer of Forteana and weird mysteries. Best known for his paranoiac classic *The Mothman Prophecies*.

In another book, *The Complete Guide to Mysterious Beings,* Keel mentioned Ortner's article. First published in 1970.

Kobek had seen a reference, scattered in Internet UFO debris, about Keel offering a contribution to *Unknown*. A fanzine published by Paul Doerr.

It was possible that Doerr had come upon the article this way, through Keel. Rather than going through issues of *Popular Science*.

†

The next thing wasn't much.
Just three lines.
It said this:

> ammoniun *[sic]* nitrate, common commercial fertilizer, mixed with fuel oil..1 gal per 100# is explosive as dynamite but only 4¢ per pound...must be kept dry

And here, Kobek knew that he was in the deepest of shit.

chapter four

the death machine
is a ready made

IN HIS 9 NOVEMBER 1969 letter to the *San Francisco Chronicle*, Zodiac wrote: "Take one bag of ammonium nitrate fertilizer + 1 gal of stove oil + dump a few bags of gravel on top + then set the shit off + will positivily ventalate any thing that should be in the way of the blast."

In his 20 April 1970 letter, Zodiac wrote: "I have killed ten people to date. It would have been a lot more except that my bus bomb was a dud. I was swamped out by the rain we had a while back."

The 20 April 1970 letter was publicized and published, but the *Chronicle* withheld Zodiac's ammonium nitrate threat of 9 November 1969. It was not in public circulation.

There's a complexity deriving from Zodiac's use of "stove oil." It's a shifting term with different definitions based on historical moment and geographical locale. The specification of "1 gal" tells the informed reader that Zodiac's using the term interchangeably with fuel oil. He's offering the formula for ammonium nitrate and fuel oil. It's common enough to have its own acronym. ANFO.

9 November 1969. It's the first substantial mailing sent after Zodiac learns that he left fingerprints on Paul Stine's cab. News of the mistake appears in the *Chronicle* and *Examiner* on 18 October 1969, seven days after the murder.

He claims 7 dead, two more than the official total. A day before he mailed the 9 November letter, he sent another communication, a greeting card. It says almost nothing, is the delivery mechanism for his second cipher. But in its short 69 words, Zodiac hints that his unknown victims were killed in August. This dovetails with media speculation from that month of Zodiac killing two teenagers. Which he did not. There's no raw material for new letters, no new death, no fuel. So the writer invents. In the 13 October 1969 letter, the one in which Zodiac claims responsibility for Stine, he threatened to shoot school children. Which set off a panic. Now, on 9 November, he returns to the idea. But it's got to be bigger and bolder. He writes that he's building a bomb to blow up a bus. He provides the ANFO formula.

Flash forward to 24 August 1970.

Eight months after Zodiac's letter. Four men pack a van full of ANFO and blow-up Sterling Hall at the University of Wisconsin-Madison. The culprits are protesting the Vietnam War.

24 August 1970.

It's the very first time that ANFO is weaponized. Later reports suggest the bombers learn of the explosive mixture from *Pothole Blasting for Wildlife*, a pamphlet published by the Wisconsin Conservation Department. But that isn't true. The formula gets on the bombers' radar when one of them visits a farm and watches its owner blast holes for duck ponds.

Wisconsin brings ANFO into the terrorist arsenal. The idea spreads. The San Jose IRS building is bombed. ANFO. Timothy McVeigh blows up the Alfred P. Murrah building in Oklahoma City. ANFO. Anders Brevik sets off a bomb in Oslo. ANFO. The Islamic State blows up the temple of Baalshamin in Palmyra, Syria. ANFO.

Zodiac has ANFO a year before anyone in the counterculture.

He understands that the formula can be weaponized.

Zodiac lives in the Bay Area. There's a radical whisper network stretching from the Haight to Berkeley, it's in Oakland, in Fremont, in Dublin, everywhere with disaffected youths. If Zodiac is young, if he's connected to the counterculture, if he hints that he knows how to make a new kind of bomb, then the idea will spread. Immediately. ANFO bombs will go off across the Bay Area and the rest of America.

That doesn't happen.

No one in the counterculture knows about ANFO bombs. Not until Wisconsin. Not until 24 August 1970.

Which means: Zodiac isn't young.

Which means: Zodiac has no place in the counterculture.

†

As far back as the 1870s, people knew of ammonium nitrate's explosive properties. The idea of carbonization via fuel oil doesn't arrive until the mid-1900s. Industrial use takes off around 1960. ANFO's principal virtue is that it's cheaper than traditional explosives. Throughout the early 1960s, the formula appears in print, but almost entirely within specialty publications that cater to individuals who work in mining and construction and demolitions. *Pothole Blasting for Wildlife.* Or military demolitions manuals.

Pioneer #9 dates from 1972. Long after Sterling Hall, after ANFO is common knowledge. There's a complication. Contemporary reports omit the mixture. After the University of Wisconsin bombing, trade publications stop spreading the formula. Kobek assumed that Doerr would've gotten ANFO from a publication predating Sterling Hall. Doerr was interested in mining, placed classifieds in *Gems and Minerals.* Presumably read trade journals.

But how did Zodiac have the knowledge? He'd specified "1 gal." He'd seen a formula somewhere.

Doerr wrote: "ammoniun *[sic]* nitrate, common commercial fertilizer, mixed with fuel oil..1 gal per 100# is explosive as dynamite but only 4¢ per pound...must be kept dry."

Zodiac wrote: "Take one bag of ammonium nitrate fertilizer + 1 gal of stove oil + dump a few bags of gravel on top + then set the shit off + will positivily ventalate any thing that should be in the way of the blast."

They'd both used "1 gal". They'd both referred to ammonium nitrate as a fertilizer. Doerr specified that the explosives must be kept dry. Zodiac demonstrates the same knowledge on 20 April 1970: "I was swamped out by the rain we had a while back."

ANFO is a misnomer. The reactive components are ammonium nitrate and fuel oil. But ANFO requires a third component. It needs a primer, something that explodes first, inside the mixture, and thereby triggers the bigger explosion. Someone could mix all the world's fuel oil into all of the world's ammonium nitrate. Buried in the earth, as depicted in Zodiac's bomb, starved of oxygen, and it's not going off without a primer. In mining and construction, people use half a stick of dynamite. Or blasting caps.

Zodiac's 9 November 1969 illustration depicts an electrical circuit that sends a small charge to bags of ANFO. The letter specifies all the components:

> The death machine is all ready made. I would have sent you pictures but you would be nasty enough to trace them back to developer & then to me, so I shall describe my masterpiece to you. The nice part of it is all the parts can be bought on the open market with no questions asked.
>
> 1 bat. pow clock—will run for aprox 1 year
> 1 photoelectric switch
> 2 copper leaf springs
> 2 6V car bat
> 1 flash light bulb & reflector
> 1 mirror
> 2 18" cardboard tubes black with shoe polish in side & oute

Missing is the primer. The third component. What sets the shit off. The bomb couldn't work. It would send a small electric charge to bags of ANFO. And do nothing. An amateur mistake, betraying a lack of practical experience. Or a lack of care. Zodiac didn't come across the formula in the course of his employment. The inexactitude reveals that this isn't a byproduct of military training. ANFO is copied out of a publication. Like everything else.

Zodiac might not know about bombs, but he did know electronics. The trigger mechanism might work, in so far as generating an electric charge sent to the inert ANFO.

There was a thing that no one apprehended in the Zodiac moment and made no sense in Kobek's own era. The writer lived in a period when anyone with a smartphone could access all human knowledge. But when information is not easily available, when it requires work, then every reference resonates with meaning. The words echo a lifetime of reading and memory. If someone read Zodiac's letters, gleaned the resonances, and put them together, an impression of the killer could be extracted. It wouldn't be exact. But it would tell you about his interests and hobbies.

Kobek couldn't help but think of a letter that he'd found, from Doerr, in a 1966 issue of *Electronic Design.* The magazine was for amateurs and professionals alike. People who made their own electronics.

Doerr's letter was the last sally in a small war. An editorialist'd stumbled across a Neo-Nazi rally. He'd been horrified and published a piece in *Electronic Design.* Doerr read the editorial, wrote to the magazine and denounced the editorialist. The editorialist wrote back to the magazine and denounced Doerr. The letter that Kobek found was Doerr writing back to denounce the editorialist who had denounced Doerr for denouncing the editorialist.

The content was irrelevant. Place of publication was everything. Doerr was reading magazines that would help an amateur design a bomb with photoelectric switch and copper leaf springs.

Kobek found Doerr's post office box and phone number in the June 1968 issue of *Oceanology International.* The entry read like this:

> Miscellaneous Inc
> Box 1444, Vallejo, Cal. 94590
>   404/646-3591
> Minerals, biological specimens, hard-wired electronic instruments, and research reports.

In *Pioneer* #9, Doerr wrote: "ammoniun *[sic]* nitrate, common commercial fertilizer, mixed with fuel oil..1 gal per 100# is explosive as dynamite but only 4¢ per pound...must be kept dry."

The 1 gal abbreviation.

The knowledge that the mixture is sensitive to water.

And what's missing?
A primer, any sense of how the thing works.
Same language. Same mistake.

†

Kobek theorized that although the Left of 1969 did not know about ANFO, the knowledge was possessed by the Right. He considered this a subfunction of class and geography. Most of the Left's bombers were urban or from affluent backgrounds. No surprise that when the formula is first used by the Left, it's after someone visits a farm.

In the early 1960s, a man named Robert DePugh, a biochemist from Missouri, founded a radical group. He called it The Minutemen. DePugh hated Communists. The loathing wasn't unusual. Other than a handful of people in New York City and Berkeley, most Americans in 1961 were hostile to Communists. It's a moment when capitalism is working for more people than ever before. Someone like Paul Doerr grew up thinking that the hardscrabble hell of the Great Depression was all they'd ever get. And then World War Two happened. America converted itself into a manufacturing powerhouse. And then World War Two ended. Most of the world's industrial powerhouses were flattened. But America was untouched. And full of new factories. There was an unparalleled prosperity boom. People who expected to be treated like dirt ended up with tract homes. And then feared that the Communists wanted to take it all away, redistribute their modest wealth. The country vibrated with loathing. And even in this atmosphere, DePugh is distinguished by the depth and caliber of his hatred. The Minutemen are absolutely psychotic about the Communist Threat.

But, in 1960, there are almost no American Communists. There are kids on college campuses, the ones who read Karl Marx and think, well, *Why not? What's the worst that can happen?* And then there's about 3,000 members of the American Communist Party, people who weren't turned off by revelations that Josef Stalin's Soviet Union was show trials, gulags, and anti-Semitic purges. And then there are the sad bastards who flirted with socialism and spent the late 1940s and 1950s being dragged by the House Un-American

Activities Committee. Most of whom weren't Communists. When DePugh founds The Minutemen, there's possibly 75,000 Communists in a country of 183,700,000. This estimate is unrealistically high and generous.

In the 1960s, the world ends every other day. The Minutemen witness the waves of transformation, feel something slipping away, and assume that the thing slips because it's pulled by the unseen hand of Communism. The most visible change is the shifting status of the African-American population. The Minutemen think that Black people are too stupid to organize, that the miracle of Martin Luther King Jr. and Bob Moses and Bayard Rustin can't be real, and thus all Black agitation is controlled by Communist forces, that the Negro Issue is a Soviet stalking horse. It's an easy explanation for something that they refuse to understand. It attracts a certain kind of person.

If you're a Minuteman, the Communist take-over of the United States is so obvious, so complete. Look at the increasingly liberal slant of the media. Enshrined constitutional rights are eroding. The only response is to form small, decentralized militias. And resist. Through violence, through weapons, through anything that embodies the principles of the founding fathers. One can't count on an infiltrated government. The Citizen Patriot will take the fight to the Commies.

In 1966, several Minutemen are arrested with an enormous cache of weapons. The police theory is that they're going to bomb Left-wing summer camps. Communist indoctrination centers. In 1968, Minutemen near Seattle are arrested for plotting to rob four banks and blow up several power stations and Redmond City Hall. The grand jury also indicts DePugh. Several months later, he's arrested on weapons charges. On bail, DePugh disappears. He goes underground. In 1969, he's captured in Truth or Consequences, a town in New Mexico named after a defunct radio quiz show.

The Minutemen organization issued bulletins and a magazine called *On Target!* Most of the time, these communications were the expected: Commies, Negroes, pinkos, end of America, resist, fight, rinse, cycle, repeat. Sometimes, most often in the bulletins, the content was practical. Sometimes the Minutemen sent out manuals on guerrilla and psychological warfare.

In January 1966, the group circulates a new bulletin.

They advertised it like this:

AMMONIUM NITRATE HIGH EXPLOSIVES
It is generally known that common fertilizer, ammonium
nitrate, can be used as the basis of high explosive compounds.
A special bulletin is available to dues paying members that
gives complete formulas for these easily made explosive compounds plus considerable information about their practical
uses.

Before this bulletin, The Minutemen had published other guides to explosives. The previous works did not include ANFO. The formula's sudden appearance allowed Kobek to date, roughly, when the idea entered the arsenal of the Far Right.

Late 1965 to early 1966.

The Minutemen were trailblazers. The Internet before the Internet, the distribution of death via mass media. 1969 was different than 2021, different even than 1971, the year when *The Anarchist's Cookbook* was published.

Certain information was hard to find.

Kobek clocked three non-Minutemen, non-trade, non-governmental publications about explosives that predated Zodiac's bomb letter.

The High-Low Boom! by Philip J. Danisevich.

Pyrotechnics by George W. Weingart.

Explosives Like Your Grandfather Used to Make by Don Sisco.[2]

Only *The High-Low Boom!* had ANFO. And offered the formula with such a degree of complexity that it was inscrutable to anyone other than chemists or pyrotechnicians.

One paragraph of the ANFO bulletin read like this: "Most people know that ammonium nitrate can be used as the basis for various high explosive mixtures. Little information has been available as to the best proportion, use and detonating of these mixtures."

---

2 Sisco, who later renamed himself Kurt Saxon, also published *The Militant's Formulary.* Sources tend to date this text's first edition as 1968, presumably based on a misreading of Sisco's 5 August 1970 testimony before the United States Senate Subcommittee on Investigations into Government Operations on Riots, Civil and Criminal Disorders. Kobek found copies of all three editions of *Formulary*. The first is copyrighted 1970. ANFO appears in the first edition *Formulary* in a ratio of 1 pint of fuel oil to 8 1/2 pounds of ammonium nitrate. This is a significantly higher ratio than anyone else, including Doerr and Zodiac, ever suggested.

Another paragraph read: "The most common and the best all around mixture consists of 94% prilled ammonium nitrate and fuel oil. In this case the term fuel oil can include No. 2 diesel fuel, kerosene, light lubricating oil..."

One can dig through the era's mining and government publications and find instructions on the manufacture of ANFO. What's never present is the suggestion of using anything other than No. 2 Diesel Fuel Oil.

The chemical properties of No. 2 diesel allow for a higher impact and lessen the chances of accidents. None of these journals recommend using kerosene, which, in the common parlance of the era, was indistinguishable from stove or range oil.

This was a Minutemen innovation.

And Zodiac did not specify fuel oil. Zodiac wrote stove oil.

†

Kobek read more Minutemen literature. Taken together, the group's bulletins and activities were like a manual on How To Be Zodiac.

In the bulletin "Family Survival Techniques," the Minutemen advised their readership on gun choice for the coming apocalypse:

> Try to buy your gun in such a way that it cannot be traced to you. If you live in a state or city that requires a permit to buy a gun, go to some other state that does not have such a requirement.

Zodiac had written: "My killing tools have been boughten through the mail order outfits before the ban went into efect. Except one + it was bought out of the state."

Later in the same bulletin:

> [A gun] may be needed as an offensive weapon in resistance warfare; in the home or carried for personal defense; possibly

as a survival weapon for living off the land. What shall it be? Though it will surprise many people, my recommendation is a .22 caliber semi-automatic pistol... As to a specific brand, I much prefer the Ruger (made by Strum-Ruger Co.)... Other good .22 automatics include the High Standard, and Colt models."

Ballistic reports on casings gathered from the Lake Herman Road crime scene, the California Department of Justice concluded: "As a result of these studies we find that the exhibits correspond only with tests fired in the J.C. Higgins Model 80, .22 semiautomatic pistol. It should not be assumed that the exhibits must have been fired in such a weapon but this is the only type presently in our files which corresponds, therefore, it appears somewhat probable that the responsible weapon was of this type."

This J.C. Higgins 80 was manufactured by High Standard and available for sale at Sears. A house brand. The Model 80 was the same gun as the High Standard M101. The only difference between the two models were their respective grips. The M101 looks space age. The models can not be distinguished via ballistics.

The notion of cryptographic communication repeats throughout the Minutemen literature. In the bulletin "Communication Techniques in a Resistance Movement," the following appears:

In communication, through a dead drop the agent receives his assignments in written form. These agent assignments must be encoded or enciphered... Therefore we must train the agent in the use of ciphers, codes, the preparation of soft emulsion film, microdot, and secret writing.

Reading through what material could be found, it appeared to Kobek that the Minutemen's methods of cryptography instruction were in-person seminars and an audio recording of DePugh. The writer could find no evidence that the recording had survived.

Interviewed after the attack at Blue Rock Springs, Michael Mageau stated that when Zodiac fired his weapon, he could not hear any sound from the gun. Which made sense when he himself was being shot. Any number of biological processes could have impeded his hearing.

But why didn't he hear anything when Zodiac shot Darlene Ferrin? Another witness, who lived several hundred feet away, said that he heard gunshots. The witness said the sounds were different than fireworks. But this claim is hard to verify. And no one reported hearing the shot that killed Paul Stine in San Francisco. Which asked a question. Had Zodiac used suppressors?

The Minutemen published another bulletin titled "Silencers." It was a guide to the construction of silencers. In all three gun attacks, Zodiac used semi-automatic weapons. In "Silencers," the Minutemen offered this advice: "When it comes to hand guns, automatics are much easier to silence than revolvers. This is especially true with anything more powerful than a .22."

There was something else. The Minutemen had circulated a bulletin entitled "Practical Security Measures." It was a list of techniques that Minutemen could employ to avoid detection. Item #4 read like this:

```
    4.  Send all letters from corner mail boxes or from post
offices where you are not known.
```

Which is exactly what Zodiac had done.

†

Regardless of their retrograde politics, the Minutemen weren't clueless troglodytes. They understood media. They knew that to really make it, one must reduce content and message. The key to mass market success is distillation, the densest amount of information transmitted in the simplest icon.

The Minutemen had a slogan, a mantra. It went like this:

Traitors beware! Even now the cross hairs are on the backs of your neck.

A symbol accompanied the slogan, one that the group recommended its members paint in public places.

The group put the slogan and the logo on stickers. The stickers were background radiation of the 1960s, visible in half the men's rooms along the Interstate Highway System. These stickers were part of something that the Minutemen described as "Psy-War Project No. 32."

A full explanation of Psy-War No. 32 read like this:

Psy-War Project No. 32

COMMUNIST TRAITORS BEWARE
EVEN NOW THE CROSS-HAIRS ARE AT THE BACK OF YOUR NECK

The words written under the cross-hairs symbol pictured at the right, published in the March 15 issue of On Target, have been reprinted hundreds of times in left-wing papers and magazines. Fourteen words that really shocked the reds and made them worry !

Psy-War Project 32 will continuously remind the traitors that those cross-hairs are still there and always will be. That sooner or later they will pay the price for selling their country out to the enemy.

STARTING IMMEDIATELY, ALL MEMBERS ARE TO PAINT OR DRAW THE CROSS-HAIRS SYMBOL EVERYWHERE POSSIBLE THAT IT WILL BE SEEN BY THE PUBLIC. In public wash rooms, on trees, on the blank side of road signs, on fences, walls, abandoned buildings, bus stop benches, etc.

In the past when we put up posters and stickers, the reds tried to tear them down as soon as we put them up. Let's put these symbols up to stay. A little bottle of finger-nail polish with a brush on the cap can be used to paint small symbols in doors, on tile, glass, etc. A pressure spray can of paint can be used to quickly paint the symbol on concrete walls, bridges, rocks, etc. A spray can of white or yellow paint will show up well on rough surfaces such as trees and telephone poles, etc. Ordinary paint and brushes are best for the backs of smooth metal signs. We don't expect many of you to be able to put the words with the symbol, and have determined that the symbol itself will be most effective at this time.

During the next few days, these signs should appear from coast to coast – put them everywhere ! The more the better ! The bigger the better ! Just be careful that you do not make people mad at us by defacing private property.

Very soon stickers will be available that will appear much as the drawing above. These may be placed in areas where paint and nail polish cannot be used too easily.

NOTICE: This is part one of a two part project. As soon as the cross-hairs symbol has been widely seen by the general public, the second part of the propaganda project will be announced. Don't wait ! Devote at least two full nights work to this project. Cover your area completely. Drive out along the highways. Work at this project all this next week end. Let's really shake the reds up. This has a greater effect on their moral than you could ever believe. We will explain more about this at a later date.

The Minutemen might've gathered weapons, and some of its members did plan attacks, but, in practice, the organization was most active through the Postal Service. Kobek read the first issue of *On Target,* dated 1 January 1963. The publication explained itself: "The purpose of On Target is not to inform but rather identify by name, address and phone number the thousands of communist traitors who are even now working to sell out their own country to the enemy... One of the primary rules of propaganda is that to be effective, it must be aimed at individuals. Organizations, general issues, and similar nebulous targets are almost immune to propaganda. Only when it is directed at some individual does propaganda become fully effective."

On Target published the names and home addresses of American liberals. Secret Communists, fellow-travelers. There'd been multiple Minutemen harassment campaigns via anonymous letters. This first happened in 1962, described in a later Minutemen bulletin. An FBI file dated 5 February 1963, sent from the Denver field office, described another bulletin: "The letter is entitled 'Psychological Warfare Project No. 8,' and contains instructions about the mailing of post cards anonymously and simultaneously from all over the United States to an individual named JOYCE C. HALL of the Hallmark Card Company, Kansas City, Missouri."

One bulletin detailed some of these efforts:

```
        When one of our members was murdered in California the
coroner quickly ruled it "probable suicide", the papers ignored
it and the whole thing was well on its way to being hushed up.
We picked half a dozen well known pinks on the West coast as
our targets.  Our members from all over the country started
mailing anonymous cards that read, "Dear Comrade:  Did your
communist friends murder Newton Armstrong, Jr.?"  These cards
created so much excitement that the whole case was re-opened,
the newspapers carried it from coast to coast, and millions of
people were given a glimpse of the truth.

        About two years ago a group of pinks, reds and "do-gooders"
started a campaign to get our government food surplus sent to
red China to help relieve the famine there.  The project was
led by a well known "one worlder" Dr. Karl Menninger, of the
Menninger Psycho Clinic in Topeka, Kansas.  The idea was given
good press coverage and the President announced on TV that he
was favorably inclined to consider the suggestion.  Here we
picked Dr. Menninger as our target.  From all over the country,
thousands of cards were addressed to Dr. Karl Menninger,
Menninger Concentration Camp, Topeka, Kansas.  They read,  "Food
for red China? Not till they send home the 463 American service
men that are still held prisoner in Chinese Communist slave
camps since the Korean War." After a few days of this one of
our members who was working as an orderly in the clinic reported
that Menninger was ready for his own nut house.  The whole rotten
scheme was dropped like a hot potato !
```

Another bulletin detailed Psy-War 42:

PSY-WAR PROJECT No. 42-Determine the home addresses of the most
notorious liberals, reds, one-worlders and chief parasites in your area
and mail them envelopes with "Traitors Beware" leaflets enclosed.

FBI file #62-6101-1A54, dated 12 July 1967, reproduced of an anonymous letter mailed to an individual whose name was redacted.

The letter and its envelope looked like this:

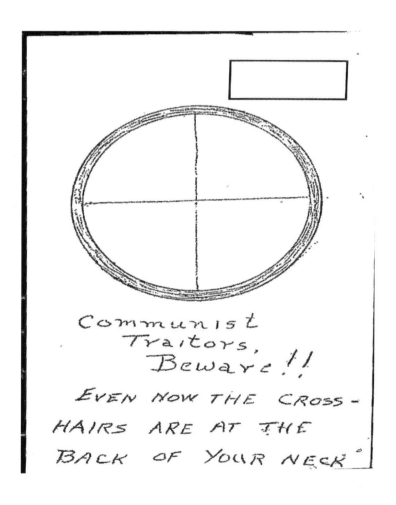

Kobek was hyperattuned to the Left. The writer could describe, without recourse to reference material, many of the 1967 freak establishments on Haight Street. But the Right was often a mystery.

So he'd missed it, ignored the obvious.

Throughout the Zodiac letters, there are hints of heavy thinking. Zodiac mentions gun control. The perennial concern of the radical Right. Almost of all letters bear stamps of American Presidents. It's even there in one of the attacks. Darlene Ferrin was killed on 4 July 1969.

Independence Day.

Zodiac copied. The cover of a comic book becomes the Halloween Card sent to a newspaper reporter. *The Mikado* becomes a list of future victims. *Popular Science* becomes Lake Herman Road.

Zodiac used a symbol to sign most of his letters.

It looked like this:

The symbol demonstrated the problem with histories of The Zodiac. Once a thing happens, once it's documented, it seems like part of a plan. But Zodiac was the same as anyone else. He was bedeviled by fuck-ups and indecision and wrong turns.

Kobek had a question.

How does anyone know what the crosshairs meant to Zodiac?

It was unanswerable, could never be solved. Other than small circulation Vallejo newspapers, the symbol wasn't reproduced in any contemporary reporting on the first three letters. No major Bay Area newspaper printed Zodiac's crosshairs, visually, until October 1969. By which point, the killer has the tradename, has sent ciphers, worn a hood, gone to San Francisco, shot Paul Stine. The narrative is in place. The crosshairs are another piece of the story. But they predate everything except the cipher. Along with slaves in the afterlife and the cryptography, they're one of three elements present before the killer knows what to call himself.

Zodiac went with whatever happened. Regardless of original intent. If a newspaper says that he committed a murder, he accepts it. The crosshairs becomes the Zodiac symbol. And Zodiac goes with it. But when the symbol is first scrawled, it's not the Zodiac symbol. There is no Zodiac. The name is only chosen with the 4 August 1969 letter.

In the initial three letters, the ones with the first cipher, the crosshairs is not the Zodiac symbol. Because there is no Zodiac.

It's only crosshairs.

Kobek had a standard policy. He always went for the shortest, least complicated route. In 1969, the shortest path to crosshairs via anonymous letters are the Minutemen.

And the Minutemen also published the ANFO formula.

Traitors beware.

†

Kobek discovered the Minutemen through researching Paul Doerr. A friend suggested that he look through the online academic databases to which her university subscribed. He found one operated by Gale Cengage. It was called *The Minutemen 1961-1969: Evolution of the Militia Movement in America, Part I.*

Kobek searched on what had, by now, become a default: "Box 1444."

When DePugh was arrested in Truth or Consequences, the authorities discovered a cache of documents and weapons. Including a list of 2,800 names. All of the people who'd been Minutemen, all of its small number on this North American continent. The ones who'd been sent its bulletins and newsletters.

And there, on page 79, unredacted by the FBI in file #62-107261-3552, was this:

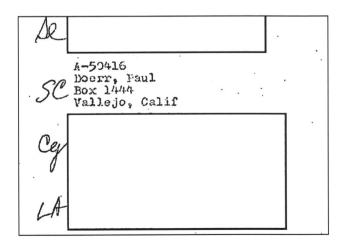

The number atop Doerr's name was a Minuteman ID, a number that the group issued to members. Once assigned this ID, Minutemen were expected to communicate through the number. The "A-" preceding the ID number was Doerr's Minutemen security classification. These various levels were documented in a bulletin entitled "Notes on Recruiting":

> The degree of frankness with which our members can recruit others will depend on the degree of security they are attempting to maintain for themselves.
>
> We classify our members into four security groups.
>
> A. Those who have been identified publicly or by law enforcement agencies as members of the Minutemen.
>
> B. Those persons not known as members of this organization but who are generally known as being patriots.
>
> C. Those persons who have kept their political beliefs hidden.
>
> D. Members who profess to be liberal for the purpose of infiltrating enemy organizations.

Now Kobek could see it.
He'd over-complicated.
Doerr didn't need mining journals or trade publications.
He didn't need *Pothole Blasting for Wildlife*.
To learn about ANFO, all he had to do was open his mail.

†

Kobek was living in a year when the United States Capitol was invaded by Far Right ideologues dressed as Northern California shamans. The writer's era labored beneath Internet cross-pollination of radicalism. But in 1969, there was a sharp division between the Far Right and the Far Left.

The Left doesn't know about ANFO until someone visits a farm. But the information circulates amongst the Right. If you're on the Left, opening a Minuteman bulletin is like putting your hands into a pile of dung. The Minutemen embodied an establishment that demanded destruction.

And then there was Zodiac. He's from the Right, maybe adopts a logo and a bomb formula from the Minutemen, but his letters also betray someone thinking and reading about the counterculture. Kobek couldn't guess at the number of people in 1969 California who easily co-existed in both worlds. He had no way to estimate. But he didn't imagine that it could've been more than 1000.

Kobek knew that some of these people were like Doerr.

They were Minutemen.

The evidence was there in "Practical Security Measures."

It was the bulletin's first item:

```
            PRACTICAL SECURITY MEASURES

     1.  Use deceptive measures.  Subscribe to one or more left-
wing periodicals or get on the mailing list of some "peace movement"
This will keep the postal inspectors guessing as to which side you
are really on.  See the December issue of On Target for names and
addresses of many left-wing organizations or write to National
Headquarters for this information.  While doing this our members
can be of great assistance in searching this left-wing literature
for names and addresses of fellow travelers and forwarding this
information for our Central Intelligence files.  We desperately
need people to assist in this work.  Please inquire as to detailed
instructions for such activity.
```

Which is exactly what Paul Doerr did.

He was a Minuteman who placed classified advertisements for communes in underground feminist newspapers.

chapter five

WANT LIST

KOBEK RETURNED to the idea that Zodiac was from Vallejo. Or the Vallejo area. He'd found supporting evidence in a 2007 report prepared by Kim Rossmo, who held a chair in Criminology at the University of Texas and directed the Center for Geospatial Intelligence and Investigation.

The report was titled *Geographical Profile: Zodiac Serial Murders.*

It appeared to have been authored, possibly without Rossmo being asked, for the San Francisco Police Department.

The first sentences read:

> Geographic profiling is a criminal investigative methodology that determines the most probable area of an offender's search base through an analysis of their crime locations....

> For the vast majority of criminals, their search base is their residence and the terms are sometimes used interchangeably. But in certain cases the search base for an offender's crimes is some other anchor point, such as their work site or immediate past residence.

Rossmo analyzed Zodiac's crimes and phone calls and letters and concluded that the killer was more familiar with Vallejo than San Francisco or Lake Berryessa.

And thus, probably, was from Vallejo.

†

In 1972, the United States Census Bureau published a population tract for the Vallejo-Napa area. The publication offered data collected during the decennial 1970 population census. It was a reasonably exact tally of the region's population. Less than a year from Zodiac's reign of terror.

The male population, aged 25 to 54, of Napa and Solano counties was 44,425. Solano County included Vallejo and Fairfield. Exclude African-American men and the number is 41,360. With individuals between the ages of 25 and 34 removed—language in the first cipher led police to believe that Zodiac was older and the cop who let Zodiac go described a White male adult between 35 and 45 years of age—and the race-adjusted population is 25,966.

In reality, both numbers would have been lower. The census tract did not estimate Asian-American or Latino populations.

If Zodiac lived around Vallejo, he was one of 25,966 to 41,360 individuals. In the raw, both numbers were huge. But could be winnowed on the basis of the letters.

Zodiac had to be someone with some rudimentary knowledge of encryption, he had to know something about ANFO. He had to have crude knowledge of electronic design and be reading *Popular Science*. He had to be an individual with some reason—recreational or religious—for dressing as a medieval executioner. Zodiac had to purchase guns via mail order.

This wasn't just a boast in the letters. Contemporary news reports state that the police attempted to trace Zodiac's guns through local dealers. And came up with nothing.

Any one of these vectors, alone, would not be enough to reduce the population pool. It was hard to imagining a large number of individuals exhibiting all of these qualities. Not just in Vallejo. Anywhere in America.

But in a pool of 25,966 to 41,360? There couldn't be more than ten. Even that felt generous.

Kobek'd found someone who fit all of these vectors, someone who worked in Vallejo, who lived near Vallejo, and who kept a mailbox in Vallejo. Who published his own cipher while referring to it as both a "cypher" and a "code." Who knew ANFO and used the same abbreviation as Zodiac and who, like Zodiac, didn't mention a primer. Who liked dressing in medieval drag. Who traded guns mail order. Who knew amateur electronic design. Who recommended articles from *Popular Science.* Who was a Minuteman.

Whatever this was, it was not the plan.

†

Kobek again wrote to Murdoch University and asked for copies of *Patter,* of which the library held two issues, and *Trove,* of which the library held one.

The library sent PDFs. Kobek started with what was labeled *Patter* #1. After the first few paragraphs, Kobek understood the nature of the thing.

Doerr was a member of the Fantasy Amateur Press Association. The group worked like any other Amateur Press Association: every few months, members received a mailing of fanzines produced by other members.

For each member to stay in good standing, they contributed some amount of money to cover the cost of postage. And, depending on their status within the group, some members were required to send in occasional copies of their own fanzine. Which were distributed to other members in the group's mailings.

Patter #1 was Doerr's contribution. Most of its text responded to other people's fanzines from the previous mailing. From internal references, Kobek dated the issue. Early-to-mid 1975. (Later, the writer would learn that this issue had been sent in the May 1975 FAPA mailing.)

Patter #1 contained Doerr's clearest reference to something that Kobek'd picked up through other sources. Somewhere around the end of 1974 or early 1975, Doerr purchased land in Mendocino County, in the town of Covelo. Doerr went there on weekends. He had a cabin without electricity or any modern conveniences. He lived an ersatz version of pioneer life. A man in wilderness. Or an approximation thereof.

Patter #1 had a curious response to *Alien Critic* #4, a fanzine from a previous mailing. It read like this:

> I wondered how many of these artificial pensises were bought by women. I received an ad recently (prices $20 to $70) for rubber(?) fullsize dolls for men (or women). One model was a female and another model had a motorized something in the vagina. The other was a male with enormous erection, cavity in the rear, open mouth, etc. I wonder if any of these are bought for use? I wonder if anyone has ever been "let down" with a terrible bang at the climactic moment?

In another response, Kobek saw this sentence: "A city cop parked at the curb pulled out after me, stopt me, gave me a ticket for driving 40mph (which, at the time & place would have been impossible."

This wasn't much, not really, but it was close to Zodiac's language in his cut-and-paste index card of 5 October 1970: "There are reports that city police pig cops are closeing in on me."

And then there was this:

> I have mentioned John Norman's series of adventure books on the counter-earth planet of Gor. In my opinion, the best of the series is Nomads of Gor. This is a nation of plains warriors who live in animal-drawn wagons with theer *[sic]* herds; freely, bravely, adventurously. I know of at least two groups of people who are trying to live like them in animal-drawn wagons, out in the back country away from all people, towns, roads, industry, etc.

Science Fiction is like any other subculture. It has its own language of neologisms and proper nouns that circulate amongst the initiated.

Gor is part of that language.

The books revolve around a central conceit. There is a tenth planet in our solar system, an equal of our own Earth. This planet is on the exact other side of the Sun. It can not be seen from Earth. Raiders from this tenth planet visit Earth and kidnap human beings. The kidnapped are brought to the tenth planet. The kidnapped women are enslaved. The men, if they can handle the counter-earth's brutal masculinity, become warriors. The Priest-Kings of Gor, an insectoid alien race who live in a mountain, have technology that ensures no one on the tenth planet ever ages. Unless they're violently killed. It was Paradise. And full of slaves.

The first *Gor* book was published in 1966. As the series went on, some of the kidnapped earthlings were ladies whose heads are filled with women's lib ideology. They arrive on Gor and are placed into slavery and learn that true feminism comes only from submission to one's master, or, as the Goreans sometimes put it, when she becomes the first to lick her chains. The women's lib falls away and the feminists become happy slaves. The bitter taste of the lash is sweet as sugar.

As early as 1975, the novels had occasioned a great deal of concern. Even then, if you wrote *Gor*, if you said that you liked the books, people wondered if something was a bit wrong.

Kobek thought that maybe Norman's novels had served as the source material for Zodiac. Slaves in paradise. The writer examined each *Gor* book published before July 1969. He found no corresponding language.

It was the second worst thing that he would do while researching Zodiac.

†

The final two pages of *Patter* #1 were singled-spaced sheets that included a vast list of everything Paul Doerr needed at the moment of composition. And all of the things that he was looking to sell or trade.

The wants were what one would expect of a man who owned a cabin without modern convenience. Tools. Woodstove. Forge. Anvil.

Most of WANT LIST's text was filled with books that Doerr sought to unload. The two pages looked like this:

```
paul doerr  box 1444  vallejo calif 94590      WANT LIST
tools;hand/blacksmith/farrier/farm/lumbering/metalworking/auto..woodstove..forge..anvil
..heavy vise..benchgrinder..treadle grindstone..aladdin & metal oillamps..bumperwinch..
bottlegastanks..rifle/shotgun..binoculars..riflescope..fruitcrusher & press..hammermill
..grain seperator..oxyacetaline torch..gas refrigerator..horse harness/implements..
bottlecutter..alternator & rechargable batteries..hives & honey extractor..gasoline gen-
erator..elect welder..canning jars & lids..brabant reversable plow..treadle sewing mach-
ine..chainhoist..chifferobe..gardentiller..sextant..barometer..chronometer..rdf..boat
compass..books/magazines;horsecare/horseshoeing/metalworking/blacksmithing/subsistance
farming/health/medicine/mother earth stuff..veterinary/medical/surgical tools..rolex
watch..good car radio..ham transmitter/receiver..44mag rifle..4 wheel drive pu & camper
or traveltrailer..small portable typewriter..cheap panel truck..chickenwire..books;
canfield,elements of farrier science/wiseman,complete horseshoeing/butler,principles o
horseshoeing/lungwitz,horseshoeing/adams,lameness in horses/army manual,the horseshoer
hoover,farriers science/armstrong 1918,commercial poultry raising/judd,poultry raising
mckay 1930,commercial poultry raising/butler,iron & forge work/bealer,art of blacksmit
hing/cooley,complete metalworking/clemens,handbook of railway blacksmithing/evans 1800s
young millrights & millers guide/holtzapffel 1900s,turning & mechanical manipulating/us
govt,ships medicine chest/us hospital corps handbook/potters new cyclopedia of botanica
drugs/national formulary/us dispensatory/us pharmacopoia..high mpg car..land
TO TRADE..wood frames for 28' sailboat..custom design/built 25' new oceansailboat..meta
detector..45# $145 bow..5 acres land 80 mi east of portland ore..concord radio diarctio
finder..stamps..zenith transoceanic radio..8mm 98 mauser..new savage 99 lever 308 rifl
mens gold rings;5 carot alexandra jewel(colorchanging red-blue),white zircon & 2 chips
black onyx diamond chip initial D..new longines stereo phono..68 ford falcon..30 tapes
7" reels 10 new..swords;blades 1x36,3x28..new sextants;davis,ebco,barker..antique gold
pocketwatch & carved horsehead fob..new down sleepingbag..new down jacket..5hp longshaf
seagull outboard motor..plans for 25' sailboat..new hunters headband batterylight..new
sears flyreel..davis handbearing compass..silva marine compass..baskethilt for sword..
dummy grenade..infkatable liferaft..crossman airpistol..throwing knives..scuba gear..li
ga scuba powerhead..delaval #15 cream seperator..prospectors chemical analysis kit..
nikonos camera..2 ft square fish breeding aquariums..
THE FOLLOWING order over $10/10% discount..over $25/25%..over $100/50% discount on cash
$5..dembeck,animals & men..heuvelmans,in the wake of the seaserpents..linton,tree of
culture..santillana,hamlets mill..cohane,the key...$4..gibson,complete illustrated book
of psychic science..benwell,sea enchantress..irving,amateur archaeologists handbook..
hawkins,stonehenge decodod..$3..ruppelt,report on unidentified flying objects..scully,
behind the flying saucers..gould,loch ness monster..sanderson,invisible residents..ger
hard,lower calif guidebook..lawrence,7 pillars of wisdom..cavendish,black arts..huson,
mastering witchcraft..hill,supernatural..shaver,hidden world..$2..leel,diary of a witc
daniken,gods from outer space..daniken,chariots of the gods..pinney,complete book of
cave exploration..$1..dring,earth is your spaceship..schenck,itzamna..myers,ancient
history..same,diff edition..myers,history of greece..grant,greece in age of pericles..
limebeer,greeks..limebeer.romans..caldwell,ancient world..zahl,to the lost world..wald
marco polo..hart,tiwi of n australia..clark,archaeology & society..campbell,jungle gow
..beals,rio grande to cape horn..cooke,blue book of crime..heinlein,stranger in a stra
land..wheeler,desert lake..troward,edinburgh lectures on mental science..winchester,
beyond this tumult..watson,indians of mesa verde..50¢..fate mag49-my,50-ag,52-a-n-d,53
j-ag,54-f,57-my,58-a,59-a-s-s,60-ag-s-n-d,61-j-f-mr-my-j-jl-ag-s-o,63-j-my-ag-s-d,65-
f-ag,66-a-jl-ag-n,67-s-s-d-d,68-j-f-f-jn-jl-o,69-j-ag-s-o-n-d,70-o-n-d,71-j-f-mr..sear
56-o-d,57-my-d,58-f-jn-ag,59-a-jn-ag,61-j-n-o-d,62-f-a-jn-ag,63-ag-o-d,64-mr-my-s-n,
65-j,66-f,67-jl-s,68-j-mr,69-j-mr-my-jl-n,70-j-n..mystic 53-n-n-n(i st ish),54-mr-ag,
55-f,56-my-jl..beyond 69-f-jl..explor unknown 61-jn,69-j-mr-o,70-mr..tomorror 55-wint..
flying saucers57-n-jn,58-f-d,59-my,61-my..fly sauc ufo peport 1967#2..levey,satanic
  want book LIVE,roger charnel,1962, prentice-hall pub
```

```
bible..gaer,how great religiond began...jones,life on other worlds..mannix,hellfire club.
smith,religious of man..traline,supernatural strangers..ley,satelites,rockets,outer s
space..jaffs,crucibles..woolley,digging up the past..barker,they knew too much..hamil-
ton,greek way..pike,strange ways of men..vroman,blood..storer,web of life..curie,madame
curie..colby,strangely enough..onstott,child of sun..keel,our haunted planet..anon, 7
maidens..stone,initiation rites..marco polo,travels..rigaud,secrets of voodoo..beller,
satellite..calder,after the 7th day..coleman,modern theories og universe..rapport,crust
of earth..calder,science in our lives..henry,strangest things in world..holzer,window
to past..braddeson,scientology..mead,coming of age in samoa..robinson,myth legends of
all nations..wells,time machine..collier,indians of america..true experiences in pro-
phecy..ikeda,japan..honegger,space..rapport,archaeology..alda,youth communes..hagen,
world of maya..binder,unsolved mysteries of past..david,flying saucer reader..sanderson
things..edwards,strangest of all..montague,man..saltman,ghosts & other strangers..
churchward,cosmic forces of mu..homer,odyssey..homer,iliad..vergil,aeneid..heinlein,
glory roys..buckland,pkt guide to supernatural..masin,kavins world..daniken,gods from
outer space..churchward,children of mu..robb,more true spirit stories..lewinsohn,hist-
ory of sexual custome..renault,fire from heaven..barnett,universe & einstein..sproul,
science book of human body..stone,lust for life..mokendrick,greek stones speak..edward
strange world..durant,philosophy..renault,mask of apollo..apuleus,golden ass..martello,
weird ways of witchcraft..caen,bagdad by bay..nzis,new zealand..evans..renault,
king must die..louys,collected works..hammel,getaway..daraul,secret societies..church-
ward,sacred symbols of mu..hervey,ufo over southern hemisphere..plutarch,lives..hoyle,
nature of universe..norman,gods demons ufos..huebner,power thru witchcraft..rand,virtu
of selfishness..rand,for new intellectual..rand,atlas shrugged..stine,earth satellites.
renault,last of wine..holiday,great orm of loch ness..gould,oddities..downing,bible &
flying saucers..earll,am revealed..renault,bull from sea..baney,search for sodom and
gomorrah..folsom,exploring american caves..jung,man and his symbols..gaddis,mysterious
lights & fires..edwards,flying saucers serious business..richards,t e lawrence..hunt,
exploring occult..smith,world of strange..fort,wild talents..fort,lo..fort,book ob
damned..fort,new lands..coleman,relativity..ley,for your information..evans,ufo report.
evans,natural history of nonsense..smith,strange abominable snowmen..steiger,strangers
from the sky..hornell,our fair flagellants..field,cinebiology..rohmen,romance of sor-
cery..kidrodstock,deportment and discipline of young men..auden,portable greek reader
..payne,splendor of greece..kitts,greeks..furneaux,worlds greatest mysteries..susann,
psychic world around us..lenders,excess of love..froumer,amsterdam..steiger,sex and
satanism..hamilton,mythology..motz,this is outer space..cottrell,bull of minos..bowra,
greek experience..adler,how love began..krutch,great cgain of life..hardon,great
religions of world..durrell,bitter lemons..lefebure,witness to witchcraft..fuller,
strange fate..decamp,world of dinosaurs..reiseberg,i dive for treasure..keel,strange
creatures from time and space..sanderson,more things..ston,witchcraft,today..wilkins,
strange mysteries of time and space..greene,100 great thinkers..daroul,secret societies
..gamow,one two three infinity..taylor,sex and marriage problems..wells,pkt history
of world..steiger,esp your sixth sense..ford, nothing so strange..doyle,edge of unknown
..tralins,children of the supernatural..henry,strangest things in the world..steiger,
strange guests..hurwood,vampires werewolves and ghouls..macklin,orbits of the unknown
..thiel,and there was light..gatland the inhabited universe..slaughter,your body and
your mind..broms,our emerging universe..goodwin,science book of space travel..plato,
dialogues..schlauch,gift of language..robinson,greek drama..mcbirne,the secret weapon
..salvidori,rise of modern communism..reichenbach,from copernicus to einstein..
the boat is double-end,twin-keel,slope-deck,stayless demountable mast, set for that
junkrig which has proved fastest and easiest for one man, built for cross-ocean work,
3/4" hull with fiberglass overlay, foam floatation, compartmented heavy anchor posts,
now, almost finished, completion cost if started today over $15,000, will consider
smaller boat and cash or land or house.
```

If *Pioneer* #9 made Kobek think that he was wading in deep shit, well, now the filth was in his lungs.

Start with the car.

On the day that Kobek became aware of Doerr, the writer learned the man's address in Fairfield, California. 225 E Utah Street. Kobek used

Google Maps and Google Street View. He looked at Doerr's home. A tract house built during the boom after World War Two. Bog-standard California.

Google Street View was part of the multinational conglomerate's attack on privacy. Google sent cars all over the world, cameras mounted on their roofs. The cameras photographed everyone's house. The pictures were available through Google Maps.

Kobek remembered when Sacramento arrested Joseph James DeAngelo as the East Area Rapist/Original Night Stalker. People on the Internet used Street View to look at DeAngelo's home. They employed a little known feature, allowing the user to view the full history of any given location. From the first privacy invasion program right through to the most recent privacy invasion. People on the Internet made a startling discovery. In a privacy invasion from February 2009, it was possible to watch DeAngelo driving up his street.

What the hell? What's the worst that can happen? thought Kobek. He opened the timeline of historical imagery and went to the oldest available privacy invasion. October 2007. Two months after Doerr died. An old dilapidated car was in the driveway. It was rusted, painted green, looked like it had been attacked by a posse of mallet-wielding rodeo clowns and then sat around forever.

2007 was early days for privacy invasion. Google used sub-par cameras. The image was too pixelated to identify the car's model. Kobek asked a friend who knew about cars. The friend could not identify the model.

But it was obvious that the car was an American compact car. In the 1950s, American cars were the size of boats. In 1961, the major manufacturers introduced smaller models. From styling and shape, it was clear that, whatever the make, the car in Doerr's driveway was from this period. Roughly.

It wouldn't have mattered. Not really. Except. The only known description of Zodiac's car came from Michael Mageau. He'd given this statement, while in the hospital and recovering from the attack at Blue Rock Springs on 4 July 1969.

Mageau described Zodiac's car like this:

Michael states that as the vehicle drove off he only saw the rear portion of it, this rear portion appearing to be a vehicle similar to or the same type as [Darlene Ferrin's] car, a Corvair. It had a very similar color, possibly a little bit lighter brown. It had a California license, however he could not tell what the numbers were.

A great number of Zodiac researchers read this passage and thought that Zodiac drove a Corvair. Another compact car from the American 1960s. But Mageau hadn't said it was a Corvair. It might have been. Or was a vehicle like it. In the dark of the parking lot, with no overhead lights. Shot through the neck and jaw. Interviewed while pumped full of morphine.

When Mageau said the car was like a Corvair, what he'd meant was: a compact car.

And here was a compact car in Doerr's driveway.

It looked like this:[3]

---

3   Reader, apologies for above photo's quality. And consolations for the fact that this experiment is not repeatable. Several months after Kobek made this discovery, a resident on Doerr's old street opted to have their house removed from Street View. This process results in Google blurring out the requested house in the most recent photograph. And removing previous historical timeline imagery. But one can rest assured that the photographs never escape the multi-national conglomerate's deepest archives. Further imagery at: http://jarettkobek.com/car/ (See Appendix E.)

On that first night, Kobek thought this coincidence. Who holds on to a car for forty years? Who keeps an old junked thing around for that long? Kobek imagined that Doerr bought the car later in life with the hopes of fixing it up. And never got around to it.

But, now, as he read WANT LIST, Kobek saw this amongst the items:

"..68 ford falcon.."

The writer returned to Google Street View's October 2007 privacy invasion. He then Googled images of 1968 Ford Falcons. He compared these images with the car in the privacy invasion. Doerr had gotten one thing wrong. The car in his driveway was not a 68 Ford Falcon. It was the 1967 model.

In 1968, Ford modified the Falcon's rear detailing, replacing its rounded taillights with squares. From the low quality privacy invasion, Kobek could make out rounded taillights.

In the early months of 1968, Ford continued to sell the '67 model. Anyone could go and buy one off the lot. Brand new. Like an American. If you bought a '67 model in 1968, you'd call it a '68 Ford Falcon. It seemed possible that Doerr had bought this car new. And kept it for forty years. If this happened, then he'd owned the car on 31 July 1969.

Kobek tried to imagine what Mageau would have seen in the darkness of the parking lot with blood leaking out of his body. It couldn't have been much. Taillights and a general sense of size. Darlene Ferrin owned a 1963 Corvair. The model had four lights on its rear, but two were turn signals. The taillights were rounded. Kobek researched every generation of every make of every American compact car from 1961 to 1969. With the exception of the 1965 to 1967 Ford Falcons, none had taillights that resembled those of a 1963 Corvair.

In the same chunk of text mentioning the Ford Falcon, Doerr listed a great number of weapons. Including guns. The full text looked like this:

```
TO TRADE..wood frames for 28' sailboat..custom design/built 25' new oceansailboat..meta
detector..45# $145 bow..5 acres land 80 mi east of portland ore..concord radio dierctio
finder..stamps..zenith transoceanic radio..8mm 98 mauser..new savage 308 rifl
lens gold rings;5 carot alexandra jewel(colorchanging red-blue),white zircon & 2 chips
black onyx diamond chip initial D..new longines stereo phono..68 ford falcon..30 tapes
7" reels 10 new..swords;blades 1x36,3x28..new sextants;davis,ebco,barker..antigue gold
pocketwatch & carved horsehead fob..new down sleepingbag..new down jacket..5hp longsha
seagull outboard motor..plans for 25' sailboat..new hunters headband batterylight..new
sears flyreel..davis handbearing compass..silva marine compass..baskethilt for sword..
dummy grenade..infkatable liferaft..crossman airpistol..throwing knives..scuba gear..1
ga scuba powerhead..delaval #15 cream seperator..prospectors chemical analysis kit..
nikonos camera..2 ft square fish breeding aquariums..
```

Kobek clocked the following: (1) 45# $145 bow. (2) 8mm 98 Mauser. (3) New savage 99 lever 38 rifle. (3) Swords. (4) Blades 1x36, 3x28. (5) Crossman airpistol. (6) Throwing knives. (7) Baskethilt for swords.

Doerr advertised his willingness to commit a felony. In print. And sent the advertisement out to an untold number of people.

Then there were the books. There were so many books in WANT LIST that the prospect of examining them was like a yawning abyss of madness, like the moment in a Lovecraft story when the protagonist apprehends the nature of cosmic entities whose multidimensional existence outpaces the human mind's ability to comprehend that apprehension.

The data dump of Cthulhu.

Kobek scanned the titles. He would investigate anything that stood out. Thirty minutes in, something caught his eye:

"..pike, strange ways of man.."

The writer knew enough about mid-century publishing to guess that the book was a collection of essayistic chapters about the quote, strange, unquote customs of people who did not live in the USA or Western Europe. He thought of the Little List letter and how the most baroque of its tortures—people in cages and fed salt beef—was lifted from *Macleod of Dare*.

Maybe something akin to this would be found in E. Royston Pike's *The Strange Ways of Man: Rites and Rituals and Their Incredible Origins*. The book was published in 1967.

There was an online copy. Kobek moved through its pages until he came to Chapter Five. "The Craft of the Head-Hunters." And it was in this chapter, on Page 61, that he found the following:

> edly to please the women. Among some tribes it was said to be an indispensable necessity for a young man to procure a skull before he could marry: the fact that a man was brave enough to go head-hunting spoke well for his ability to protect and provide for a wife and family. Some tribes believed that the persons whose heads they had taken would become their slaves in the after-life: head-hunting was thus a wise precaution for the future. A vendetta or blood-feud was a very common reason for

The context and the language was a near duplicate of Zodiac's first cipher. "All the [text missing] I have killed will become my slaves I will not give you my name because you will try to slow down or stop my collecting of slaves for my afterlife."

Pike named his source material. Kobek tracked down the old publications, most from the Victorian era. Pike had changed their language. None referred to slaves in the afterlife. On page 141 of Volume 2 of Henry Ling Roth's *The Natives of Sarawak and British North Borneo,* this paragraph appeared:

> "The Uru Ais believe that the persons whose head's they take will become their slaves in the next world." (Brooke Low.) Bishop Chambers speaking to the Banting Dyaks of Heaven in accordance with Christian ideas was once interrupted by one of them to tell him of "their belief, that the persons whose heads had been taken in this world would in the next become the servants of the warriors who had taken them." (Miss. Field, 1868, p. 222.) The Ida'an also believe "That all whom they kill in this world shall attend them as slaves after death... From the same principle they will purchase a slave, guilty of any capital crime, at five-fold his value, that they may be his executioners." (Dalrymple, p. 42.)

Pike's book was the first time that the phrase had appeared in the context of a murderer and their victims. It was published around May 1967. Two years and some change before Zodiac's first cipher. Kobek was in this mess because he thought that his friend Dave might recognize the phrasing. Dave had given Kobek the info to find Doerr. Doerr had given Kobek the info to find *Strange Ways of Man.*

Chapter Four of Pike's book was about the Thuggee, a quasi-mythological sect of murderers who roamed the Indian sub-continent during British colonialism. Since publication of *Strange Ways*, scholarship had begun to doubt the existence of the Thuggee. They'd become seen as the Satanic Panic of the Raj. Pike wrote before this historical revision. He relayed everything that he could find. In Chapter Four, on Page 55, six pages before slaves in the afterlife, this text appears:

> speak.' Few answered; those who did reply merely requested as a dying favour that their bodies on being taken down might be burnt. One hardened villain, however, as he was turning to leave the court, disturbed the solemnity of the scene by muttering, 'Ah, you have got it all your own way now, but let me find you in Paradise, and I will be avenged!'

Kobek had found the apparent source material. It came through learning about Doerr. Just like with the Minutemen. It was what would happen if you discovered a credible Zodiac. Details of the suspect's life would enhance knowledge of original mysteries. No information was being bent. There was no hearsay. There was no attempt to solve a cipher. New and easily available information solved old mysteries.

In a way, this was the easiest route to Zodiac. Find the source material for slaves in the afterlife and the source material for the crosshairs, the two things predating the Zodiac tradename, determine that these are not common materials, find a person in possession of both, discover that they have a knowledge of cryptography, and you've found Zodiac.

And here was Paul Doerr. A Minuteman who owned *Strange Ways.* And a knew a thing or two about codes and cyphers.

Strange Ways had appeared in 1967. Hardcover. A paperback in 1970. Kobek couldn't tell which edition Doerr was trying to sell. If it were the latter, Doerr might have come upon the book after Zodiac sent in the 31 July 1969 cipher. But even this was murky. Doerr could have owned the hardcover and the paperback.

Kobek decided this was unnecessary obstruction.

A Zodiac mystery had been solved.

Because of Doerr.

†

Kobek suspected that Murdoch University had mislabeled the issues of *Patter.* #1 contained references to at least one previous issue.

(Later, the writer learned that this assumption was correct. Doerr failed to number either issue. What Murdoch University labeled #1 was composed and distributed after what the institution labeled #2. The earlier publication, Murdoch's #2, appeared in the February 1975 FAPA mailing.)

In *Patter* #2, Doerr wrote: "its not easy to reduce. ive dropped to 150 and plan eventually to get down to 140-145. its healther im told. where did you say that you found all those females? i could do with just one...the right one...out in the mountains."

Every description of Zodiac suggested a man between 180 and 220 pounds. If Doerr was reducing, then from what weight? How much do you lose before you trumpet the loss in a fanzine?

Then there was this: "ive been hunting for a copy of vampirella comix. ive heard it was pretty good."

Kobek thought of the Halloween Card. Kobek thought of *Tim Holt* #30. Kobek thought of something in the August 1968 *The National Fantasy Fan.*

The passage read like this: "Paul Doerr wants information about clubs and apas, some of which should be in the article on apas in this issue; and says he wants to reach the comic collectors. The best way to reach comic collectors, I suppose, is to subscriber to a number of comic fanzines."

Doerr wasn't just into Science Fiction.
Doerr was into comic books.

†

On 27 October 1970, Zodiac mailed what has come to be known as the Halloween Card to Paul Avery, the reporter at the *San Francisco Chronicle*. It looked like this:

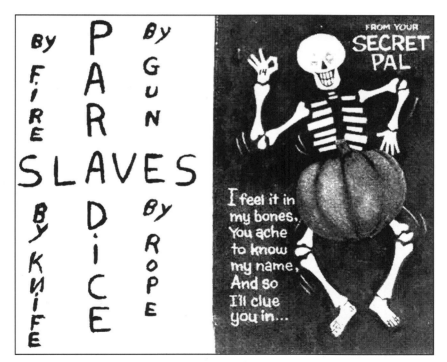

(exterior)

(interior)

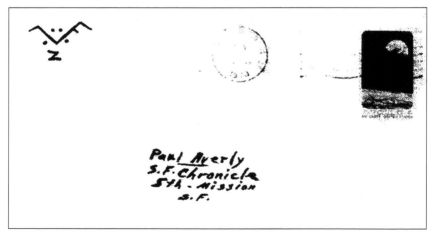

(envelope)

The exterior skeleton was part of the original design. The interior skeleton was a Halloween decoration glued in by Zodiac. The pumpkin atop the exterior skeleton was also glued by Zodiac. The Secret Pal writing was original design. Zodiac added the following: the 14 written on the exterior skeleton's hand, 4-TEEN written above the interior skeleton, PEEK-A-BOO YOU ARE DOOMED!, twelve of the interior's thirteen eyes, the V symbol, the Z accompanied by the Zodiac symbol, and the PARADICE/SLAVES acrostic on the card's exterior.

The latter quoted from the cover of *Tim Holt* #30, a comic book published in 1952.

The relevant detail looked like this:

As soon as the card was received, it was perceived as a threat against Paul Avery, the *San Francisco Chronicle* writer to whom it was addressed.

But it'd been mailed 27 October 1970.

That morning, Avery published an article. A 'JACK THE RIPPER' THEORY ON SLAYINGS. It was about a new pattern of killings in San Francisco. African-American women sex workers butchered. Assailant unknown, not captured until several years later. The most recent victim discovered on 24 October 1970, four days before the article.

Her name was Jackie Truss. She was 16-years old.

Her body was found in Presidio Heights on Laurel between Jackson and Pacific. One block north, four blocks east of where Zodiac killed Paul Stine. Avery linked the slaying to the London crimes of 1888. His article's final paragraph read like this:

> During the year he prowled Whitechapel, the Ripper would stalk his victim, kill and disappear into the fog. He then would post letters to police and newspapers boasting of his latest slaying. After the seventh murder he was never heard from again.

Which sounds an awful lot like someone else.

And that someone was reading.

The evidence is the card itself.

Beyond the timing, Zodiac's added details on the card make sense in the context of the article. Jackie Truss was disemboweled in Presidio Heights. Zodiac glues a cartoon pumpkin over the exterior skeleton's torso. It looked to Kobek as though the cracks on the interior skeleton's head were drawn on by Zodiac. There were no other cracks anywhere on the skeleton. Truss's skull had been crushed. 4-TEEN. Jackie Truss was 16-years old.

The card was more important than anyone realized. If Zodiac sent it after seeing Avery's article, and it was postmarked that same day, then all of Zodiac's source material—the greeting card and *Tim Holt* #30—were items that were on hand. That Zodiac owned. Or were in his house.

Kobek knew that Zodiac had guns, that the killer had a hood, an American compact car, a knife. But beyond vague ballistics reports, there was nothing to know about the guns. The hood couldn't be traced. Good luck with the knife. The car is a ghost in a wounded boy's eyes.

In 2013, online Zodiac researcher Tahoe27 discovered the *Tim Holt* connection. Kobek was not surprised that its implications hadn't been absorbed. It was so recent.

†

For all of their obsessiveness, the comic book people had never figured out a reliable method of establishing scarcity. The best attempt arrived in 1989 with *The Photo Journal Guide to Comic Books.*

Authored by Ernst and Mary Geber, *Photo Journal* was a two volume edition visually reproducing the covers of almost every comic book published between the years 1935 and 1965. But the Gebers went beyond the camera. They graded each individual issue of each comic book title along a Scarcity Index. Every issue was assigned a number between 1 and 10.

1 stood for **Very common**. In Ernest Geber's words: "likely every comic store in the country has copies." 10 stood for **Unique.** In Geber's words, "Less than 5 known copies in existence."

The Gebers assigned *Tim Holt* #30 the midpoint value of 5. It stood for *Less than average.* Geber described the ranking: "Generally between 200 and 1000 still exist, this one is more difficult to find. Diligence should pay off after several weeks and checking with most dealers and following most ads in comic newspapers."

After the Internet transformed the sales of back issue comics, there was some debate about the Geber Scarcity Index.

How accurate are the numbers in an era when eBay has unearthed scores of previously unknown issues? No one had a good answer but some people came up with an ad hoc solution. The Geber estimates, on the whole, remained broadly accurate. But, for safety's sake, one should take their numbers and double them. It's not perfect, but it's workable. The approach would mean that there are somewhere between 400 to 2000 copies of *Tim Holt* #30. In the whole wide world.

A handful of people proposed another metric: determining how often a book appears in online auctions. Between 2006 and 2019, eight copies of *Tim Holt* #30 were offered by Heritage Auctions. In contrast, the archives of Heritage Auctions lists 25 sales of *Superman* #76, published a month before *Tim Holt* #30 and also receiving a 5 in the Scarcity Index. The disparity suggests an underestimation of *Tim Holt* #30, that it might better be ranked as 6, or **Uncommon,** described as: "Between 50 to 200 still exist." Double these numbers, and one arrives at the rough estimate of 100 to 400 copies of *Tim Holt* #30. In the whole wide world.

But there was a problem with online auctions.

In December 2013, Tahoe27 identified *Tim Holt* #30 as Zodiac source material. Word trickled out. From 2014, any auction is tainted. People who'd bought *Tim Holt* #30 in 2003 for $15 now possessed something they could off-load onto a new market. By 2021, copies were moving for in the $750 to $3000 range. And the prices kept rising. Which meant some copies were showing up in online auctions more than once, skewing the numbers. Pump and dump.

It was possible, just, to get a sense of the pre-Tahoe27 rarity.

In response to Doerr's inquiry, *The National Fantasy Fan* recommended that he subscribe to *Newfangles*, a fanzine published by a husband and wife team Don and Maggie Thompson. History has come to see the Thompsons as main progenitors of comic book fandom. They were there before almost anyone else.

The June 1970 *Newfangles* contains Don Thompson's "Rummage List." Comics that he was looking to off-load. One item is *Tim Holt* #11, the first appearance of the original Ghost Rider. It proves that copies of *Tim Holt* were traded in the Zodiac moment.

Newfangles #53, dated November 1971, contains Thompson's comics WANT LIST. At the very bottom of the page, he lists TIM HOLT. He's looking for issues #20 through #31. Kobek could see the import. The June 1970 issue makes it apparent that Thompson is collecting *Tim Holt*, has at least one issue to spare. And seventeen months later, roughly a year after Zodiac's Halloween Card, in November 1971, Thompson still doesn't have a copy of #30. And he's one of the best connected people in comics.

Another indicator came on 17 June 1995, when Sotheby's held an auction called *Comic Books and Comic Art*. In the catalog, there's lot #647:

□ 647
Group of M.E. Western Comic Books, comprising *Red Mask* Nos. 42–44, 46–54; *Straight Arrow* Nos. 2–55; *Tim Holt* Nos. 18–24, 26–29, 31, 32, 33, 36–39, 40; *Durango Kid* Nos. 1–27, 29–41; *Best of the West* Nos. 1–12; and *B-Bar-B Riders* Nos. 1–13, 16, 17, 19, 20; *A.C.G. fine plus—71.* (approximately 155)

Provenance:
The Mohawk Valley Collection
                              $2,000–4,000

No #30.

None of the above was hard evidence. But it did seem to indicate that #30 was a rare comic. During the Zodiac moment and after.

†

Kobek believed establishing scarcity was of the utmost importance.

The reason was simple.

Tim Holt #30 is the sole determinant of the Zodiac era. Regardless of Doerr or any other suspect. The comic is the single most important thing known about the killer. And it's rarer than gold, if not as valuable. There are between 100 and 2000 copies. In the whole wide world.

This is what *Tim Holt* meant: for someone to be a plausible candidate as the killer, or at least the letter writer, there must be a demonstration of how and why they are in contact with an object that is rarer than gold. That exists in 100 to 2000 copies. That, in 1970, almost everyone considers as less than garbage. It's a practical disqualifier for most of the named suspects.[4]

The Gebers estimated that the number of back issue collectors in 1970 was roughly 2,500 individuals. For the entire country. 0.00122% percent of the United States population. Like the Scarcity Index, it's ad hoc. But as with the Scarcity Index, the estimate is roughly reflective of reality.

In 1970, Brooklyn teenager Joe Brancantelli published *Fandom's Fans*. It was a Who's Who of comics fandom. Listing collectors' names and addresses and interests. Brancantelli gathered these names through a simple mechanism. He advertised in other fanzines.

Not everyone had responded. Paul Doerr isn't listed. Brancantelli received responses from exactly 431 people in the United States. There was a broad self-selecting mechanism in the numbers, but Kobek had a feeling that the distribution by location was, roughly, proportionally representative of the overall distribution of comic book fans throughout America. The largest section in *Fandom's Fans* was New York City, while some states, like Alabama, were in the single digits. California had 51 people, roughly 12.53% of 431.

For the sake of argument, Kobek assumed that the Gebers' 2500 number was accurate. Which it was not. And he assumed that the 12.53% percentage of California collectors was correct. Which could not proven. Calculating the ratio, it came out to 313 comic book collectors in California. This number wasn't too bad. In 1970, the very first San Diego Comic Convention had about 300 attendees. For safety's sake, Kobek doubled the number and assumed there were 626 comic book collectors in California in 1970. This was about 0.0031% of California's population.

In the year of 1970, the entire population of Napa and Solano counties, unadjusted for race or sex or age, was 249,081. And 0.0031% of that number was 7.7 individuals. With women removed, the number was 3.9 individuals. Accounting only for males between the ages of 24 and 54, the number was 1.37.

The numbers were guess work. But Kobek thought that they got to a certain truth. In the whole of the Vallejo area, there was probably no more

---

4   This does not include Arthur Leigh Allen. He was, apparently, a reader of Science Fiction.

than five collectors of back issue comic books. Probably two to three. Maybe just one. Find whoever collects *Tim Holt* and you've found Zodiac.

Kobek lived in a time when everyone knew there was an inherent value in the old ratty publications. Prior to about 1975, this idea wasn't on the radar. Most people bought the things and threw them out. In 1954, a psychiatrist convinced the United States Senate that comic books caused juvenile delinquency and sexual disorder. It lead to a huge number of publications being destroyed for American purity. The Gebers estimate a less than 2% survival rate for comic books published in 1952.

October 1970 is eighteen years from the publication of *Tim Holt* #30. It's not impossible that someone could find an old junked copy up in the attic, anything is possible, but this is a possibility in the same way that being hit by lighting is a possibility. A far likelier scenario is that Zodiac's copy came through the nascent channels serving collectors. Or that he bought it when it appeared and kept it for nearly two decades.

And if, by some chance, lightning does strike, and it's found at a yard-sale? One still has to make the decision. One still has to buy it. One still has to take it home. One still has to decide that this object is worth consideration. Most people, back then, couldn't see it. They looked at a comic book and saw trash.

In 1970, anyone with *Tim Holt* #30 has made a consumer choice.

They are a collector.

The knowledge was there with the first cipher.

Slaves in the afterlife.

†

Trove #1 was dedicated to treasure hunting. It established that Doerr understood maps. It wasn't proof of Zodiac, but it suggested someone capable of drawing a modified Zodiac logo over Mt. Diablo. Which had happened with the letter 26 July 1970 letter.

And then Kobek read the following:

A while ago I was reading one of the treasure hunting slicks and saw a note which rung a bell. After a few months researching in the local libraries, I drove out into the country near Lake Berryessa and located some landmarks and dug up a small posthole bank containing a handful of gold coins including some California gold coins, so it can be done, with luck and effort.

There it was.
Lake Berryessa.

chapter six

from the hell
beneath the hells

NOW KOBEK DUG as if he were hunting posthole banks. He discovered an article by Doerr in the June 1972 issue of *The Explorer's Journal*.

"A New Cave is Found." It was a short account of Doerr exploring Heater Cave in Calaveras County, southeast of Sacramento. Doerr went inside with associates from the National Speleological Society's Diablo Grove chapter. The article included an image of its author, flash photography taken in darkness from a strange angle. Doerr stands beside a naturally formed pillar, wears a safety helmet, gloves, and a hooded sweatshirt. Other than demonstrating that Doerr had an unusually large chin, the photograph was useless for physical identification. But it did indicate one thing. Doerr was neither a giant nor a dwarf. His height was perfectly average. Like every description of Zodiac.

Buried deep in Google results, Kobek saw that Doerr contributed to *REHUPA* #15. This was a mailing of another Amateur Press Association, one dedicated to the life and works of the Texas writer Robert E. Howard, a contributor to *Weird Tales* and best known for creating Conan the Barbarian.

Unrelated to Zodiac, Kobek had just finished reading the autobiography of S.T. Joshi, the foremost scholar of the weird tale and the man who had, with a little help from his friends, revolutionized academic study of H.P. Lovecraft. It occurred to Kobek that he could kill two birds with one stone. He sent an email to Joshi, complimenting the book and asking if the scholar knew anyone with a copy of *REHUPA* #15. Joshi wrote back and suggested that Kobek get in touch with Bobby Derie, who'd written a book that the writer admired. *Sex and the Cthulhu Mythos.*

Kobek sent Derie an email, explaining that Doerr was a distant relative and wondering if there were any way to get a copy of *REHUPA* #15.

That night, Derie sent the PDF.

†

REHUPA #15 was dated May 1975.

Its final two pages were labeled "Paul Doerr's Supplement." Unlike all of Doerr's other work, the supplement was handwritten. Doerr explained why: "Please forgive the format but [a previous REHUPA mailing] just arrived thanx to someone, and I just wanted to get into #15. I am at 'work' locked in my office, sans typewriter, busily (they think) preparing documents on the repair of a nuclear submarine. I work at Mare Island Naval Shipyard. Don't let anyone tell you we aren't at war, and suffering occasional hurts."

An impulse mailing, tossed off. There wasn't anything new in the content, not really, just Doerr recycling the same stories that appeared in his letters and fanzines. Another mention of John Norman and *Gor*. Another mention of comic books. A notable paragraph read like this:

> How many of you can handle a sword, spear, lance, bow, etc
> Anyone want to hear how I hunted tigre with sword +
> spear? I got one but I doubt if I'll put too much time
> on the opposite end of a blade, with one of the big cats
> on the other. They object to being punctured. I've often
> considered going after a boar the same way. I imagine
> it could be a chore too. a "little" 100 pound pig is
> big and solid, as you know if you've ever tried to
> move one around. Those hides are packed solid with
> pig. I can imagine a full grown boar with his big
> tusks facing me. exciting, you might say.

Kobek was fighting confirmation bias. He couldn't help thinking that this sounded like Zodiac's first decrypted cipher. And it exhibited a verbal tic that appeared in all of Doerr's writing. He was always hunting things. He was hunting new weapons, books, comics, farming equipment. The final sentence reminded the writer of a line in the 9 November 1969 letter: "I was leaving fake clews for the police to run all over town with, as one might say, I gave the cops som bussy work to do to keep them happy."

Kobek did not believe in handwriting analysis, felt that the principal point of the pseudoscience was putting poor people in prison. The technique worked on the assumption that any given document was the crystallization of individual. But the pseudoscience lacked context, lacked evidence of everything written before, all the pieces of paper that went unseen, the things that weren't mailed, items thrown into the trash. Each new document was the last installment in a continuum. And the handwriting analyst could only see a fragment of time.

Kobek believed that it was possible to ignore the letterforms. He'd noticed that Doerr had the habit of ending lists of objects with "etc." There was an example in the section about hunting tigres: "How many of you can handle a sword, spear, lance, bow, etc." Another *REHUPA* #15 example read like this: "If anyone is interested in recipes for preparing whole grain, acorns, etc into food, I will gladly respond."

Zodiac had done the same thing. 9 November 1969: "... when I commit my murders, they shall look like routine robberies, killings of anger, & a few fake accidents, etc." 28 April 1970: "Every one else has those buttons like [peace], black power, melvin eats blubber, etc."

There was another tic. When Zodiac wrote, he tended to substitute the word "and" with ampersands that resembled plus symbols. Like this:

Examples of this symbol had appeared in the 20 December 1969 letter to Melvin Belli. In this communication, Zodiac employed a different script. It was neater, more controlled, radically altered from the previous letters.

For comparison, here are the first three lines of both the 15 October 1969 letter and the Belli letter:

Dear Melvin

This is the Zodiac speaking I wish you a happy Christmass.

This is the Zodiac speaking. I am the murderer of the taxi driver over by

The first page of the Little List letter starts in the Belli script and, as the killer writes more, degenerates into the more familiar Zodiac script:

This is the Zodiac speaking

Being that you will not wear some nice ⊕ buttons, how about wearing some nasty ⊕ buttons. Or any type of ⊕ buttons that you can think up. If you do not wear any type of ⊕ buttons I shall (on top of every thing else) torture all 13 of my slaves that I have wateing for me in Paradice. Some I shall tie over ant hills and watch them scream + twich and squirm. Others shall have pine splinters driven under their nails + then burned. Others shall be placed in cages + fed salt beef untill they are gorged then I shall listen to their pleass for water and I shall laugh at them. Others will hang by their thumbs + barn in the sun then I will rub them down with deep heat to warm

Even though Zodiac used a different script in the Belli letter, he'd kept the ampersands. They looked like this:

Years earlier, Kobek had picked up a little knowledge about the history of American handwriting. Throughout the 19th Century, children were instructed in what is known as the Spencerian Method. It's the flowery cursive found in just about every major document prior to the 1910s. The Spencerian Method relies on hand and finger movement to form letters.

The advent of the typewriter changed how people thought about writing. Another method developed. The Palmer Method of Business Writing. Its innovation was a reliance on arm movement to form looping letters. It put less strain on the hand, and, in theory, allowed the practitioner to compose at the same speed as a typewriter. From about the 1910s until somewhere in the 1950s, this was the dominant method of American handwriting instruction. Then the focus shifted away from early instruction in cursive to what is technically called manuscript but better known as printing. Simple block letters. The dominant method of the day was Zaner-Bloser, although its prominence has been overstated. In later grades, children were still taught to write in longhand, but as has become obvious with time, the shift to manuscript had the effect of murdering cursive. Good riddance.

The Little List letter is the Rosetta Stone of Zodiac's handwriting. As Zodiac's writing degenerates across the first page, he demonstrates that the Belli script is unnatural.

The Belli script is an exact duplicate of the letter forms taught in Zaner-Bloser. Some of Zodiac's letters are less well formed than others, but with the exception of the Z in Zodiac, they're all replicas of what was being taught to children in elementary school. The Zaner-Bloser method did not teach its disciples to use an ampersand in the place of the word "and." The symbol's usage is a holdover from the Spencerian period. And it's something that shows up in the letters of people who learned Palmer.

This was what Kobek meant by stylistic tics. A thing that Zodiac can't stop doing. He can fake a new script, he can write in elementary school manuscript, but he can't change what he learned in the beginning. Spencerian ampersands appear in Zaner-Bloser.

No one ever identified, successfully, Zodiac's handwriting as belonging to an individual. There was an obvious reason.

All of Zodiac's handwriting is fake.

But there are tics. It's possible to tell that Zodiac was trained in Palmer. The method instructs its pupils to base their looping lower case Ds and Gs on the lower case A. There's variation in each individual letterform but examine enough Zodiac examples and the Ds are pure Palmer, they've got the same base form as the lower case As, and the while the writer modifies the loop on the G, he's using A as its basis. Unlike the Belli script, the default handwriting is almost always slanted. The Palmer Method required turning the paper at an angle. It was a necessary condition for relieving tension and allowing fluidity of movement.

The following illustration demonstrates the technique:

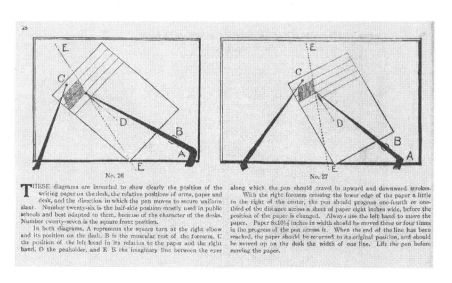

No. 26   No. 27

THESE diagrams are intended to show clearly the position of the writing paper on the desk, the relative positions of arms, paper and desk, and the direction in which the pen moves to secure uniform slant. Number twenty-six is the half-side position mostly used in public schools and best adapted to them, because of the character of the desks. Number twenty-seven is the square front position.

In both diagrams, A represents the square turn at the right elbow and its position on the desk, B is the muscular rest of the forearm. C the position of the left hand in its relation to the paper and the right hand, D the penholder, and E B the imaginary line between the eyes along which the pen should travel in upward and downward strokes.

With the right forearm crossing the lower edge of the paper a little to the right of the center, the pen should progress one-fourth or one-third of the distance across a sheet of paper eight inches wide, before the position of the paper is changed. Always use the left hand to move the paper. Paper 8x10½ inches in width should be moved three or four times in the progress of the pen across it. When the end of the line has been reached, the paper should be returned to its original position, and should be moved up on the desk the width of one line. Lift the pen before moving the paper.

This is exactly what Zodiac does. With the exception of when he uses Zaner-Bloser, he always writes at an angle. The default Zodiac script is the manuscript printing of a man who first learned Palmer.

The 9 November 1969 letter contained four instances of Zodiac lapsing into Palmer cursive. Two were on the fourth page. These occurred when Zodiac drew the horizontal bar of a T followed by an H.

They looked like this:

On the final page, Zodiac only wrote twenty-five words. Two of them, the word "am" and the final two letters of the name "Zodiac," lapse into Palmer cursive, into what is presumably Zodiac's actual handwriting:

To prove that I am the Zodiac, Ask the Vallejo cop about my electric gun sight which I used to start my collecting of slaves.

The adoption of Palmer and Zaner-Bloser varied by school district, so these stylistic relics do not allow an exact gauge of Zodiac's age. But the ampersand is older, it's much less common with writers who learned penmanship after 1950. If the younger generations do substitute a symbol for "and," it's a simple plus symbol. +. A best guess is that Zodiac learned to write in the 1930s or 1940s.

In *REHUPA* #15, Doerr's handwriting is absolute Palmer Method. He's not the clearest writer but the letterforms are exactly those taught during the 1930s and 1940s.

In many of Doerr's published letters, Kobek had noticed that the typeset representations often included a plus sign instead of "and." Kobek had seen no example of this in Doerr's typed fanzines. Which made sense. People write differently with different implements. In *REHUPA* #15, Doerr's got the ampersands.

They look like this:

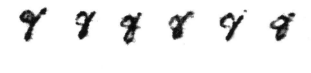

†

The special collections of the University of Iowa held three Doerr fanzines that Kobek had not seen. *Pioneer* #1, *Unknown* #19, and something labeled, simply, "Paul Doerr."

The writer got in touch with the library and was sent PDF scans.

"Paul Doerr" was *Pioneer* #10.

One could forgive the mislabeling. Doerr didn't announce the fanzine's title or issue until halfway through its sixteen pages.

The publication starts with a description of Doerr's plan to buy 10 acres of land in Northern California.

He wants to live on this land and hunt Bigfoot.

Doerr wrote that he had a way to capture Bigfoot. He did not elucidate the method. Doerr wrote about seeing UFOs through his bedroom window in Fairfield.

And then there was a long jag about prehistoric survivals, two book reviews, and something about Doerr visiting the Headless Valley along Canada's Nahanni River.

Just before the mid-point break, Doerr returned to the topic of postal rates. Which would affect the nature of *Pioneer*. The passage read like this:

Costs keep rising. Amateur publications continue to cease publication with no warning. Many come out only once or twice a year and may only consist of a single sheet. Living expenses still rise. I expect to not be working in the future if the job-cutting continues. Some of my writing has been questioned by various authorities (and some of my other activities as well), so this will be an excellent opportunity to lose me legally. Postage is high and is expected to higher. The same for paper costs, etc. My boat building and equipping costs are increasing. I am trying to save some money for expenses and living later. I have been doing a lot of figuring, and between tears, my crying towell *[sic]* is soaking wet, I have come to some decisions, which I dont *[sic]* particularly like, but which may stave off disaster for a while longer.

†

Some of my writing has been questioned by the various authorities.
And some of my other activities as well.
Doerr liked to boast about his exploits.
He made things up. That much was obvious.
Except. The last authentic Zodiac letter was sent on 13 March 1971 to the *Los Angeles Times*. In this letter, the killer claims Cheri Jo Bates, the Riverside co-ed who was murdered in 1966, and who, in 1970, was spuriously attributed to Zodiac. In the letter, he writes: "I do have to give them credit for stumbling across my riverside activity, but they are finding the easy ones, there are a hell of a lot more down there."
And some of my other activities as well.

†

Kobek turned to *Pioneer* #1. The cover looked like this:

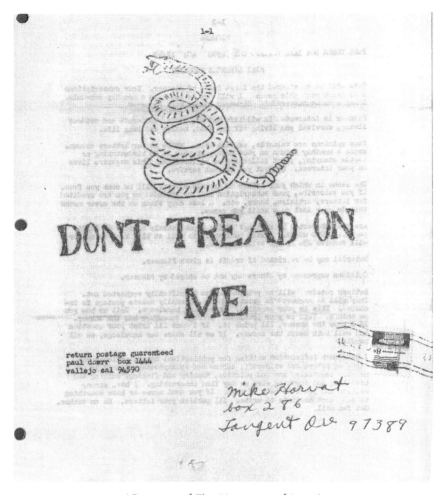

return postage guarenteed
paul doerr box 1444
vallejo cal 94590

mike Horvat
box 286
Sargent Ore 97389

(Courtesy of The University of Iowa)

The stamp was an upside down flag. In 1942, the United States Congress made public law of a previously informal National Flag Code. Section (4)(a) stated: " The flag should never be displayed with the union down save as a signal of dire distress." Kobek had seen other upside down flag stamps on Doerr's fanzines. But until he saw it with paired with the snake, the ubiquitous symbol of Libertarianism, he hadn't realized that this was expressive placement. Doerr sending a message. Distress. The world's gone wrong. The Minuteman emerges.

In the text of *Pioneer* #1, Doerr explained what he hoped to achieve with the fanzine: "Do you wonder about the name of this magazine? Pioneer. We are pioneers in a return to a better way of living. If food quality continues to depreciate we may be the only health people. Or perhaps the only ones." He also suggested what some of the content might be like: "I have much information writing for publication; notes, articles, and plans on nature and wildcraft, cabins and shantyboats, deadfalls and molotov cocktails, man and polotics *[sic]*, hunting and fishing, sailing and traveling and anything else we may find interesting."

Doerr saw a planet of pollutants and criminality and crises and violence. *Pioneer* stood in opposition, argued for the cabin life Doerr would establish later in Mendocino county. There were six pages about the perils of water fluoridation. Followed by a collection of survivalist tips. These weren't far from *Pioneer* #9. It was a publication for people who could not tolerate the modern world.

And wanted to escape.

†

Kobek had seen a few passing references to *Unknown*, a fanzine in which Doerr explored the paranormal. *Unknown* began publication in 1970.

The postmark on *Unknown* #19 was 15 October 1972, the same day that Doerr mailed Marquette University's copy of *Hobbitalia* #3. The flag stamps on both were upside down.

Unknown #19 had collaborators. A woman named Ramona Clark was the associate editor. She was the author of *The Truth About The Men in Black*, published in 1970 by Galaxy Press of Kitchener, Ontario. A man named Wayne Ruple contributed a slightly paranoid column about the origins of the peace symbol. The rest of #19 was random factoids about UFO sightings and the history of ancient religions and civilizations. Apparently the issue was substandard. Doerr acknowledged this by writing: "This issue isnt *[sic]* the usual 20 pages, its very late and it isne *[sic]* the all-mib issue promised.

Sorry about that. Problems beyond my control. Perhaps they will have been solved by next issue."

Kobek found nothing of note in *Unknown* #19. Standard early 1970s paranormal paranoia.

But the cover?

It was simple, no illustrations, only Doerr writing the names of different supernatural phenomena. In a variety of different scripts. It proved that Doerr could write letterforms that looked nothing like what appeared in *REHUPA* #15.

Kobek did not believe in handwriting analysis. He did believe in tics. He looked at the cover of *Unknown* #19 and thought of the Halloween Card, the text appropriated from *Tim Holt* #30. That looked like this:

The cover of *Unknown* #19 looked like this:

(Courtesy of The University of Iowa)

Doerr did not capitalize his Is.
Just like Zodiac.

†

Something about *Unknown* reminded Kobek of the executioner's hood and the Society for Creative Anachronism. As an organization, the SCA was subdivided into regional chapters. The original was from Berkeley, could only be from Berkeley, and was founded in 1966. But in a very short time, the basic idea—the sheer thrilling fun of dressing like the shit-encrusted nobility of the medieval era—caught on. The group rapidly expanded across America and then the world, dividing itself into regional "kingdoms." The original Berkeley SCA became known as The Kingdom of the West.

The Kingdom of the West had its own website, which was exceptionally well tended and organized, offering a dizzying array of historical data about the group and its activities. Someone had written a history of the Kingdom's first eleven years. Kobek looked through it and found no mention of Doerr. This did not surprise him. Doerr was always on the periphery without ever being noticed. He'd only gotten attention when editors published his letters. Those were easy to find. But in the multitude of fanzines written by other people, Kobek found no mention of anyone who could attest to the Doerr's physical presence, who'd hung out with him at Science Fiction conventions.

Kobek assumed that this quality also belonged to Zodiac. With the passage of five decades, it'd become a self-evident historical fact. He was the kind of man that you saw and forgot.

Digging through the Kingdom of the West's website, Kobek found mention of its members participating, unofficially, in the Third Annual Renaissance Pleasure Faire and Ha'penny Market.

In 1967, the SCA began issuing its own fanzine. *Tournaments Illuminated.* Kobek thought that, maybe, if he looked at *Tournaments,* he'd find some evidence of that participation, maybe someone would have written something about an executioner's hood.

As he moved through the issues, they only reinforced his sense that Zodiac must be linked to this general milieu. The 1969 issues of *Tournaments* document an idea as it comes into being, a new concept not yet interfaced with mass market production. If participants want to dress like a medieval baron, they have to make their own outfits or find a tailor. Zodiac couldn't buy the hood off a shelf. *Tournaments Illuminated* detailed the manufacture of weapons and costumes. In the early issues, the makeshift nature was evident. People are finding sewing patterns for children's Halloween costumes and scaling them to adults.

The Fall 1969 issue of *Tournaments Illuminated* had a letters column. And, there, Kobek found the following:

SIRS:

Re: THE BASKET HILT— I believe they were in use (if not common) so far back as the Roman Empire. They are more difficult to make than the bare hilt and take more material. Each age made that which it was most capable of making. As a matter of fact, the ancient Roman Empire also had the steam engine.

—Paul of Sunriver

Kobek had translated Doerr's Cirth Elvish at the bottom of the final page of *Hobbitalia* #1. PLDR E ORANORTUIN.

Paul Doerr of Sun River.

Kobek went to the Internet. He discovered that the SCA had taken medieval life to its furthest extension. Members could register Coat of Arms. The SCA kept detailed rolls of these heraldic registrations.

Paul of Sunriver registered his Coat of Arms in August 1982. It was described as: "Azure, a compass star Or." It was a compass rose.

It looked like this:

The Kingdom of the West's website also hosted issues of *The Page*, a kingdom-specific internal newsletter. Originally, *Tournaments* served the same function. When the SCA went metastatic, *Tournaments* became an official organ for all kingdoms. After this, each demesne, if it so chose, began issuing its own internal publications circulating amongst its respective serfs. First, the Kingdom of the West had *Tournaments*. Then they had *The Page*.

Kobek turned to *Page*. The earliest mention of Doerr was in the June 1971 issue. It looked like this:

```
    And yet further announcements.....
The Land Fund of the Kingdom of the Mists has been disbanded and re-
funded.  I put it to the bote of the membership, and only myself and
a member of the Eastern Kingdom contributed, so I figured that the
rest of the membership was not terribly interested.  If anybody has
objections, they can write Felice of Mayhem House (Felice Rolfe),
762 San Ramon, Sunnyvale, Ca. 94086.  I would be perfectly happy to
reactivate the fund, provided there is sufficient interest shown.
My particular apologies to Paul of Sunriver, who was very interested
in finding us land at a ridiculously low price.  Unfortunately, when
he wrote me he failed to include his address, so I couldn't reply.
I am sorry, and I am sure Paul of Sunriver is too, to see this project
fall through.  If enough other people are, perhaps we can do it after
all.
```

It demonstrated, yet again, Doerr's mania for the acquisition of land. Evidence was apparent across the decades—Doerr writing about land in Washington state, land in Humboldt County, land in Mendocino County. In the archives of the Sierra Club at the University of California, Berkeley's Bancroft Library, there is a letter from Doerr in which he tries to convince the environmental organization to buy 1,000 acres of redwood forest. So of course, obviously, when hearing of a land drive, Paul of Sunriver would be very interested.

The lack of return address indicated an assumption on Doerr's part. That the SCA people would know him by his sobriquet. And yet they had no idea. Kobek saw this as confirmation of his read of the Kingdom of the West's early history. Doerr was eminently forgettable.

Kobek found three other Doerr appearances in *Page*. One was from September 1988. Doerr sent in a letter, attempting to form an SCA fencing group. Another was from April 1973. Doerr placed a small advertisement that said, only, "WANTED: BAGPIPES." Followed by his Vallejo post box address. The third was from October 1970. It looked like this:

Paul Doerr, Box 1444 Vallejo, Ca. 94590, would like to meet with anyone who can teach fencing in his area. He is also looking for someone who can construct him a Viking battle-axe.

This pre-dated the October 1988 fencing letter by seventeen years.

Kobek had learned something about Doerr. The man was consistent in his obsessions. Over time. Over years. Over decades.

He wants to fence in 1971. He wants to fence in 1988.

What caught Kobek's eye was the request for the Viking battle-axe. It proved that Doerr wasn't just an on-looker. He was someone who wanted and collected the gear, the accoutrement and matériel of an earlier era.

And what, in the common conception, is the weapon most associated with a medieval executioner?

chapter seven

vonu rhymes
with "so new"

IN *F.A.P.A. PSYCHOTIC* #2, dated February 1973, Kobek came across a response to Doerr's *Pioneer* #9: "I like this odd collection of wit, wisdom, facts and speculation. I wish you'd mimeo it better so I could enjoy it better. I remember you from a letter or two you had in GREEN EGG. Ever get that land you were looking for? Ever start that commune/tribe/whatever you were thinking of? Or am I confusing you with someone else?"

Founded in 1968 by a man named Tim Zell, *Green Egg* began as the house newsletter of a Neo-Pagan religion called the Church of All Worlds. The inspirations for this religion were Ayn Rand's bibles of greed and Robert Heinlein's *Stranger in a Strange Land*.

Stranger had it all: free love, a mystery religion, telekinesis, a horny Martian. It's been said that Heinlein wrote the novel as a parody of New American Spirituality. When it was published in 1962, people read it as deadly serious. The Martian in *Stranger* comes to Earth and teaches the planet's inhabitants how to get groovy. He says Martian things like: "Thou Art God." He teaches them Martin words like *grok*. "Do you *grok* this sexy groovy time?" asks the Martian. For hundreds of pages, the Earthlings answer yes. They *grok* the sexy groovy time. He names his religion The Church of All Worlds.

As a college student, Zell and a friend founded a secret society. They used *Stranger* as their society's defining text, aped the novel's rituals. Upon graduation, Zell transformed the group into a religion. He borrowed its name from *Stranger*. He named his religion the Church of All Words.

Green Egg began as the Church's one-sheet bulletin. By the 1970s, the publication had become a magazine that explored nearly every aspect of New American Spirituality. Issues ran into the high dozens of pages. It was the most influential magazine on the development of American Neo-Paganism.

Green Egg was familiar territory. In his widely over-acclaimed novel *I Hate the Internet*, Kobek had made fun of Zell and his future wife for inventing the word polyamory—Latinate nonsense for fucking as many people as possible—while also practicing the fine art of torturing goats.

This wasn't comic exaggeration. The Zells really had tortured goats, cutting open the heads of newborn animals and fusing their dual horn buds into a single structure. The purpose of this torture was the production of ersatz unicorns, mythological beasts that had something or other to do with sorcery and magick. Once, as a child, Kobek had seen one of the Zell's unicorns. The poor thing was named Lancelot. It was part of a circus.

The Zells drifted so far into goat torture that Tim Zell patented the process. (US4429685A.) One of its accompanying illustrations looked like this:

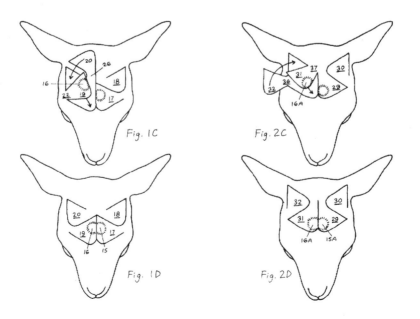

Fig. 1C

Fig. 2C

Fig. 1D

Fig. 2D

†

Doerr first appeared in *Green Egg* #38, dated 7 May 1971. His letter looked like this:

Hi,

Bob Rimmer suggested I write you about a Harrad type place. I have been trying to start my own in the country. If you're interested in corresponding, please write.

Thanx,
Paul Doerr
Box 1444
Vallejo, CA
94590

Doerr didn't realize that he was writing for publication. Zell published every correspondence that he received, regardless of whether or not the correspondent intended their letter for public distribution in *Green Egg*.

Kobek gave this editorial policy a name.

Paul Doerr's Dream.

The disastrously named Bob Rimmer was a novelist from Boston. He was not a good writer. His work exhibited the tics of a polemicist who disguises their ideology in fiction. Unrealistic dialogue, tone-deaf attempts at colloquial language, one dimensional characters that react poorly to the writer's underlying beliefs before accepting these beliefs as gospel truth. An author who wraps the message in a fictional world that they alone control and who refuses to admit the existence of that control. Kobek had used this technique, intentionally, in *I Hate the Internet*. He knew the scam when he saw it. Rimmer's best-known book, published in 1966, was *The Harrad Experiment*.

It was about an academic experiment in Cambridge, Massachusetts at a liberal arts college. The students are brought together, given roommates of the opposite sex, taught about human sexuality, and asked to make love. The book's characters become stronger, more realized people as they throw off the shackles of monogamy.

Kobek imagined Doerr sending a letter to Rimmer, a mixture of fannish admiration and inquiries. Does the author possess knowledge of any Harrad-type experiments on the West Coast? Rimmer recommends that Doerr get in touch with Zell. This could have been a genuine interest in opening communication or, more likely, the author making Doerr someone else's problem.

Doerr's first *Green Egg* letter demonstrates that, in 1971, he is interested in what would have been called mixed-marriage. Or free love. There was a purpose to the communes advertised in 1970. It was more than subsistence farming in Oregon. Doerr wanted to establish a space where people, including himself, could experiment with sexuality.

When Doerr wrote the letter, he'd been married since 12 September 1949. He lived with his wife in Fairfield. They would remain married until the day that he died.

†

Starting with issue #40, dated 1 July 1971, Doerr became a *Green Egg* fixture. It was as if Tim Zell fed a stray dog. The situation became so absurd that another correspondent later wrote and complained: "One thing I've noticed about the GE - every month "Paul" has a "letter" - Ad in it - asking for something? (money for land - money for house-boat - or if not money, he has things to trade.)"

In issue #40, Zell ran two of Doerr's letters. One of these correspondences read, in part, like this:

> In the beginning, things were not as they are now. People were intended to be happy. This is repeated again and again in the holy books of all religions. We were intended to have

long, health, happy lives. It was this way in the beginning, is now and ever shall be. It is our choice...

...Man was given fine motives and sensibilities. He was intended to be kind, gentle, loving, to live in peace and sharing with his neighbors. He was not intended to lie, cheat, steal, rape, torture, kill and war. It was not intended for one to roll in luxury and another to starve in poverty.

True, man is unequal in size, strength and intelligence and some must be in authority and some under authority, but it was not intended for one to be master and another, slave.

This was not the Paul Doerr that Kobek had read in fanzines and letters to other publications. Barring the references to torture and slaves, he sounded nothing like Zodiac.

Green Egg #41, dated 4 August 1971, ran an article by Doerr. Entitled "The Naked Truth." Three pages of advocacy for throwing off the tyranny of clothing.

In issue #42, dated 27 September 1971, Doerr sent in an advertisement for his fanzines.

It looked like this:

```
PIONEER (woodcraft, survival)
UNKNOWN (ufo, psychic, bigfoot)
TROVE (treasure hunting, prospecting)
HOBITALIA (hobbits, smials, Tolkien)
30¢ each - 12/$3.00
Doerr, Box 1444, Vallejo, Cal. 94590
```

Kobek could now date *Trove* #1, the treasure-hunting fanzine in which Doerr mentioned Lake Berryessa. At the very latest, it was published in September 1971.

Doerr's letters from 1971, 1972 and 1973 were meditations on paganism and a fallen world. As the months went on, the letters started exhibiting trademarks of Doerr's other writing. The jagged content, the pointless sharing of knowledge, the desperate requests for people to join him in his adventures. But, for these three years, Doerr did not sound like an insane person. Just a Libertarian who thought that maybe the counterculture had some good ideas. He preached harmony and tolerance and the rise of a paganism. Doerr hated Christianity and thought that the Catholic Church was conspiring to take over the world. None of this was atypical of the milieu. The early days of American Neo-Paganism were as much about anti-Christianity as anything else.

In issue #49, dated 11 August 1971, a letter from Doerr extolled the virtues of living on a boat: "I could live in San Francisco for about $20/ month berth fee. This includes water, electric & garbage. Probably 1 day's work/week would provide plenty of money. Anyone could live this way. I've heard from a couple of girls who are interested but thought that they couldn't. Of course, a girl is weaker but, if your boat is not much over 25', very little strength is needed."

Kobek guessed how Doerr heard from the girls. The 8-14 August 1969 *Berkeley Barb* classified, the ad that ran a few days after Zodiac established the tradename.

In *Green Egg* #45, dated 3 February 1971, Kobek found the first instance, in all letters and all fanzines, where Doerr wrote anything close to the topic of Zodiac:

> The zodiac is an imaginary belt in the heavens, 16° broad which includes the paths of the moon & the principle planets. Its centerline is the ecliptic or sun's path. Though few consider it, other heavenly bodies enter this zone and their influences should be considered.
>
> A good time to begin or end a ceremony, if it is the type for dawn/dusk observance, is in the zodiacal light, that

nebulous luminosity seen in the west after twilight & in the east before dawn.

There was nothing knowing in this passage, no wink, no hint.
Kobek was looking to exclude Doerr.
These letters felt like the way.
This was not a spotty record dependent upon library survivals. This was a month-to-month picture of Doerr, almost a running diary of his thoughts and interests.
It sounded nothing like Zodiac.

†

With *Green Egg* #60, dated 1 February 1974, the tone of Doerr's letters started to shift. One paragraph stood out: "I have been doing research into another field and need some info. Does anyone in the Sacr/SF area have files or back issues of Craft or Satanist magazines?... I am interested in the subjects called, variously: incubi, succubi, ecotoplasm, psychokinetic projections, mind traveling, demonic appearances, etc. I have been corresponding with people who claim to have been "visited or transferred to "other worlds." *[sic]*
Doerr's next letter appeared in #63, dated 21 June 1974. He'd written the following: "There are many kinds of attacks. Some are psychic. Like a freezing wind, howling around a castle on a crag, seeking a crack in the wall, an uncemented crevice in a rock, an empty chimney, where it can creep in and clutch someone within with icey fingers, perhaps causing a fatal chill, the psychic attack comes. Keep your fires burning. Some are physical. Like the armies surrounding the battlements. Don't just sit there. Counterattack!"

†

Issue #65, dated 21 September 1974, contained no letter from Doerr. But there was scandal in the letter pages.

An italicized note on page 52 relates details of a 20 July meeting of the Church's Board of Directors, discussing issues of concern to the Priesthood.

One such issue was Michael Hurley, a Priest from the Church's early days, and his lack of responsibility in personal relationships. The board decided to rescind Hurley's status as a Priest. The board gave him ten days to respond.

Hurley sent a response on 23 July.

Zell printed Hurley's letter below the italicized note. Although Hurley uses a dialect of peace and brotherhood and Pagan spirituality, his underlying message is plain ol' American. *Go fuck yourselves.* Hurley states that he is building a tribal family, a community of brothers and sisters, at Spring Farm.

Another note follows Hurley's letter. Tim Zell writes and explains that between 25 July to August 1, his wife Morning Glory's daughter was left in the care of Michael Hurley's wife Leslie. The daughter was 4-years old and named Rainbow. On 3 August, Tim and Morning Glory picked up Rainbow. The girl's hair had been cut short. To the ears. Rainbow and Leslie were staying at Spring Farm. Someone fed Rainbow a dose of LSD. The four year old had a bad trip. The dose was administered on the orders of the farm's guru, a character named Gridley. Zell writes that Gridley is running a Masonesque mindfuck. Spring Farm is a bunch of bikers and people whom the Zells believed were friends. Leslie doesn't care what happened to Rainbow. Neither does anyone else at Spring Farm. Part of Gridley's mindfuck is the eradication of parental bonds. When Rainbow was on her bad trip, she was told that Tim and Morning Glory were dead. Zell expresses his frustration. Other than pounding the shit out of Gridley, they have no recourse. None of the residents at Spring Farm will testify against their guru. The only evidence is the word of a 4-year-old child.

The italicized note ends like this: "*We would welcome suggestions from any of our readers... What would YOU do? -TZ*"

In the next issue, #66, dated 1 November 1974, Paul Doerr answers Zell's question. *What would YOU do?* The relevant part of his letter reads like this:

Tim... if something like what you describe at Spring Farm had happened to my child, I would have three impulses... One, I would destroy him. When "Uncle" sends millions of men out to destroy people they don't know and have no grievances against, I see no reason to spare those who would give dope to a 4 year old girl...Two, possible rethinking would produce, instead of One, a formal charge & statement with the police (you help pay for them, why not use them). Of course, probably with the quality of judges we have today, very little would happen to the criminals...

....Third, my social consciousness, concern for others, love of my fellows, whatever you call it, would require action on my part to prevent this from happening to other children, including those other children you mentioned...

...Finally, and I won't put this on paper, but I can suggest to you *personally*, various physical procedures that you could carry out.

I would be very sure I was right first, then I would take action against such a menace.

It might be better if you don't print this part of my letter. As you can see I'm not the turn-the-other-cheek, don't-get-involved typed. I was in a vaguely similar situation some years ago and there are fewer people here because of it now. The Law is not dependable. Also, in a personal situation, I'm all in favor of definitive personal action.

The only good enemy...

Kobek had gone through Doerr's literary remains. The writer looked for overlaps with Zodiac. But he'd never suspected that this was coming down the line. He never imagined this as a potential commonality.

A letter in which the writer confesses to multiple murders.

†

In the same issue, *Green Egg* published a letter from Richard S. Hack a/k/a Thor Xavier Challenger a/k/a Master Satan a/k/a The Complainer. Master Satan writes with the express purpose of freaking out *Green Egg*'s readers. Before he gets there, he greets two of the magazine's correspondents. One is Al Greenfield, whom Master Satan knows from UFOlogy.

The other is Paul Doerr, whom Master Satan recognizes from a publication called *VONU LIFE.*

†

VONU LIFE came into being in 1971. It was the descendant of two other publications.

The first was *Liberal Innovator*, founded in 1964 as a newsletter of the Forum for New Ideas.[5] Despite *Innovator*'s masthead claiming that it, and the Forum, were owned and operated by a young woman named Cara Leach, the publication was the brainchild of a man named Tom Marshall.

Depending on which account one reads, *Liberal Innovator* was either the print expression of a small Libertarian study-group in Santa Monica called Preform, dedicated to the idea of setting up an island nation state, or the causation of that group's formation. Whatever the structure, most of the publication's contributors were involved in Southern California's aerospace industry.

Back in 1964, there was still confusion about basic things like nomenclature. "Liberal" could mean classic liberalism—a belief in the paramount ability of a free market to sort social problems when the individual is unshackled by restrictive laws. The root belief of what is now called Libertarianism. Hence the *Liberal* in *Innovator*.

Before the advent of *Liberal Innovator*, American Libertarianism tended to be cloaked in the accouterments of pseudo-academe. It was Ayn Rand holding Manhattan salons. It was Murray Rothbard talking about some old bullshit he learned in Austria. Milton Friedman. *Liberal Innovator* seized arguments from these rarefied circles and attempted practical application.

---

5   Kobek could find no evidence this organization's existence beyond the pages of *Liberal Innovator*.

It was where every crazy notion that defines Twenty-First Century America was first presented to an unwashed hoi polloi. Reading its initial three years, Kobek could not distinguish the material from cryptocurrency Twitter. *Alas*, thought the writer, *without these words, Elon Musk would not be.*

If the publication was, as seems uniformly agreed upon, the idea of Tom Marshall, and financed by him, then it makes Marshall one of the most important figures in the intellectual development of the Twentieth and Twenty-First Centuries.

And totally unsung. And unstudied.

With its November 1964 issue, *Liberal Innovator* became *Innovator*. Cara Leach was off the masthead, replaced by new editor Kerry Thornley. A year later, the two would marry.

Thornley wasn't aerospace. He was an aspirant writer with a raging hard-on for laissez-faire capitalism. In later years, he'd be somewhat well-known for his co-authorship of *The Principia Discordia*, the ur-text of joke religions. In 1964, that's not why he stood out. He was known for one thing. And one thing only. He'd served in the Marines with Lee Harvey Oswald.

For a few months, Kerry had a warm acquaintance with the oddball loner. They traded politics, books, talked some shit inspired by George Orwell. Thornley found Oswald remarkable enough that the former wrote an unsaleable book about the latter. Prior to the Kennedy Assassination. It lead to Thornley testifying before the Warren Commission.

In 1964, Oswald was megamyth. He'd shot the President and then, streaking like lightning, scarred the psychic landscape with his arrival and disappearance, himself shot two days later. On television. Where everything became more real than real. (As opposed to the Internet. Where everything became less than real.)

If you were Thornley, if you'd known the man before the myth, you were sub-mythology. You'd played pool with the devil. Or God. In an article from 1970, Thornley suggests that he experienced a name change. People began introducing him as "Kerry-who-knew-Oswald."

Thornley was hopped up on Ayn Rand, traveled in Libertarian circles. At its core, this milieu was opposed to American governance. Kennedy was the once-living personification of that governance. Thornley knew the man who killed the personification. It gave Thornley real juice, got him in the door, an offer from Tom Marshall to edit *Liberal Innovator*. No one ever said any of this aloud. But it was there. Thornley knew the man who killed a king. And every good Libertarian lusts for a regicide.

Liberal was gone. Now the publication was *Innovator*.

The Forum for New Ideas became a subdivision of the Institute for Social Progress.[6] Marshall contributed articles.

Under both his own name and the pseudonym El Ray.

Somewhere along the line, Marshall sold *Innovator* to someone named Richard Bray. The sale may have happened as early as January 1966, when Bray is listed as editor and Thornley and El Ray become contributing editors. This masthead is stable throughout 1967.

The March 1968 *Innovator* heralds a sea-change. It's a special issue edited by El Ray, has contributions from Marshall and others. And is about a very different idea. If the early years were about escaping American governance by establishing a new government, now Marshall/El Ray no longer believe in the viability of this alternative. Instead, one must simply disappear from the strictures of control. One must become a nomad. The best way to do this is through mobile living, by buying a motor home and hiding in the woods. #vanlife.

Kobek clocked the timing. It was something missed by the scant subsequent commentators. Although Marshall had hinted, anonymously, at nomadism in an earlier issue of *Innovator*, the idea doesn't emerge until March 1968. Three months earlier, on 9 January 1968, Thornley was subpoenaed by New Orleans District Attorney Jim Garrison to testify about whether or not the would-be writer associated with Oswald in 1963. The idea is not implausible. In 1959, Oswald and Thornley were something like friends. Both men spent some of 1963 in New Orleans.

But as with everything in Garrison's one-man's crusade, the idea rested on a misunderstanding of his own city. Garrison comprehended neither urban demimondes nor their overlapping circles of freaks and misfits. If a random homosexual knew another random homosexual who knew a waiter who knew a busboy, Garrison saw conspiracy.

---

6   Again, Kobek found no evidence of this organization's actual existence beyond the pages of *Innovator*.

Rather than people trading sex and drugs to alleviate malaise while pretending they're artists.

It's possible, via old classifieds, to demonstrate that Marshall shared a post office box with Thornley, and it's also possible, via other writing, to demonstrate that the two men were close.[7] Or as close as Marshall could be with anyone. Thornley's writings of the mid-1970s highlight 1967 as the year when he caught wind of Garrison's interest. Before he left Los Angeles in Autumn. And there's Tom Marshall. A paranoid, a man who believes that the greatest evil on Earth is government. He's hearing about Garrison, about what's coming. Then his close friend is subpoenaed. A close friend who was also a former employee. With whom he shares a post office box in Santa Monica. The alarm starts ringing.

In February 1968, Thornley testified before a grand jury. In April, Garrison indicted Thornley for perjury. The idea was that Thornley, in his testimony, had lied about meeting with Oswald in New Orleans in 1963. Thornley's sole accuser, a woman who said she saw the two former Marines talking once in the Bourbon House, was a practicing witch.

There was no way to interpret the indictment as anything but Garrison getting ready to incorporate Thornley into *Le Grand Récit*. Marshall's friend and former employee was about to get fingered for killing the President.

In June 1968, Marshall began publishing *Preform-Inform*, dedicated to ideas floated in the March 1968 *Innovator*.[8] He still contributed to *Innovator*, was responsible for most of its 1969 content. But *Preform* was the main effort.

The dream of escape from America has been present for as long as there's been America. But Marshall occupied this territory with better reasons than most. He knew Thornley. He witnessed state coercion at a micro-level. If Garrison could reach out, the long hand of the law stretching through time, how long before the District Attorney or someone else started inquires into the would-be writer's former employer?[9]

---

7   For this purpose, the most helpful work is an essay by Thornley that appears in issues #11 and #13 of Samuel Edward Konkin III's *New Libertarian*.

8   An initial volume of *Preform-Inform* was published in an unknown number of issues throughout the middle 1960s. Kobek had only seen issue #14, dated 19 January 1965, of the original run. The 1968 *Preform-Inform* was more like a reboot than an entirely new publication.

9   In the files of Harold Weisberg, one of the progenitors of JFK Assassination con-

†

In *Perform's* first issue, Marshall provides a rare biographical insight while offering his Libertarian credentials:

> TO PREFORM: I am & consulting engineer, 36 years old, no family. For about eight months I have been living full time in a large camper. Utilities include cooking stove, floor furnace, hot-water heater, shower, DC-to-AC converter; all "self contained." I use a trail motorcycle, which can be mounted on the back, for auxiliary transportation both in wilderness areas and cities.

This was supplemented with more information in *Preform #4*:

> BACKGROUND INFORMATION ON THE EDITOR
>
> An engineer by profession, I have been an explicit libertarian for about eight years; the most influential single book I have read is Ayn Rand's ATLAS SHRUGGED.
>
> Libertarian character references whom I have known for four years or more: Don and Barbara Stephens, Atlantis Enterprises (mailing address same as mine); Kerry and Cara Leach/ Thornley (write c/o OCEAN LIVING, listed above).

---

spiracy theory and a Garrison associate with a quasi-formal investigative relationship, there is ample evidence of attempts to collect back issues of *Innovator* and, like, you know, dig its meaning. The most effective effort, unrelated to Weisberg, is an FBI report (NARA Record Number: 124-90125-10026) relaying details of a low-level Bureau investigation into *Innovator*, which the agency misinterpreted as part of the New Left. Reading the report's five pages, Kobek experienced the wisdom of Tom Marshall. While Cara Leach is named, and subsequent editors and owners are subject to perfunctory investigation, Marshall is never mentioned. The report closes with the Bureau shrugging its shoulders and moving on.

Relevant, verifiable activities: active participant in (original)
Preform -- a laissez-faire-freeport study group, 1963 - 1965;
contributor to INNOVATOR (March 64, Sept. 67); general
manager, then editor of INNOVATOR, April through Dec.
1965; lectured at Atlantis Enterprises' "Self-Liberation" and
'Retreat" seminars in Spring 1968.

Preform was a mimeographed newsletter in which its editor and readers,
who sent in letters, shared information about techniques to live off the grid.
And told each other about different places to squat.

But it was something else, too. It was also the diary of a romance. In
Preform #3, dated January 1969, there's a letter from a woman named
Roberta. It reads like this:

Saw your ad in December THE GREEN REVOLUTION
and want to learn more about you! Can't say that I myself
am & nomad now. (On second thought maybe I am, since I
haven't ever stayed anywhere permanently. Last year I was in
Connecticut as a psychiatric aide. This year I'm in California
as a phys. ed. teacher. I do some foraging, especially for
mushrooms, and want to learn more about living off the
land. I do & lot of rummaging too. However, I wouldn't
call myself a nomad, probably because I couldn't just get up
end go anytime I happened to feel like it.) So I don't feel
that I can trade you a situation summary but I've enclosed
$1.00 for "four issues." .... Roberta (Northern California)

The second line of *Preform* #6, dated September 1969, heralds a change.
It reads: "Tom and Roberta, Editors." Later in the issue, there's a multi-page
article entitled EVOLUTION OF A LIBERTARIAN or HOW I GOT
HERE FROM THERE. It's by Roberta. She gives a little background on
herself—Russian Jewish extraction, red-diaper baby, New York region—and

details how she received a letter from Tom, asking if he could stay with her as he heads up north for the Summer. Roberta said yes, Tom showed up, they spent a week together, she took off on the road with him and read *Atlas Shrugged* by campfires. Love blossomed in their laissez-faire hearts.

Robert and Marshall became each other's "freemates," a word they'd coined to replace husband/wife and marriage. Roberta embraced nomadism, ascended to co-editor of *Preform*. Much of the remaining issues are dedicated to their dual pursuit of freedom and, in essence, their pursuit of each other.

Both contributed to *Preform* under their own names.

And pseudonyms.

Marshall was El Ray, at least, and Roberta was, amongst other things, Haelen Hygeia. *Preform* never breaks face. Tom and Roberta exist alongside El Ray and Haelen Hygeia. On the page, all four are distinct entities.

Preform continued until May 1971, when its subscribers received copies of *VONU LIFE* #1, which billed itself as, "formerly Preform-Inform." The first page describes vonu, a contraction of Voluntary and Not vUlnerable: "invulnerability to coercion—coercion being physical attack by a volitional being against another volitional being or his non-coercively-acquired property." This term was coined in the final issue of *Preform*, dated March 1971.

Vonu was different than liberty, which is exemption from coercion. Vonu was about transforming the self. Liberty was about transforming others. Enduring peace and freedom can only be achieved through vonu, through the small transformations of multiple individuals that becomes The Transformation of everything.

The first page also contains this note: "Thanks to Tom and Roberta of Preform for much advice and assistance on this first issue, and to all who have sent materials. RAYO." This was the removal of Marshall and Roberta from the *Innovator* lineage—replaced by Rayo and Dr. Naomi Gatherer, editors, and someone named Mike Freeman, listed as publisher. Rayo, of course, was Marshall himself. Dr. Naomi Gatherer was Roberta. The best guess is that Mike Freeman was another Marshall pseudonym.

By this point, Tom and Roberta were practicing vonu up near the California and Oregon state line. What's remarkable about the pretense of a schism between Tom & Roberta and Dr. Gatherer & Rayo is that, apparently, no one noticed. One nomad couple swapped out for another. And the readers seemed to accept and believe the story.

A passage on the front page of *VONU LIFE* #4 gives a sense of the occasional weirdness this created:

> Your letter to Tom and Roberta came to me, in their absence. I am publishing portions of it in case some readers may be able to help you.... RAYO

In practice, *VONU LIFE* wasn't much different than *Preform*. Rayo and Roberta wrote their articles about vonu, nomadic living. And the readers wrote in with their own accounts. Rayo, sometimes, responded.

In issue #7 of *VONU LIFE*, Rayo announces a change. It reads like this:

VONU LIFE CHANGES EDITORS

> Lan, a vonuan of considerable experience, is now editor of *VONU LIFE*. Dr. Gatherer and I are quitting so that we can devote more time to shelter and food. Last Winter we failed to accomplish many of the things we intended because we didn't have a shelter that was both warm and roomy. (Our lay foam-hut is warm but not roomy; our poly tent is roomy but not warm.) We want better shelter before another Winter comes. Also we intend to forage more, to see if we can economically reduce our dependence on food imports. We intend to write for *VONU LIFE* occasionally. Please address any personal mail for us to *VONU LIFE* (G) or *VONU LIFE* (R). RAYO

The announcement is followed by a long letter from Lan, explaining who he is and his plans for *VONU LIFE*. The normal vonu posturing. Kobek couldn't help but ask the obvious: *was Lan an actual person?* Evidence cut both ways. Lan sounds different than Rayo. But Marshall had used previous decoys—Cara Leach listed as the owner and operator of *Liberal Innovator* when, from available evidence, she was the publication's secretary. Lan could be Marshall. But it was impossible to say.

In issue #9, Lan announces that *VONU LIFE* is splitting into two publications. There will be *VONU LINC*, a continuation of the existing *VONU LIFE* under a new name. And *VONU LIFE* will become a yearly annual. One issue of the latter was published in 1973. It's roughly 80,000 words long, printed in minuscule type and four column pages.

VONU LINC functioned much as *VONU LIFE* and *Preform-Inform*. A handful of notes and ideas by the editor. Most of the content written and sent in by the readers. It'd been this way from the beginning, writ on the very first page of *VONU LIFE* #1: "*VONU LIFE* guarantees to publish without editing at least six photo-ready pages (per subscriber per year) if relevant to invulnerable living, one-half page on almost anything."

It was a call across the wilderness.

And Paul Doerr heard the sound.

†

Doerr first appeared in *VONU LIFE* #4, dated November 1971. It's an enormous letter, about 2500 words, printed in double columns and occupying an entire page. Kobek felt that it was possible, based on a letter in *Green Egg* #42, dated 27 September 1971, to establish Doerr's discovery of *VONU LIFE*: "Write VANU [sic] LIFE, Box 607, Grants Pass, Ore. 97526 for a mobile nomad pub." Early in September 1971.

The letter in *VONU LIFE* #4 was the Doerr that Kobek knew. Every paragraph its own miniature essay. It was *Pioneer* territory, a long list of survivalist tips and the usual questions about finding land in Northern California. Most of the survivalist tips were refactored, directed towards vonu.

Doerr appeared again in *VONU LIFE* #5, dated January 1972, with reprinted material from *Pioneer* #8. An issue that Kobek had never seen, could find in no library. The reproduced article was nothing more and nothing less than Doerr going on about the building of smials, the homes of Hobbits.

This dovetailed neatly with something that Marshall had proposed in *Preform* #6, dated March 1970. Tom calls the idea Libertarian Troglodysm, a name coined to describe people who live in underground hidden chambers. Preferably on public land. Marshall writes that he and Roberta plan to adopt this tactic.

The next appearance was *VONU LIFE* #6, dated March 1972. A letter and an article. The article was about soddies. These were houses built in the 1800s. With wood at a premium, pioneers dug sod from the earth and used it as material for their crude makeshift shelters. Doerr believed the soddy to be an excellent choice for vonu.

Doerr's letter in *VONU LIFE* #6 was as long as the midsummer day. Well over 2,000 words. Its three major themes were tax avoidance, radiation, and fluoride in the water supply. It was utterly paranoid, a crank letter that could only be published in a survivalist fanzine with generous editorial policies.

Kobek saw something of interest.

Doerr had written the following two-line paragraph:

> If the Cryptoscript is any kind of substitution system its easy
> to break just by frequency of letters/ratio.

This was a response to something that had appeared in several issues of *VONU LIFE*:

```
CRYPTOSTRIPS provide a relatively simple yet difficult-to-break
cipher.  Privacy is realized by use of individual, easily-remembered
key phrases;  a communication cannot be deciphered through knowledge
of the Cryptostrip system alone.  Messages of moderate length are
secure without change of key, and are easily disguised to avoid
arousing suspicion.  Spaces and punctuation marks are included to
aid deciphering in the presence of transmission errors.  And the
strip format makes for rapid ciphering.  One set, $1;  two sets, $1.50.
VONU LIFE.
```

Doerr's response was an exact description of Zodiac's first cipher. And how it had been cracked.

One of the few definitive facts about Zodiac, one that could be neither avoided nor reasoned around, is that the killer knew a thing or two about cryptography.

Which created a problem. All previously identified suspects had no relationship to encrypted communications. They were movie buffs, they were homosexuals, they were house painters. Theories were invented, baroque ideas floated. *They learned about it during their obligatory military service! They told friends that they were going to take books out of the library!*

As far as Kobek knew, no one, not once, produced evidence that any of these individuals had, in their entire lives, demonstrated even the rudiments of enciphering messages.

And here was Paul Doerr.

Writing about frequency analysis.

†

Doerr appeared in every subsequent issue of *VONU LIFE*. He had an article in *VONU LIFE 73*, the digest-sized version of the original publication, and he appeared in several issues of *VONU LINC*, which wasn't much more than the original *VONU LIFE* under another name. His most significant appearance occurred in *VONU LINC* #12, dated May 1973.

Doerr sent in a letter that, even by the usual standards, was unbelievably long. It took up an entire page and then ran on to half of the next. It was about 5,000 words long. And had no paragraph breaks. Solid columns.

The letter was beyond summary. Kobek saw several points of note, not the least of which was Doerr's claim that he'd written 100 pages of a book about his adventures and a boast of correspondence with the Science Fiction writer Robert Heinlein.

But that wasn't the major thing.

The major thing came at the end. It was a few words, not much, but it said this:

```
govt to notzi, communist, whatever. i usually give address for clips once
with 1st reference in ish, or try to...except for paper.  a letter to s f
examiner, s f will reach it without street address.  livabord will have more
```

Kobek started his investigation with hopes of disproving that Doerr was Zodiac. The writer dug into this historical anonymity, a man of no particular importance. As Kobek made his way through *Green Egg* and *VONU LIFE*, he found an individual with a Vallejo return address, a man who'd confessed to multiple murders in print and demonstrated a working knowledge of base-level cryptography.

And now there was this.

It mattered for a very simple reason.

One of the first three Zodiac letters arrived in an envelope that looked like this:

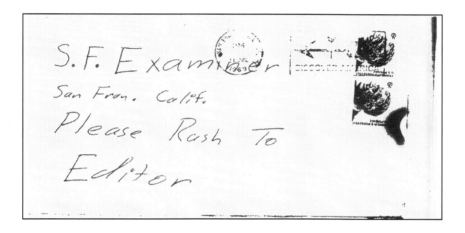

By the time that *VONU LINC* #12 was published, Doerr had managed to get two letters printed in the *Examiner*.

One was dated 10 April 1972. The other 24 January 1973.

VONU LINC #11, which seemed to elicit Doerr's comments about Heinlein in #12, was dated January 1973. But the 5,000 word letter also responded, directly, to content in much earlier issues. Which, like #11, included a discussion of Heinlein. It was possible that the #12 letter was written before the publication of Doerr's January 1973 *Examiner* letter.

This had been an actual letter to the editor, an inquiry about removing Supreme Court justices. The previous *Examiner* letter was sent to Guy Wright, one of the paper's conservative columnists. And thus could not have been addressed, simply, to "s f examiner, s f."

It was possible that the #12 letter referenced the second *Examiner* letter, a demonstration of recent knowledge.

But.

Here was a man who'd confessed to murder.

Who'd described how the first Zodiac cipher was constructed.

And who now described how Zodiac letters were mailed to the press.

If one wrote a letter to "s f examiner, s f" there was only one way to know that it'd gotten there. When it was published.

Otherwise, it'd be nothing but a missive tossed off into the wind. With no evidence of delivery. Editors didn't write back to every crank correspondent.

By the time of *VONU LINC* #12, almost none of the Zodiac envelopes had been published in the press. Only the Melvin Belli letter, which had a full home address. And the address-side of a 5 October 1970 post card mailed to the *Chronicle*, which read: "San Francisco Chronicle, S.F."

The Zodiac *Examiner* envelope was never published by the press.

There was only one way for Doerr to know that the technique worked. Practical application.

If he'd done it himself.

†

Kobek imagined Doerr first reading *VONU LIFE*, and when, as is made apparent from subsequent letters, he received copies of *Preform-Inform*. Assuming that Doerr didn't realize that Dr. Gatherer and Rayo were Tom and Roberta, he would have found evidence of two men interested in living underground. Both of whom had convinced a woman to live off the grid.

Kobek made a late discovery, one that escaped earlier efforts. A classified in the 20-26 October 1967 *Berkeley Barb*:

> MAN, 40, wants attract fem sex
> hike travel perhaps live in N woods
> cbn no mod conveniences send
> pic PO B 1444 Vallejo 94590.

This predated the nomad debut in *Innovator*.

Doerr had the idea first.

It wasn't the only overlap. Kobek found a letter from Marshall in the January 1967 issue of *Boating* magazine, sent under the expanded pseudonym of Elton Ray. It read like this:

Live-aboard Sea Boat

I plan to live aboard a boat with the immediate objective of becoming internationally mobile and the eventual hope of being able to live in a floating community.

I seek information as to the most suitable type of boat. Everything from steel-hulled motorboats to molded fiberglass trimarans has been recommended to me as a floating home. If you know of any specialized books of living aboard?

Elton Ray,
Los Angeles, Cal.

This was almost word-for-word identical to Doerr. *VONU LIFE 73* reprinted a piece from *Pioneer*. "A Small Boat for Live Aboard." The article's first sentence reflects the overlap: "Soon, maybe by the time that you read this, I will be living aboard a small boat."

Kobek wasn't paranoid. He didn't find great significance in the concordance. People have wanted to escape America for as long as there's been an America. But the overlap had a certain implication, a resonance with the imagined moment of Doerr's first vision of *VONU LIFE*.

Doerr was a bullshit artist, someone who spent most of his life dreaming and writing about things that he never did. And here were Tom and Rayo, two distinct entities, people who'd gone ahead and done those very things of which Doerr dreamed. Tom and Rayo went into the woods. They'd picked up women. They lived without amenities.

Doerr's *VONU LIFE* #4 letter is the first time that the publication uses the word smial. The Hobbit-hole that one can build into the Earth. From what material Kobek could find, Doerr first mentioned smials in *Hobbitalia* #2.

Included in the September 1971 mailing of N'APA, dispatched on the 15th of that month. Marshall had introduced Libertarian Troglodysm in *Preform*. Before Doerr was aware of the publication's existence.[10] All of which indicated, yet again, another instance of both men spontaneously generating the same idea.

After Doerr's appearance in *VONU LIFE*, Marshall wrote multiple letters and essays in which he discusses his attempts to build smials. He uses the word. Repeatedly. (The first attempt flooded.) Beyond a stray comment in the fanzine *Aspidistra* #9, dated June 1972, in which a letter writer laments that no one signed up for Doerr's attempts at building a "hobbit village," Marshall's letters and essays were the only evidence of anyone, ever, taking Doerr seriously.

Doerr never built a smial. He said so in *VONU LINC* #12: "have i build any smials? no. im a cavecrawler..." Just theorized about them. It was like the boat that he was going to sail around the world. Fantasy. Half-realized, never completed, bullshit.

Kobek imagined how Doerr felt when Rayo—an actual engineer in actual wilderness with an actual woman—wrote about experimenting with smials.

Total validation. Someone, anyway, could make it work.

†

As he researched, Kobek compiled Doerr's appearances into a spreadsheet.[11] Well over three hundred entries, but this wasn't reflective of the actual number. There were multiple instances, in multiple issues of multiple publications, when Doerr had mailed in multiple items. A letter and a classified. Three classifieds. Multiple letters. Kobek stuck these in the same entry. Most were quotidian requests, like a letter in the March 1989 issue of *VIDEO* magazine. Doerr asks the editors if it's possible to watch television on his computer monitor.

---

10   It's possible to deduce Doerr's ignorance of both *Innovator* and *Preform*. The absence of Doerr letters in either.
11   See Appendix B.

There were few of real significance. If Doerr were Zodiac, these were the letters where the killer revealed something that he shouldn't. With one exception, all appeared in either *Green Egg* or *VONU LIFE*.

Kobek saw concordance between the two publications. Both were edited by men who'd achieved something that Doerr wanted.

Rayo was obvious. He was the character of Paul Doerr, the one who existed on the page and in classifieds and letters, made real.

Tim Zell, editor of *Green Egg*, was a practicing pagan who'd founded a church based on Heinlein's *Stranger in a Strange Land*. Heinlein spent most of his life as a free love radical. (Like anybody who was everybody in post-war Southern California, it's possible that the Grand Master of Science Fiction engaged in group sex with L. Ron Hubbard.) Zell named his church after the church in the novel, the conceptual pulpit from where a groovy sexy Martian preached about *groking* how to get down and dirty. And *Green Egg*, at first, was the bulletin of that church. Free love was everywhere.

Green Egg #46, dated 21 March 1972, demonstrates the omnipresence. The issue contains an article by Zell. "Ero-Ethos: Neo Pagan Sexual Morality." It's a fairly well-reasoned, if naive, argument for everyone fucking everyone else as much as possible. It's where the message is made most obvious. But even the most casual reader of *Green Egg* would pick up on the theme. The publication gives the distinct impression of Zell as a Magickal Cocksman, someone living in quasi-communal micro-societies where genitalia and seminal fluid serve as the basis of an ad hoc barter system.

Exactly what Doerr wanted. Classified ads for communes. Hobbit villages. This desire drew him to *Green Egg*. He arrived on the recommendation of the disastrously named Bob Rimmer, author of *The Harrad Experiment*. Forget Heinlein. Kobek considered *Harrad* to be the most Science Fiction-y of all American novels, one that rested on an impossibly fantastical conceit beyond the ken of mortal man: that it was possible to have rewarding sex in the spiritual wasteland of Boston, Massachusetts.

"Ero-Ethos" was written before Zell met his wife, the woman who'd coin the word polyamory while her husband was torturing goats. But it was an early vision of the same thing. Do your crazy thing in every baby, crazy baby.

What Doerr wanted.

More than anything.

Same thing as Rayo and *VONU LIFE*. Someone wasn't just writing. Someone'd done it. Doerr must have imagined the mythical Zell, out there in Middle America, the brim of his wizard's hat slanted at a rakish angle, removed only for circumstances of heavy Pagan sex, when the fucking was too intense to balance chapeaus hand-embroidered with anthropomorphic depictions of the Moon and the stars.

Doerr's worship was there in *Green Egg* #46. Two letters. One of them read, in part: "I do admire the superb quality of your thinking, Tim, in your Biothanatos. I believe you will develop to become of of *[sic]* the Great." Another read, in part, like this: "I wish, someday, that Tim Zell would publish a list of the books he has studied. It must be fantastic."

Kobek *groked* how this explained the *VONU LIFE* and *Green Egg* letters.

Write to Tim. Write to Rayo.

To the men you admire. Who've achieved what you want.

Whom you want to be.

Like a child performing magic tricks at the dining room table.

Trying to impress the adults.

Go ahead.

Tell them every thing you know.

chapter eight

chainsaw party

Kobek found *Hoom* #2, a Tolkien-themed fanzine distributed as part of the Neffer Amateur Press Alliance (N'APA). Its author responded to Doerr's appearance in the group's June 1968 mailing. Then there was *Pioneer* #9, with ANFO, and *Trove* #1, mentioning Lake Berryessa. Whenever Kobek found *Pioneer* #9 in a library, it was almost certain that the same institution would also possess *Trove* #1. *F.A.P.A. Psychotic* #2 indicated that *Pioneer* #9 was sent with FAPA's November 1972 mailing. Given the overlap, Kobek suspected that *Trove* #1 was distributed by FAPA.

It suggested more extant Doerr material, the stuff distributed as his contributions to Amateur Press Alliances. APAs worked like this: each member received a mailing of fanzines produced by other members. To stay in the group, each member had to produce a certain number of pages every year.

Kobek reached out, yet again, to the world's beleaguered librarians. He received copies of Doerr's contributions to N'APA and FAPA, a period that spanned from June 1968 through May 1976.

†

In June 1968, N'APA listed Doerr as a new member. He contributed two items. One was *Pathan* #1. The other was called *CHAMPAGNE NEWS*.

Pathan #1 was printed on two sheets of standard sized paper, folded in half, with text columns on either side of the fold. A total of eight half-pages. Kobek thought this the earliest of Doerr's fanzines, predating even *Pioneer* #1.

In the November 1968 *Magazine of Fantasy & Science Fiction,* Doerr advertised both:

BURROUGHS fanzine 25¢. Wildcraft magazine 4/$1.00. Doerr, Box 1444, Vallejo, Cal. 94590.

Pathan #1 looked like someone's first effort at self-publishing. Its two exterior facing pages sported Doerr's drawings of dinosaurs. The six interior pages were printed on a sub-standard mimeograph machine. Doerr typed in ALL CAPITAL LETTERS.

The first text page looked like this:

Pathan #1 was dedicated to the writer Edgar Rice Burroughs. Doerr was uninterested in Tarzan, Burroughs's most famous creation. He focused on John Carter of Mars and, in particular, Pellucidar, a series of books about the Hollow Earth. Venture beneath our planet's surface and there's a secret world of prehistoric survival, where dinosaurs roam beside men.

After his introductory material, Doerr wrote: "Could [Burroughs] have been writing about real people and places and just took artist's license to weave in a little romance? All writers of historical romances do. Well, if he was re-incarnated, he is probably with John Carter now. When I see him again, I'll have a lot of questions to ask."

In several letters published by *Green Egg,* Doerr made multiple references to reincarnation. This one felt more explicit, more obvious. And weird. Doerr wasn't just suggesting that he and Burroughs would be reborn, but so too would John Carter of Mars. A fictional character. It opened a possibility. Could Zodiac have believed the claptrap about slaves in the afterlife? From the dawn of literacy, people had read impossible things in books and thought them true.

The quote demonstrated the nature of Doerr's attraction to Burroughs. The man believed Tarzan's creator to be a vessel of truth. The Pellucidar books were slightly fictionalized documents of the hidden world.

Doerr elucidated the possibility. He started with obvious. The survivals that can't be denied. The cockroach, the shark, the crocodile. Then he moved to more recent scientific discoveries and more speculative creatures. The mammoth, the coelacanth, the plesiosaur, the giant minnow of Colorado, the komodo dragon, the Missing Link and Bigfoot, and, using Burroughs's Pellucidarian word of *thipdar,* the pterodactyl.

Kobek remembered the September 1959 *Popular Science* article referenced in *Pioneer* #9. "Do 'Extinct' Animals Still Survive?" by Everett H. Ortner. Excluding the shark, the cockroach, the crocodile, the ones that everyone knew had not gone extinct, Doerr had referenced seven newly discovered or possible prehistorical survivals. Five, arguably six, including the pterodactyl, also appeared in Ortner's article. There was no direct quotation, but it suggested that Doerr read this article before John A. Keel's 1970 reference.

†

The final lines of *Pathan* #1 demonstrated that Doerr had not produced the fanzine exclusively for N'APA. He asked people to subscribe, he provided a return address, and marked it with POSTMASTER: RETURN POSTAGE GUARENTEED *[sic]*. None of which was necessary for the group's internal distribution.

CHAMPAGNE NEWS seemed to be a N'APA exclusive. It was one-sheet, printed only on its front side. The text was a joke, a pretend newspaper reporting on Doerr's pretend candidacy for the 1968 Presidential election. A series of questions and answers, a parody of the interviews that befall anyone with the naked ambition to assume the nation's highest office.

Of the 22 questions, six were related to killing people and four were about punishing people from the counterculture. A few examples:

> **Q.** One of your fellow candidates says "Make Love, Not War". What do you think of this?
> **A.** I think it is stupid. We have too many people now. Make war and reduce the excess population.

> **Q.** What percent of the population do you think is excessive?
> **A.** 90%

> **Q.** What about crime?
> **A.** Reorganize the vigilantes and offer free rope.

> **Q.** What is your platform, Mr. Doerr?
> **A.** Peace by 1970 with or without people.

> **Q.** There are many protestors *[sic]*, drop out, etc, who wish to leave our world and our society. What do you have for them?
> **A.** Poison.

Doerr next appeared in the September 1968 mailing of N'APA. The very first issue of *Patter*. Although the mimeography was better than *Pathan* #1, Doerr hadn't abandoned his habit of typing in ALL CAPITAL LETTERS. And, in a way, he'd moved backwards. *Pathan* #1 had employed multiple paragraphs. *Patter* #1 was a single paragraph. The first and final pages were illustrations. The interior was four pages of text, solid columns. At the top of the first page, Doerr typed: **WALLACE IN 68**.

On each subsequent page, Doerr included **WALLACE IN 68** as a header above his columns of text, accompanied by additional content. In order, these headers read like this:

WALLACE IN 68   CIVIL RIGHTERS HATE WALLACE
WALLACE IN 68   HIPPIES HATE WALLACE
WALLACE IN 68   ONE WORLDERS HATE WALLACE
WALLACE IN 68   POVERTY PROGRAMERS HATE WALLACE

On the final page of *Patter* #1, Doerr drew multiple illustrations of bats, written BATS TO YOU beneath his artwork, and included the following in the upper right hand corner:

WALLACE IN 68
NOONE SO MAY PEOPLE HATE,
CAN BE ALL BAD

DOERR IN 68
PEACE BY 1970
WITH OR WITHOUT
PEOPLE

The Wallace in question was former Alabama Governor George Wallace, infamous for standing in a doorway while attempting to block the college registration of African-American students. It was a publicity stunt staged with the help of the Federal government, an event with a predetermined outcome. Wallace would make a last stand and then give in to the federal troops. The feds went along with the plan because Wallace promised to prevent local violence. All he asked was for the photo-op. The image made Wallace the nation's most valiant crusader against integration. This was the appeal of his 1968 Presidential campaign. A former Democrat, he ran as a candidate for the third-party American Independent Party. His distilled platform was *segregation now, segregation forever.* Wallace knew that he couldn't win the Presidency, but, like the photo-op, victory was never the point. He wanted to capture enough electoral college votes to deny either major party's candidate a majority and throw the Presidential selection into the House of Representatives. In theory, this would have turned Wallace into a power-broker who guided Congress towards choosing a President more favorable to segregation. It didn't happen. Richard Milhous Nixon triangulated against it. And won. But as Paul Doerr put together *Patter #1,* the idea seemed plausible.

It was one of the ugliest Presidential campaigns.

And Doerr supported it.

†

On *Patter* #1's first page, Doerr wrote the following:

> Speaking of nice places, I lay here 'neath a blooming lemon tree, the waxy cream blossoms drenching me in their delicious perfume, the bees busily buzzing as the *[sic]* extract of their golden tribute, I occasionally reaching up to pluck a bright yellow globule of delicasy *[sic]* and thoughtfully eat it skin and all, and reading SF, the bright sun reaching through the fluttering leaves to dapple my page with light and shadow... I enjoyed Fringe as a prestidigious presentalion *[sic]* of profound performance by one of the shy flowers that bloom quietly and prettily in a secluded corner of the napan universe, tho there was muchly of matrimony, maturnity

[sic] and like that which I avoid as I understand it might be catching...

An eruption of Nineteenth Century diction. The beginning felt like a mannered English novel, while the end—marriage might be catching—was akin to American popular journals of the late 1800s.

Kobek wondered if the material was original to Doerr. He attempted to find a source. The best that he came up with was the beginning of Chapter VI in *The Devil's Due,* an 1888 novel by Grant Allen:

> It was once more a glorious August day, and the joy of the summer pulsed full and free in Harry Chichele's bounding veins. He sat out in a garden chair under the big lime tree on the rectory lawn, reading a novel, and hearing the hum of the myriad bees, busily buzzing among the heavy-scented flowers.

It was possible that Doerr's writing was a quotation that Kobek could not find. But given how little sense the first sentence made—lemon trees don't have waxy cream blossoms, Doerr certainly did not eat lemons skin and all—it was easy to believe that this was original material.

To pastiche language, a writer must have encountered that language, must have read enough of the old to make the new. Kobek thought of Zodiac's Little List letter, with one of its six torture methods copied from a Nineteenth Century work.

The rest of *Patter* #1's first page was Doerr writing about the *Berkeley Barb* and another underground newspaper, *The Southern California Oracle.* By the time that he'd composed *Patter* #1, Doerr had placed classifieds in the former. It didn't stop him from complaining that the paper was in favor of race riots, LSD, dirty books, and dirty words. Another excuse to bitch about The Hippie, though Doerr noted that he did approve of their excessive nudity. He saw *The Southern California Oracle* as a distinct contrast to the *Barb.* It wasn't a paper of hippies, it was a paper of spiritual seekers. He ended by writing the following: "I'd like to visit [Southern California communal experiments] if they were closer. The last few weekends, I've been driving thru Antelope Valley, Mohave, Death Valley, King's Canyon, Sequoia, Yosemite grabbing my spring pictures." These two sentences contradicted one another. Half of the places driven through were in Southern California.

The wording was almost the same as something that Doerr wrote six years later in *Pioneer* #13: "I used to fly and I drive a lot (Ill *[sic]* go from s f fri eve thru Joshua, Mohave, Death Valley, Kings Canyon, Sequoia, Yosemite and back to work mon morn for work to take pictures...)"

On Page 3, Doerr offered a few hundred words on the nature of fandom and responded to comments on music in the previous N'APA mailing. He denounced rock music for its primitive nature: "The same kind of screaming and hollering can be heard at any Caribbean voodoo meeting or any Mau Mau or Cannibal meating *[sic]* in Darkest Chopmeup. But folk, classic, some opera and the older popular is nice."

Followed, almost immediately, by this:

> And there <u>are</u> too many people. What shall we cook up to rectify the situation? Poison everyone's hootch but ours? Witchcraft is returning. In some force, I might add. There are thousands of covens in England and it is rapidly spreading here. I would like to know of one here. I think there is one in San Francisco... Get a couple big geese, turkeys, swans or peacocks to protect your chickens from dogs (and sometimes your home from you), or a 22.

A .22 was used at the first Zodiac attack.

Towards the end of Page 4, Doerr moved, randomly, to another topic:

> Why don't we burn some flag burners? I'll furnish gas and matches... Its *[sic]* not that a piece of dyed cloth is more important than a man's life, it is that that piece of dyed cloth is symbolic of our people and our nation (if its *[sic]* our flag burning) and my safety and security. You may not give a damn about your safety. That is your business. You

may not care about your family. I have seen what happens to women and children unprotected. They are mistreated, robbed, overworked, raped, killed and eaten. This will not happen here if I can help it and this like everything (including flag burning and race riots) starts small and builds up. If war must come, better in your yard than mine. If someone must die, better thousands of you than one of me.

Doerr's next fanzine was *Patter #2*, published in the March 1969 N'APA mailing. It was like *Patter #1*: two illustrated pages accompanied by four text pages. At last, Doerr had abandoned ALL CAPITAL LETTERS. And was again using paragraph breaks.

The fanzine began with Burroughs fan fiction, presumably written by Doerr, about characters from Pellucidar attacking each other with bagels and how one of these characters, a fellow named Hoojah the Sly One, got together with hippies from Haight-Ashbury district and sailed to Pellucidar and how Hoojah had been banished back to the Haight-Ashbury. It was a shift, of sorts, from the earlier publications. Doerr wasn't threatening to poison hippies. Or burn them alive. He was just making fun of them.

Responding to previous N'APA mailings, Doerr wrote this:

> Panthan #1 was printed on a Press-n-Print flatbed press. Dont [sic] ever buy one. Patter #1 was another mimeo. Maybe I'll learn to operate it right someday.

If Doerr were Zodiac, Kobek understood why he hadn't been found. It wasn't only that the information appeared in sources too diffuse to collate during the original era. It was that so many of the things touched upon by Zodiac's letters, or Doerr, remained unexplored. There was no cellular analysis of Minutemen newsletters and bulletins. No one had traced the dissemination of ANFO in underground literature. There was a lack of documentation of Amateur Press Associations in the 1960s and 1970s. And, other than a flawed effort in the 1980s, no one had attempted to discern the scarcity of any individual comic book.

And now the writer must learn about the Press N' Print.

†

The machine appeared in 1962, offered by Edwards Creative Products of Cherry Hill, New Jersey. The company's driving force was a man named Ed Cohen, who invented new products, never patented his devices, flooded the market, and then stopped manufacturing when a competitor's knock-off appeared or the novelty evaporated.

The Press N' Print was a mimeograph machine for the home user, bringing duplication to the masses. It retailed for $29.95, later reduced down to $19.95. These were the 2021 equivalents of $263.48 and $175.50. By contrast, the low average of other small mimeograph machines was around $125. The equivalent of $1,114.22. In 1962, the median family income was about $6,000 a year. The Press N' Print was advertised widely, particularly in the northeast. The advertisements tended to look like this:

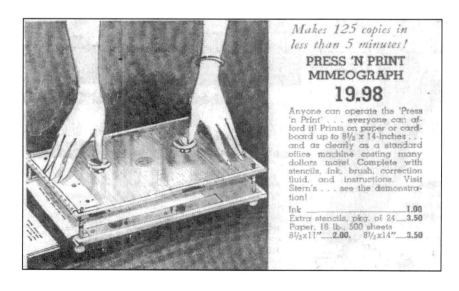

The Press N' Print was a large ink pad that the user pressed down upon mimeograph stencils, pushing ink through the perforations and openings.

The idea was ingenious. The only problem? The machine did not work. As demonstrated with *Pathan #1*, the Press N' Print produced almost unreadable documents.

At some point—Kobek guessed early 1964—Edwards Creative Products stopped manufacturing the device. (Production would not resume until the 1970s.) One of the device's last 1960s newspaper appearances was on 28 July 1966. It was part of a larger advertisement for the junk products that a department store wanted to unload, the things that'd been purchased and turned out to be disasters. The top of the advertisement looked like this:

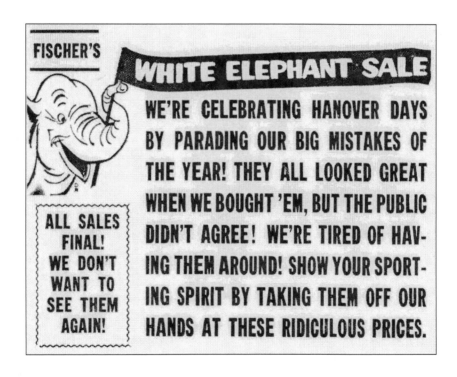

FISCHER'S

WHITE ELEPHANT SALE

WE'RE CELEBRATING HANOVER DAYS BY PARADING OUR BIG MISTAKES OF THE YEAR! THEY ALL LOOKED GREAT WHEN WE BOUGHT 'EM, BUT THE PUBLIC DIDN'T AGREE! WE'RE TIRED OF HAVING THEM AROUND! SHOW YOUR SPORTING SPIRIT BY TAKING THEM OFF OUR HANDS AT THESE RIDICULOUS PRICES.

ALL SALES FINAL! WE DON'T WANT TO SEE THEM AGAIN!

The listing for the Press N' Print read like this:

> **PRESS-N-PRINT STENCIL DUPLICA-TORS**—New York papers ran full page ads and stores sold thousands at $19.50. The theory is wonderful, but you'd better wear a wet suit when you use them if you don't want to be black all over. Only 2, each 4.44

By the time that Paul Doerr printed *Pathan* #1, the Press N' Print was no longer manufactured, no longer advertised, no longer sold by stationary stores. The machine bloomed, briefly, in 1962 and 1963. In 1968, when Doerr put his first fanzine together, the unit was no longer for sale through traditional channels. Disappeared from stores and advertisements.

It was possible to date, approximately, when Doerr composed *Pathan* #1. There was a note in the May 1968 *The National Fantasy Fan*: "Paul Doerr asks, 'Do you have any addresses of publishers of ERB zines, ERB clubs, etc?'"

Kobek knew why Doerr was asking. He wanted to send out copies of *Pathan* #1. This was a pattern of behavior demonstrated with *Hobbitalia* #1. Kobek had seen two individual copies of the fanzine, both postmarked 23 April 1970. Each sent to Tolkien related institutions. Publishing 101.

Once you've made the thing, where do you send it? To those most interested in its topic. Considering the *Fantasy Fan* contributor's deadline of 1 May, it suggested that *Pathan* #1 was either finished or near complete by this date.

In all of 1967 and 1968, only one person was selling Press N' Prints. A man from Simpson, Pennsylvania named Robert Evancho. Kobek dug around a little on Evancho, discovered someone whom the writer would classified as an operator. One of those admirable individuals who's always got something cooking. With no evidence, Kobek suspected that Evancho had bought some number of the discontinued item, cheap, and was trying to off-load them at their original price.

Evancho made his wares available through classified advertisements. A few ads appeared in *Coin World,* a newsletter dedicated to numismatics. These appeared in late May and June issues. Evancho moved to *Coin World* after advertising in another magazine. The previous advertisements appeared for five months, running from December 1967 through April 1968.

The other magazine was *Popular Science.* The first advertisement appeared in the December 1967 issue. The issue from whence Zodiac cribbed his material for his letter of 4 August 1969.

Evancho's advertisement looked like this:

**82   TYPEWRITERS,
         DUPLICATORS,
      OFFICE EQUIPMENT**

MIMEOGRAPH Machines $30.00. Brochure 25c. Robert Evancho, John Street. Simpson, Penna. 18407.

He next advertised in the January 1968, February 1968, March 1968 and April 1968 issues. These adverts differed from that of December 1967. They looked like this:

**82   TYPEWRITERS,
         DUPLICATORS,
      OFFICE EQUIPMENT**

PRESS'N'PRINT   mimeograph   machines. $29.95. Robert Evancho, John Street, Simpson, Penna. 18407.

It was possible that Doerr had gotten his Press N' Print somewhere else. Remaindered at a local stationary store. But Kobek'd read enough to know that Doerr's major purchases came through the mail or classifieds.

Evancho was still alive. Kobek found a phone number. The writer was terrible at making cold calls, botched them whenever pressed into the situation. He asked a friend for help. By the time that Kobek finished writing this book, the friend would be dead, and the writer would receive the gift of rescuing a traumatized cat, eyes of the LAPD and the coroner upon author and feline alike, from a foul and stained apartment that reeked of death, light & time refracted through the grey omnipresence of corpse-released gas. One more statistic in the opioid crisis. Ne plus ultra motor spirit, mama.

The friend called Evancho, who said what Kobek imagined: that he'd bought the machines from the manufacturer and then had a hell of time getting rid of them. Evancho also said that he was certain he had never sent a machine to California. Most of his sales had been in Pennsylvania.

Kobek remembered that Doerr was from Pennsylvania, and that Doerr was still doing business in the area. The 16 February 1968 *News-Herald* of Franklin, Pennsylvania reported that Doerr had just concluded a property deal in the area. This tallied with something in *Patter* #1: "I saw a parade in the east a year or two age *[sic]*."

Kobek's friend called Evancho back and asked about records. Evancho said that he'd look around and get back in touch if he found anything.

And then the friend was dead.

†

Three texts—*Pathan* #1, *Patter* #1, and *Champagne News*—predated the first attack attributed to Zodiac. 20 December 1968. Lake Herman Road. Done with a .22 semi-automatic pistol. Recommended by the Minutemen. And Paul Doerr in *Patter* #1.

Regarding this attack, the evidence that Zodiac offered in his letters of 31 July 1969 and 4 August 1969 was scant, half of it stolen from the December 1967 *Popular Science*. It left Kobek on the fence about whether or not Zodiac was responsible. He gave it 50/50 odds.

In two of Doerr's three texts, the ones predating Lake Herman Road, there was a commonality. Whatever their stated topic, what stood out was Doerr's anger towards hippies and the counterculture. And his threats of violence against the young, the drop-outs, the freaks.

Of Zodiac's seven known victims, five were students.

The remaining two were 19 and 22 years old.

With *Patter* #2, the first publication after Lake Herman Road, the threats disappear. Doerr might make fun of hippies but he's stopped writing about poisoning them.

The theme does not reoccur in any subsequent mailings or fanzines.

†

In *Patter* #2, Doerr mentioned that he'd attended the 1968 Baycon. This was another name for the 26th World Science Fiction Convention, or Worldcon, an event that took place, each year, in a different city. Every Worldcon had its own localized name, chosen by people organizing the event. Thus the 1968 Worldcon was also Baycon.[12]

Doerr gives some flavor of the event:

> Baycon 68 I'm glad you enjoyed your visit to the Bay. Has any other con <u>ever</u> offered so much? A con, a tourney, a riot, shootings, cops lining the route of your travel, confrontations between fuzz, hippies, yippies, commies, inexpensive drinks... what else do you want? Sorry we didnt *[sic]* manage to burn down a block or two near the consite but...well..cant *[sic]* have everything.

Baycon opened Thursday 29 August 1968 and ran five days through Monday 2 September 1968.

---

12 Technically, Baycon was also the twenty-first West Coast Science Fantasy Convention, or Westercon. But this is rarely discussed.

29 August was the final day of the Democratic National Convention in Chicago, the one where the counterculture definitively lost, the one where an unchecked police riot broadcast images of peace officers beating the living fucking shit out of the nation's youth. Which was going to flavor any gathering in its aftermath. But other things were afoot. 29 August was the beginning of a brutal heatwave. Baycon was hosted near the Berkeley city limits at the Claremont Hotel. The establishment lacked air conditioning. Or working elevators. The food served in the hotel restaurant was poisonous, sickening a great number of attendees. Which says nothing of the infestations of that prehistoric survival, the cockroach. Reverberations of the Democratic Convention came over the weekend. The inevitable riots and protests. A cop shot at Telegraph and Durant, about a mile from the Claremont. The persistent smell of teargas. If some of the attendees, the older generation, had arrived expecting the oasis of fandom, they were disappointed. Baycon was under siege from the outside world.

But something was happening inside, too. The original models of Science Fiction fans were working and lower middle class people who'd lived through the Great Depression. There are stories of fans riding the rails to early Worldcons and then, having arrived, eating out of hotel dumpsters. The newer fans were better educated, grew up with less poverty. And popular culture had taken notice of the genre. *Star Trek* was on television. LSD made Science Fiction dreams seem real. And Baycon was in the Bay Area. The epicenter of American youth hedonism. Baycon 68 was when Science Fiction fandom met the counterculture, when it became undeniable that the genre had changed.

As part of the convention, the Society for Creative Anachronism held a tournament on 2 September. Kobek was certain that Doerr was at this event and that it was his first encounter with the group. That same day, the Tolkien Society of America presented a program dedicated to its eponymous fixation. Given the lack of Tolkien in Doerr's publications pre-dating Baycon, it seems possible that this was another first encounter.

While digging through Internet detritus, Kobek found a fanzine that Doerr published in August 1985. This was the latest of any Doerr's material that the writer would find. Entitled *Filkin,* it was about a subculture of Science Fiction. This subculture, and its practices, fell under the general label of *Filk*. Its practitioners were *filkers*.

Filkers either wrote original songs about things related to Science Fiction or took the melodies and poetic meter of pre-existing songs and modified the lyrics to reference things related to Science Fiction. Sometimes the songs were about books. Sometimes the songs were about television shows and films. Sometimes the songs were about well-known figures in Science Fiction, both writers and fans.

A filker might take Bob Dylan's song "With God on Our Side," with its lyrical deconstruction of American warmongering reinforced by belief in the divine presence, and adapt the lyrics into something called "With the Force on Our Side." A condensed history of the first six *Star Wars* movies.

Filkin was two pages. It was created for the August 1985 mailing of APA-FILK, another Amateur Press Association. It said almost nothing. But it showed that Doerr was interested in the subculture. The February 1986 mailing of APA-FILK states that Doerr produced another fanzine entitled *The Filk Fiesta*. It appears that there were at least three issues.

Doerr encountered filk at the Baycon. Kobek saw the reference in *Hobbitalia* #2:

> Last issue, I suggested you read "The Wierdstone of Brisingamen" by Allen Garner (If anyone as other of his books, could I borrow them?), so this issue I'll add "Three Hearts and Three Lions" by Poul Anderson. The filksong on it is excellent as sung by Lady Diana or Randall Garrett (Lord Hightower).

The filksong in question was a calypso number. When Doerr composed *Hobbitalia* #2, the song had not appeared in print and was performed on only one occasion. During the annual Hugo Award banquet at Baycon 1968.

There was another event at Baycon. A live performance of something called *HMS Trek-a-Star*. It was an attempt to write an episode of the original

Star Trek—Captain Kirk, Spock, Bones, Uhura—in the style, and using the music of, a light opera by Gilbert & Sullivan.

The Baycon performance of *HMS Trek-a-Thon* was its second. It debuted a year earlier at Westercon XX, a convention in Los Angeles. It was one of two operettas performed at that convention.

The other was *Captain Future Meets Gilbert & Sullivan*.

Here was another aspect of Zodiac lost to the mists of time. If you took *Tim Holt* #30 in conjunction with the Little List letter, which had recycled "And Some Day It Might Happen" from Gilbert & Sullivan's *The Mikado*, and you knew something about Science Fiction fandom, you couldn't help but think that Zodiac had some connection to the genre.

It was a thing that might exist beyond research. Gilbert & Sullivan were in the DNA of fandom. You only had to look for the genetic markers. References were littered through fanzines, through convention performances. In 1960, a man named Hal Shapiro published *STF & FSY Songbook*, widely considered the first filk book. It contained many of fandom's then extant filksongs. Of its fifty-five songs, ten are based on Gilbert & Sullivan.

Including "I've Got a Little List," by the aforementioned Randall Garrett.

Isaac Asimov, one of the genre's leading lights, was an obsessive. His *Foundation* series was inspired by Gilbert & Sullivan, and, in 1958, he'd published a story about the duo, followed by another story in 1978, followed by his edition of the *Annotated Gilbert & Sullivan* in 1988.

An early plot point in the best Science Fiction novel of the 1960s—Philip K. Dick's *The Man in the High Castle*—involves a character decoding a reference to Gilbert & Sullivan's *H.M.S. Pinafore*.

And this appears in Robert Heinlein's *Stranger in a Strange Land*:

> Jubal looked very thoughtful. "If this method ever becomes popular, we'll have to revise the rules concerning corpus delecti. 'I've got a little list... they never will be missed.'"

In the February 1962 issue of the fanzine *Yandro*, another filk version of "And Some Day It May Happen" appeared:

Fannish Executioner's Song
BY *marion zimmer bradley*

As some day it may happen that a victim can be found
I've got a little list - I've got a little list
Of fandom's worst offenders who might well go underground ---
And they'd none of 'em be missed - they'd none of 'em be missed!
There's the pestilential neofans who boast of autographs,
.All candidates for Worthy Causes, Special Funds and TAFFs,
All people who yell loudly for more S*E*X in stf,
And surely every member of the (censored) N3F;
All FAFAns who on pubbing bibliographies insist --
And the whole damn' waiting list - I'm sure they'd not be missed.

Kobek thought that an argument could be made that the Little List letter, with its appropriation of a song from the *Mikado*, functioned as filk.

†

In his communication of 28 April 1970, Zodiac introduced an idea that would reoccur in the following three letters. He writes: "I would like to see some nice Zodiac butons wandering about town. Everyone else has these buttons like, ☮, black power, melvin eats bluber, etc. Well it would cheer me up considerably if I saw a lot of people wearing my buton. Please no nasty ones like melvin's..."

In his letter of 26 June 1970, Zodiac writes: "I have become very upset with the people of San Fran Bay Area. They have <u>not</u> complied with my wishes for them to wear some nice ⊕ buttons."

In his letter of 24 July 1970, Zodiac writes: "I am rather unhappy because you people will not wear some ⊕ buttons." In his letter of 26 July 1970, he writes: "Being that you will not wear some nice ⊕ buttons, how about some nasty ⊕ buttons. Or any type of ⊕ buttons that you can think up. If you do not wear any type of ⊕ buttons, I shall (on top of every thing else) torture my slaves that I have waiting in Paradice."

In the 28 April letter, Zodiac states that he wants to see these Zodiac buttons but fails to specify any defined visual appearance. How, exactly, would he know what to look for as he wanders around town? Subsequent letters refine the demand. The buttons become crosshairs.

This was yet another thing, Kobek thought, that was lost in history. The writer lived in a time of reified button ethos. His country's political apparatus distilled its heady positions into clever (apparently) aphorisms and humorous (supposedly) wordplay that fit within 280 characters. Bumpersticker morality on a Ford F-150. Or a Toyota Prius. Pick your allegiance, choose your car. Distill your concerns about social justice into a phrase that says nothing. Via a smartphone manufactured under the auspices of a genocidal regime. Then pretend there's a partisan divide. Good luck with the future.

Even in 1970, buttons were old news, totally accepted, part of the package. But those times moved fast. The buttons were a relatively new phenomenon. The earliest discoverable article on the topic, "Bugging by Button," ran in the 1-15 September 1966 *The East Village Other*. Written by Janet L. Wolfe, who reports that the craze is emerging from two places: The Big Store at 112 MacDougal Street and Underground Uplift Unlimited at 28 St. Mark's Place. Wolfe argues that the buttons represent the ethos—and sometimes the actual phraseology—of toilet and subway graffiti. Infecting a new medium, the piece of tin pinned to a breast.

No surprise that first word came from Manhattan. The entity driving the button craze, which would soon go nation-wide, was an Upper West Side outfit named Horatio Button Company. Founded by a writer and bookseller named Irving Weisfield.

Given Weisfield's pedigree and the company name, it's no shock that Horatio's products went beyond the expected confines of graffito—politics, sex, celebrity, money—and incorporated literary allusions. One of the company's first buttons said: SHAKESPEARE EATS BACON.

An old joke found in journals of the Nineteenth Century.

Wordplay about a quintessential English conspiracy theory. Adherents believed that Sir Francis Bacon was the author of works attributed to William Shakespeare. Because ol' Bill was too low class to write big boy words.

The SHAKESPEARE button was, apparently, a great success. For confirmation, Kobek only need look at new product. Subsequent Horatio buttons adhered to the oldest mass market formula: take an initial success, modify it slightly, and produce a recognizable but less coherent iteration of the original. Horatio issued other pieces of tin. They said things like: SOCRATES EATS HEMLOCK.[13] And: MELVILLE EATS BLUBBER. The latter is the button on which Zodiac makes his pun in the 28 April communication.

MELVIN EATS BLUBER.

Another reference to Melvin Belli.

†

By the mid-1960s, the literary works of J.R.R. Tolkien were an underground phenomenon. This wasn't limited to Science Fiction people. Groovy acid kids loved hobbits, an idea demonstrated in Chester Anderson's poem "Buena Vista Park is Middle Earth." Issued as part of the *Digger Papers*, the poem transposes Tolkien's fantasy landscape onto the eponymous park bordering Haight-Ashbury. Mostly a site for drug deals and anonymous homosexual assignations, the park becomes, somehow, a transposed vision of Rivendell. And although the poem was printed on a mimeograph machine, it was not intended the for small worlds of Science Fiction. It was for wild children of the Haight.

Wolfe's article references a button that reads, "in Elvish": GO GO GANDALF. And there were the buttons produced by Horatio, found in its period advertisements: GANDALF FOR PRESIDENT. SUPPORT YOUR LOCAL HOBBIT. COME TO MIDDLE EARTH.

These were not for Science Fiction people. These were for groovy kids.

Here Kobek reached an unknowable. The two earliest known Tolkien buttons—GO GO GANDALF and FRODO LIVES—were designed by a New York fan named John Closson. About whom almost nothing else is known. The first mention of Closson and his buttons, including visual reproduction of the objects, appears on page 81 of the fanzine *Niekas* #16, dated June 1966.

They looked like this:

---

13   The historical Socrates didn't eat hemlock. He drank it. But, in this context, inaccuracy is meaningless. The point is to produce a commodity fetish that pings off the frisson first felt by encounters with the original issue. Wash, cycle, rinse, repeat.

Perhaps the second earliest article, appearing on 24 December 1966 in *The Courier-Post* of Camden, New Jersey reports on a button that says, simply, FRODO LIVES.

No mention of Elvish. Did Horatio attempt to corner Closson's market, or was this a case of simultaneous spontaneous generation?

Provisionally, Kobek took this as evidence of how button DNA was introduced into Science Fiction fandom.

Which mattered. Because fandom went harder, and longer, on buttons than any other American subculture. The interface was notable enough to produce at least two scholarly works: "'Reality Is a Crutch for People Who Can't Deal With Science Fiction': Slogan Buttons Among Science Fiction Fans" by Stephanie A. Hall in *Keystone Folklore* 4(1) and a chapter in *Enterprising Women: Television Fandom and the Creation of Popular Myth* by Camille Bacon-Smith.

Kobek contemplated charting how this had happened. He would use old issues of *Niekas* and accounts of the 1967 Westercon XX in Los Angeles, where a small button war broke out amongst attendants.

But he didn't have to do that.

In the November 1968 issue of *The National Fantasy Fan*, Doerr placed a classified offering copies of Pioneer.

It looked like this:

```
NEW MAGAZINE on woodcraft, survival,
politics. Sample 30¢ or 4/$1. None
free. Pioneer, Box 1444, Vallejo, Cal.,
94590.
```

On the same page, exactly one column to the right and two classifieds up, there was another advertisement.

It looked like this:

```
TOLKIEN BUTTONS. Frodo Gave His Finger
for You. Gollum Eats Goblins, Sauron is
Alive in Argentina. 25¢ ea., 5/$1 or 20/
$3.25. Include 6¢ for postage on any size
order. Mike Montgomery, 2925 Pennsylvania,
N.E., Albuquerque, N.M., 87110.
```

†

With a handful of friends, Kobek discussed the possibility of Paul Doerr being Zodiac. He showed them some of the collected material. To a person, they asked the same question: *If what you claim is true, how was it that no one noticed?*

The answer was simple. The material hadn't appeared as Kobek presented it. Even as late as 2015, it would have been impossible to gather everything. In the original historical moments, people would've read Doerr's appearances, maybe one, maybe three, but no one could have encountered them all.

The question missed the point. The real question wasn't how Doerr had gone unnoticed.

The real question was how no one in Science Fiction noticed Zodiac.

By now, Kobek had gone through what seemed like an infinite amount of fanzines. Either by hand or via digital process. The writer had found exactly zero references to Zodiac. It didn't mean that they weren't there. Kobek hadn't seen everything. But he'd read enough to know that if these references did exist, they were the exception and not the rule. He assumed the same was true of police files.

If Gilbert & Sullivan and the buttons weren't enough, there was the Halloween Card. Putting aside the reference to *Tim Holt* #30, the Card had another thing that should have been recognized. It was the strange symbol drawn on the envelope and the interior.

It looked like this:

After his first read of *Hobbitalia* #1, Kobek theorized that this symbol was comprised of letters from Tolkien's Cirth. Which Doerr used for his cipher. Kobek recognized the check-mark on the left side and F on the right side. They were the Cirth letters for, respectively, TH and D.

Tolkien himself used double and single dots as punctuation. Two vertical dots, resembling a colon, indicated the beginning of a sentence. The single dot represented a space between words. There was an even a Z in Cirth. It resolved to an ampersand. With the possible exception of the four dots, every element of the symbol was present in a visual alphabetical chart within Appendix E in *The Return of the King*.

If it were Cirth, Kobek hadn't been able to guess what this could mean. Thursday? Thand?

The writer examined other Tolkien fanzines from 1965 to 1970. Throughout this period, fans evidenced a great deal of concern about using Tolkien's alphabets to write phonetic English.

One problem facing fandom: Tolkien's alphabets didn't really work. They were incomplete accessories to a fictional world. Throughout the 1960s, people proposed various methods of solving this problem.

Cirth was easiest. It had vowels. Whereas Tengwar, a script used by Tolkien's elves, represented its vowels through diacritics placed around and near consonants. And Tolkien hadn't provided enough vowels to represent the full range of English.

(The cipher in *Hobbitalia* #1 was a crudely representative example of these efforts. In his brief text, Doerr asks two questions but comes up against a serious issue: Tolkien failed to supply characters that function as punctuation. Doerr borrows the fifth character from Tengwar, which represents a phonetic "d" sound, and uses this as a question mark.)

March 1970 saw the release of *The Best of Entmoot*. A compilation of articles from a mid-1960s fanzine titled *Entmoot*. One article was about adapting Tengwar to English. Another article was about adopting Cirth to English, dropping Tolkien's vowel glyphs and adapting the diacritics from the previous article about Tengwar. The article about Tengwar had suggested using two dots—either vertically or horizontally—as the diacritic to indicate "EA."

The Best of Entmoot made sense of the symbol. The check-mark, the double dots, the F. The single dots were, as in Tolkien's original use, punctuation.

Read backwards, the symbol spelled DEATH. This was close to what Zodiac had done in the final lines of the Z340, his second cipher mailed in November 1969. There, he'd spelled several words—LIFE, PARADICE—backwards. And ended with the word DEATH.

But to make a connection, one didn't need fandom's critical revisions. In Chapter Ten of Book One of *The Fellowship of the Ring*, Frodo receives a much delayed letter from Gandalf. It gives the young hobbit the lay of the land and contains several postscripta. The main body and each postscripta are signed with the Cirth rune that corresponds to the English letter G. The final postscriptum is signed with a much larger and more stylized version of the rune. It is surrounded by four dots.

It looks like this:

Given how Zodiac used the symbol on the Halloween Card—a signature on the inside and his return address on the envelope—Kobek saw another argument about the connection between the two symbols. Each contained only elements from Cirth, and each was stylized by a surrounding four dots. [14]

Considering all of this, Kobek remembered a passage from a Doerr letter that ran in *VONU LIFE* #5:

> An artificial language could be made with the ancient runes as used by Tolkien in his Hobbit and Lord of the Rings stories or even with the cursive form he used aldo. This would have the advatage of appering to be a kids or sciencefiction club thing...,much soul be done with a lotr or hobbit club (a shire) cover that would attract attention if not done with such a cover. This is very popular now.

---

14   Despite a fairly exhaustive search, Kobek could find no explanation of Gandalf's variant rune. Given the obsessitivity of Tolkien fans and scholars, this is rather surprising.

None of this was proof that the symbol employed Tolkien's Cirth or its variants circulating in fandom.

It simply meant that, visually, *The Lord of the Rings* could provide a plausible answer.

A symbol appearing in a mailing that referenced a comic book. Sent less than a month after it's reported that Zodiac transcribed Gilbert & Sullivan. All in the month of October 1970. After a Summer of button letters.

Between 1967 and 1972, the Tolkien Society of American issued a newsletter called *Green Dragon*. Issue #11, dated December 1970, ends with this small note in its right column: "HOBBITALIA is available free for postage (an 8¢ stamp) from Box 1444, Vallejo, CA 94590."

Exactly beside this note, in the left column, appears this text: "You can get the following buttons through the TSA: COME TO MIDDLE EARTH, FRODO LIVES (in Roman Script or Tengwar), Support Your Local Hobbit, Gandalf for President, Join the Hobbit Habit, and Go Go Gandalf (in Cereth with Gandalf's fire-lighting charm in Tengwar)."

Green Dragon #7, dated June 1969, is only two pages long. On its first, the following note appears: "MIKE MONTGOMERY [8804 Delamar Rd, Albuquerque NM 87111] has some buttons of questionable taste for sale at 25¢ each, plus reply envelope. These are Gollum Eats Goblins, Sauron is Alive and Well in Argentine *[sic]* and Frodo Gave His Finger For You."

At the very bottom of #7's second page, this appears: "I also edit, with the Browns, a more informal & personal magazine, NIEKAS which is about imaginative literature in general plus anything else that happens to interest us, such as Gilbert [&] Sullivan or Georgette Heyer."

Irrespective of Doerr, the 1970 Zodiac letters scream fandom.

Someone should have noticed.

As far as Kobek could tell, no one had.

That was the real question.

Why not?

†

Fandom was forged by misfits. Out-of-place working class individuals with odd interests, organizing themselves around a body of writing that was motivated, supposedly, by the interrogation of ideas that could not be found in *The Saturday Evening Post*. This origin baked in a tolerance for the oddball, for the outcast. Fandom was a self-consciously accepting place, a zone that existed in opposition to the judgments of the outside world.

On the surface, this sounded perfect.

But what happens when one of the oddballs is a malign actor?

For example: consider the case of Marion Zimmer Bradley, author of the "Fannish Executioner's Song," and her husband Walter Breen. The full details can be found, *ad nauseum*, on the Internet. The short of it is that she was a lesbian, he was a pedophile with homophilic leanings, they met through fandom and fanzines. They married and had children. When the 1964 Worldcon was being planned, a scandal erupted. It came to be known as the Breendoggle. Several organizers of the 1964 Worldcon were from Berkeley, where Breen lived, and they knew that Breen had molested young boys. Some of whom were the children of other fans. The Breendoggle exploded when a Worldcon organizer, a man named Bill Donahue, published a fanzine detailing Breen's activities and suggested that Breen should be banned from that year's Worldcon. The ban did happen but not without a huge amount of controversy, and, ultimately, the whole affair ended up vindicating Breen. He was kicked out of one convention but enshrined within fandom. Many decent and well-meaning individuals mounted his defense. Open knowledge of Breen's proclivities no way alienated him, or Bradley, from Science Fiction fandom or publishing. Bradley was a resonating wave through the Bay Area and greater Science Fiction. In the year 2000, she was awarded, posthumously, the World Fantasy Award for lifetime achievement. Breen never hid his inclinations. He'd written, semi-pseudonymously, a book about pederasty. He was an active member in the North American Man Boy Love Association. In 1990 and 1991, he was charged and then convicted on multiple counts of child molestation. He died imprisoned in 1993. Fandom and Science Fiction never rebuked Bradley.

After the Breendoggle, the story didn't surface, not in any meaningful fashion, until 2014. Courtesy of the Internet. Bradley and Breen's now-adult daughter Moira Greyland came forward with accusations of abuse. She said that she had been sexually abused not only by Breen but also Bradley. These accusations were supported by a subsequent interview with her brother Mark Greyland. (People who didn't read the interview claimed it as 100% corroboration. In a shocking development, the text is less clear than its digital summaries.) Then things got more complicated. Moira Greyland decided that the root cause of her suffering was her parents' homosexuality. And became a crusader against gay marriage and gay rights.

As part of a civil lawsuit in the 1990s, Bradley and her lover/assistant gave depositions about Breen and the goings-on in Berkeley. Even if one discounts the sexual accusations, the openly admitted physical and mental abuse are overwhelming. Read enough of the depositions and one thing becomes clear. The Bradley home, often seen as a Mecca of fandom, was living Jahannam. It was one of the worst places where a child could be raised.

The problem wasn't that Moira Greyland's parents were homosexuals. The problem was that her parents embodied fandom. They embraced all the worst things that Science Fiction people believed about themselves. *There's an outside world and then there's us, the special ones, the genius people, the unique beings who see through society's lies, the ones who really know what's important, to whom the rules of the outside world do not apply. Charlie Manson was right, baby. There is no time. And thus no morality.*

There is a counterpoint to Breen, a young man from the 1940s named Claude Degler. He has the distinction of being the First Bad Fan.

Degler, a former and future mental patient, came up with a new idea. He believed that fandom people were the next stage of human evolution. Which he then promulgated via a series of pseudonyms, organizations, and fanzines. He left his hometown of New Castle, Indiana and visited other fans, arriving unannounced and unwashed, eating their food, abusing their hospitality, and commandeering their mimeograph machines. Sometimes he claimed that well-known fans were members of his organizations, an idea promoted in print and without these individuals' knowledge.

Read Degler's fanzines now, in the future, and they're more creative than anything else published in the moment. Yes, they're the work of a man who's as mad as a hatter, and yes, they're not exactly paragons of type-setting or design, but word for word, line for line, Degler is a much more interesting writer than any of the Good Fans of the Golden Age. His work always fascinates, something that cannot be said for arguments regarding the nature of Science Fiction and debates about the most recent novella published by *Amazing Stories*.

Degler achieved something that Breen did not. He got kicked out of fandom. It happened when everything was embryonic, before anyone learned to dissemble. Which means that it's possible to find the exact reason for his expulsion.

In 1943, Los Angeles fan T. Bruce Yerke issued a fanzine entitled *Report to Science Fiction Fandom: The Cosmic Circle*. It was a public catalog of Degler's sins. Here are the passages that account:

> It was these two items [carrying out general education programs for non-fans, and placing articles in *Time*, *Life*, *Liberty*, and *The New Yorker*] which prompted my instant decision to find out the true extent of Degler's machinations. For if this were Degler's intent, here was another ill-guided, ill-timed attempt to contact professional magazines, which would at the very least cause further guffaws from the professional editorial field, and lay open the way for further ridicule should fandom in the future wish to present serious material to any limited amount of persons...

> The factors contributing so far to the impression made [by Degler] on the fan field and the public have been outlined as definitely unacceptable not only to the fan field but from the standpoint of the general publishing field...

> ...In contacting non-fans, try to impress them with the fact that your hobby is worth your effort, that you are not "nutty," that there are intelligent persons devoting their time to it, and that the efforts sum up to something which gives a commensurate return for the time and energy spent. There are enough half-baked publications existing in fan magazine collections today. Don't contribute to this rubbish pile....

Degler's expulsion wasn't about fanzines or egregious behavior or bad personal habits. Yerke's worry is elemental: how does Degler make fandom appear in the eyes of the outside world? He's threatening to place articles in *The New Yorker*!

This is classic group decision making, Freshman-year introductory Psych, and something that, in the abstract, explains most dubious choices of public and private organizations in American life.

An insecure in-group always makes its decisions based on the imagined perceptions of the out-group.

Kobek suspected that this principle, which expelled Degler from fandom, also prevented Breen and Bradley from being thrown out.

The writer doubted this was conscious.

It rarely is.

Hiding the beast within means that the exterior world won't know of the scandal, of the reality of a well-networked individual, with a famous wife, using his access to find new victims. If the field is scrambling for respectability, nothing could have been more disastrous than the outside world knowing about the presence of a pedophile.

Breen stays. For the same reason that Degler is expelled.

†

Why did no one notice?

If you were a monster, there was no better place to be than fandom.

chapter nine

how to monetize
mental illness

PANTHAN #2 APPEARED in the September 1969 N'APA mailing. Its
name changed from *Pathan*. The new spelling being from the writings of
Edgar Rice Burroughs. The Martian word for 'mercenary.'

Panthan #2 was Doerr's one discoverable fanzine publishing during the
1969 Zodiac era. N'APA's September mailing had a contributor's deadline of
10 September. It'd been preceded by the June mailing, which had a contributor's deadline of 10 June. The September mailing listed all of its contents
in order of receipt. *Panthan* #2 is eleventh on the list, indicating receipt in
late July or mid August. After the Zodiac attack of 4 July 1969 and near
the letters of 31 July 1969 and 4 August 1969. *Panthan* #2 makes it clear
that Doerr wrote to fulfill the requirements of N'APA membership: "Well
I'm running out of space in this so I'll continue in the next ish." "This is it
for real this time. The thrilling continuation of this exciting adventure will
be in *PANTHAN* #3."

The first paragraph read like this:

> Well, here it is....the thing you have all been waiting for....
> *PANTHAN* #2. Surprise, you can read this one, I hope.
> Another mimeo and typer may make some difference, or
> perhaps I should have started practicing sooner. The delay

between #1 and #2 was not caused by laziness. It was caused by....well....ah....forget it.

In the next few paragraphs, Doerr hits the constant themes of his fanzines. He's building a new boat. He sailed another boat from Lake Erie to San Francisco. And something that appears *Trove* #1: how a dying man gave Doerr an old coin. This coin, punctured with holes, was a treasure map.

In the fourth paragraph, Kobek saw the following run-on sentence:

> Well, now I'm started on my new boat, I'm hunting and running around on weekends so that is why my mags are slow coming out, but they will come out.

In his first three letters, Zodiac made a threat. The language was different in each letter. But they all said the same thing.

Quoted from the letter to the *Vallejo-Times Herald*:

> I want you to print this cipher on your frunt page by Fry Afternoon Aug 1-69, If you do not do this I will go on a kill rampage Fry night that will last the whole week end. I will cruse around and pick of all stray people or coupples that are alone then move on to kill some more untill I have killed over a dozen people.

Quoted from the letter to the *Chronicle*:

> If you do not print this cipher by the afternoon of Fry. 1st of Aug 69, I will go on a kill rampage Fry. night. I will cruse around all weekend killing lone people in the night then move on to kill again, untill I end up with a dozen people over the weekend.

†

I'm hunting and running around on weekends.
well....ah....forget it.

†

At the end of *Panthan #2,* Doerr mentioned that he'd paid a visit to the Headless Valley in Canada, rumored to host paranormal phenomena. Doerr reported that he'd found nothing of the sort.

†

Doerr appeared in the March 1970 N'APA mailing. Another issue of *Patter.* For the first time, the issue was not numbered, a practice continued with all subsequent *Patters.* A policy designed to cause confusion in the library catalogues of the world.

Other than an opening paragraph that recommended people in Seattle join the Society for Creative Anachronism, the majority of *Patter* was Doerr responding to previous N'APA mailings. There were two pages about treasure hunting. Another complaint about efforts at gun control. Another attempt to trade old junk for guns. And then, in the middle, there was this:

> I brewed 5 gallons of plum a while back, then fortified it. Been disposing of it ever since. A long, slow, hard job, even if many friends have kindly came over and helped me in the evenings. They say I shouldn't have to do ALL the work alone. They also say I should have a wife but that's rediik. *[sic]* They know women don't drink. And then I might be stuck with a permanent job and couldn't sail away when I finish my new boat. By the way, if you want a really good job, come here and get a job helping me design the govt's new nuclear submarines. Have you ever worked in a place

where you must check through four locked doors to get to the you-know-what? With pretty secretaries to identify you too. Sometimes I wonder, if we are really expected to do much planning. I won't tell you how we get coffee.....

Doerr sent out other fanzines and letters and classifieds that made obvious his sexual availability.

Those felt like an old horndog. This was a flat-out lie.

As Doerr wrote this paragraph, he'd been married for almost twenty-one years. To a woman with whom he lived in a house that they'd owned since 1965. Working a job which he would keep until retirement.

Kobek'd researched the Mare Island Naval Base. Entrance to the facilities was impossible without security clearance from the federal government. This brought to mind the operative sentence in *Pioneer* #10: "Some of my writing has been questioned by various authorities (and some of my other activities as well), so this will be an excellent opportunity to lose me legally." And the final Zodiac letter of 13 March 1971: "I do have to give them credit for stumbling across my riverside activity, but they are finding the easy ones, there are a hell of a lot more down there."

Losing security clearance was easy. Get into trouble. Of any kind. The newspapers of the 1970s are stuffed with stories of clearance revoked from homosexuals, the idea being that their homophilic desire opened them up to blackmail.

If Doerr had come under scrutiny, he would have imperiled, and probably lost, his employment.

When he discovered Doerr's name, Kobek did something that had become reflexive. He sent a Freedom of Information Act request with the Federal Bureau of Investigation, asking for material that the Bureau had on Doerr.

In late June 2021, the writer received a response:

U.S. Department of Justice

Federal Bureau of Investigation
Washington, D.C. 20535

June 28, 2021

MR. JARETT KOBEK

LOS ANGELES, CA 90027

Request No.: 1491787-001
Subject: DOERR, PAUL ALFRED

Dear Mr. Kobek:

        This is in response to your Freedom of Information/Privacy Acts (FOIPA) request.   Based on the information you provided, we conducted a search of the places reasonably expected to have records. However, we were unable to identify records responsive to your request.   Therefore, your request is being closed.   If you have additional information pertaining to the subject of your request, please submit a new request providing the details, and we will conduct an additional search.

        Please see the paragraphs below for relevant information that may be specific to your request. Only checked boxes contain corresponding paragraphs relevant to your request.   If no boxes are checked, the corresponding information does not apply.

☐   Please be advised that your request was reopened based on the additional information you provided.   A new search was conducted, and we were unable to identify responsive records.

☐   Records potentially responsive to your request were destroyed.   Since this material could not be reviewed, it is not known if it was responsive to your request.   Record retention and disposal is carried out under supervision of the National Archives and Records Administration (NARA) according to Title 44 United States Code Section 3301, Title 36 Code of Federal Regulations (CFR) Chapter 12 Sub-chapter B Part 1228, and 36 CFR 1229.10.   Please be advised that the General Records Schedule (GRS) disposition authority for FOIPA records is DAA-GRS-2016-0002-0001 (GRS 4.2, Item 020).

☐   Records potentially responsive to your request were transferred to the National Archives and Records Administration (NARA).   If you wish to review these records, file a FOIPA request with NARA at the following address:

                National Archives and Records Administration
                Special Access and FOIA
                8601 Adelphi Road, Room 5500
                College Park, MD 20740-6001

☐   Potentially responsive records were identified during the search.   However, we were advised that they were not in their expected locations.   An additional search for the missing records also met with unsuccessful results.   Since we were unable to review the records, we were unable to determine if they were responsive to your request.

☐   The portion of your request concerning an FBI identification record – commonly referred to as a criminal history record or "rap sheet" – has been forwarded to the Criminal Justice Information Services (CJIS) Division for processing.   For additional information, see the enclosed FBI FOIPA Addendum General Information Section.

☐   Requests for expedited processing are not applicable when a final response is issued within ten calendar days.

☐   Police departments should be aware that the search conducted was limited to FBI records. Requests for criminal history records or rap sheets should be directed to Criminal Justice Information Services (CJIS).   Information regarding CJIS is listed in the enclosed FBI FOIPA Addendum General Information Section.

The lack of a file labeled DOERR, PAUL ALFRED gave weight to Kobek's theory about the sentence in *Pioneer* #10. That it couldn't be about the letters or the fanzines. When Kobek saw the sentence, he thought that if Doerr were Zodiac, it was as close as he'd get to a confession.

But that was before *Green Egg*.

In July 1969, the Minutemen's founder Robert DePugh was captured in Truth or Consequences, New Mexico. Amongst his possessions was a list of names. Everyone who was a Minuteman. Including Doerr.

On 23 September 1969, the Kansas City field office sent copies to headquarters and every FBI field office in America.

On 30 September 1969, a dictate came from J. Edgar Hoover, Director of the Bureau. (File #62-107261-3552.) It included a note at its bottom:

NOTE:

By referenced letter Kansas City submitted for indexing purposes a 142-page list of individuals as obtained from Minutemen underground headquarters records. This list has been furnished to pertinent field offices with the instructions that since the exact nature of the list is unknown, it is not to be described as a membership list, mailing list, contact list, etc. It is being utilized strictly for lead purposes.

In other words: don't investigate.

This was square in the middle of Zodiac's reign of terror. Two of the crimes had been committed. Two had yet to happen. If Doerr were Zodiac, the authorities had him. But the Minutemen's membership, like the FBI, hated Communists. And thus was not investigated.

It was hard to imagine other groups being shown the same courtesy. What if the FBI had discovered a membership list of the Black Liberation Army?

†

Doerr's next appearance was in the June 1970 N'APA mailing. Rather than produce new material, he'd sent *Pioneer* #1. Which Kobek had received previously from the University of Iowa. The issue with the coiled snake cover. *Don't Tread on Me.*

The N'APA version was different than the Iowa version. Done in the style of Doerr's early fanzines. Folded pages, ALL CAPITAL LETTERS, much worse mimeography. The Iowa version was reasonably well duplicated, full pages, and typed in lower case letters.

Doerr had made a second issuance of *Pioneer* #1. Retyped the original onto new stencils. That's what ended up in Iowa.

The writer compared the texts. Most of the original was present in the redux. The biggest change in the Iowa version was the inclusion of several pages dealing with water fluoridation.

†

Doerr next appeared in the June 1971 N'APA mailing, sending in another unnumbered issue of *Patter*. Four pages. The final two were another want and trade list, with an almost completely different set of books from the 1975 list.

Kobek spotted two things. The first was the sheer number of manuals related to electronics. *Electricians Mate 3C*, USN. *Basic Electricity*, USN. *Basic Electronics*, USN. *Basic Course Semi State Electronics*, reprinted from *Machine Design.*

And, then, on the twentieth line of the second page:

"....ford times...."

In 2012, an individual named Rebecca Dean Swensen made *Ford Times* the subject of their doctoral dissertation. It was entitled *Brand Journalism: A Cultural History of Consumers, Citizens, and Community in Ford Times.*

Chapter One explained *Ford Times*:

For most of the 20th century, a corporate magazine called the *Ford Times* was a linchpin in the Ford Motor Company's advertising and public relations efforts. With each new model of car, Ford consumers received an owner's manual that described the mechanics of the new vehicles; they also received a subscription to the *Ford Times,* which described how the cars operated in the larger social world.

Kobek read this as confirmation that Doerr purchased his Ford Falcon in 1968. The vehicle that matched Michael Mageau's description and appeared in Google Maps privacy violations. If someone purchased a used Ford, they weren't subscribed to *Ford Times.* The writer was fairly certain that the subscription couldn't have come with another Ford, as Doerr had, in the May 1975 *Patter,* described his other cars: "I dunno about those furrin cars. I had a renault dauphine once once *[sic]* and that thing shed internal parts ever *[sic]* time i druv *[sic]* it down the rud. *[sic]* ive had vws, 4 or 5 different models. they just dont *[sic]* hold up to 500 or so miles/week on our speedways." And the May 1968 issue of *Rod & Custom* had printed this inquiry: "Where can I purchase a shop manul for my old 1955 International Metro Van?"

†

Doerr's first appearance in the Fantasy Amateur Press Association dates to the November 1972 mailing. He's sent in *Pioneer #9.* His next appearance was February 1973. *Trove #1.* His next appearance was May 1973. *Hobbitalia #3.*

None of this material was original to FAPA. From Kobek's ad hoc dating, *Hobbitalia #3* was completed around October 1972. *Trove #1* dated to somewhere in 1971.

Doerr's first original material appeared in the May 1974 mailing. It was an issue of *Patter.* Eight pages long, it touched upon Doerr's major themes—the boat, gun control, wanting to trade items, the rising cost of postage. The only thing that stood out was the top of the first page. Doerr had misspelled his own last name. *Deorr.*

Not long after this *Patter* appeared, Doerr achieved a dream. He purchased acres of land in Covelo, California. Covelo was in Mendocino County, several hours north of the Bay Area.

Because Paul Doerr was Paul Doerr, this event caused him to establish a new fanzine. It was called *Mendocino Husbandman.*

Kobek found three issues of *Mendocino Husbandman.* Each bore a 10¢ stamp, dating the issues to between 14 September 1974, when the first class rate was hiked to 10¢, and 31 December 1975, when the rate became 13¢.

The issues said little, recycled the same themes with a little information thrown in about the county and Doerr's troubles with its authorities. He'd been trying to build a cabin and come up against zoning ordinances.

†

Doerr's next appeared in FAPA's February 1975 and May 1975 mailings. These were the issues of *Patter* mislabeled by Murdoch University as #2 and #1. The May 1975 issue contained WANT LIST.

Both issues started the same way.

DOERR FOR PRESIDENT typed three times at the top of the first page. When Kobek discovered *CHAMPAGNE NEWS,* with Doerr's parodic Presidential campaign, he remembered these *Patters* and thought that it was the same thing. Doerr lining himself up for a pretend run in the 1976 election.

But this was wrong.

Almost all Amateur Press Associations had officers who kept the entities afloat. People tended to assume these positions after elections in which the membership voted. In the case of FAPA, the offices were: President, Vice President, Official Editor, and Secretary/Treasurer.

The offices with juice were Official Editor and Secretary Treasurer. The former compiled and distributed the mailings. The latter kept track of the group's finances. These positions were the organization's heart and lungs. President and Vice President were, mostly, vestigial appendages.

The President's duties included appointing members to offices that became vacant before an election, appointing individuals to tally the votes of each new election, and appointing auxiliary officers for other purposes. The Vice President was there to interpret the group constitution and assume the Presidency upon the President's disappearance.

Doerr was campaigning for the Presidency of FAPA. The ballot went out in the August 1975 mailing.

It looked like this:

Doerr won. He had no opponent.

By 1975, the Fantasy Amateur Press Association wasn't that important. But it was the oldest organization of Science Fiction self-publishers, it had been consequential in earlier decades, a handful of professional writers were involved, notable fans were contributing members, and FAPA still had influence. The victory wasn't nothing. This was the moment when Doerr, finally, joined the insiders.

News of this victory appeared in the November 1975 mailing. Doerr wrote a President's letter that read like this:

> I would like to thank everyone who voted for me. I would like
> to thank everyone who voted, no matter who they voted for.

Unfortunately, I have had to disallow the Vice-Presidential election and a order rerun with all names added, on two counts: a protest... and section 7.3 of the FAPA Constitution, which requires a plurality to elect. Unless a plurality was, in fact, obtained, no one was elected, and the election is null and void. The two listed Vice-Presidential candidates finished in a dead heat.

Other than that... Through violent exertion and extensive cogitation, brilliant intellect and supreme excellence, I have settled all problems brought to me during this particular part of my Presidential Rain. *[sic]* What's that? You say I've had no particular problems? Well, then, you see what a superb job I've done.

A man named Roy Tackett had submitted himself as a Vice Presidential candidate but been left off the ballot. The ballot for the new Vice Presidential election was included in the November mailing. Tackett won, became Vice President with the next mailing.

As President, Doerr appointed the person who would tally the new vote. And he had chosen none other than Walter Breen. Who was from Berkeley. And remained a long-term contributor to FAPA, despite an attempt to expel him after the Breendoggle.

†

The next FAPA mailing was February 1976. Its minutia noted that Doerr had given up his postal mailbox in Vallejo, the one that he'd had since somewhere around 1964, and changed his mailing address to that of his Fairfield home. He otherwise had no contribution.

Doerr appeared twice in the next mailing. May 1976.

The *Fantasy Amateur,* a fanzine that accompanied all FAPA mailings and where official business was conducted, included a handwritten letter from Doerr. He'd had heard from Bill Evans, FAPA's Secretary-Treasurer, and been told that Redd Boggs, the Official Editor, could no longer serve. Personal problems.

Doerr wrote a letter of extreme complexity, calling for a crash election. And one that was unnecessary. The same issue of *Fantasy Amateur* asked its members to disregard the President's message. Sometime after the letter was written, a new Official Editor was appointed in Boggs's place.

The letter was, thus far, the clearest and most sustained example of Doerr's penmanship. Kobek still disliked handwriting analysis. But there were several features that the writer could not ignore.

Doerr had a tic. When a word ended in a T, he formed that terminating T as an ampersand. Doerr's ampersand-T was visually close to many ampersands found in the Zodiac letters. The ampersands of the 15 October 1969 letter, the one in which Zodiac claims Paul Stine as his kill, were useful. They made the penstrokes visible:

Zodiac started at the top of the vertical line, drew down, reached the bottom, went back up, curved around to the left, and then drew the horizontal line.

Allowing for their cursive connections to previous letters, which angled the line, Doerr's ampersand-Ts followed the same path:

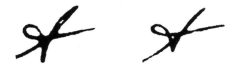

Doerr's letter was written with either a pencil or a ball-point pen. Kobek was dubious about comparing printed manuscript letters written in felt-tip against cursive written in ball-point or pencil, particularly when the examples were six and a half years apart. A lot can happen in six and a half years. But the writer did see one potential place of comparison. In the letter, Doerr wrote the word "and."

It looked like this:

Kobek thought of the last page of the 9 November 1969 letter, where Zodiac had broken out into cursive.[15] He'd written the word "am." It looked like this:

Doerr's other contribution to the May 1976 mailing was an issue of *Patter*. The first page explained a new situation:

> I have enjoyed my time here and made some good friends but things change. I have about completed my new boat... It is almost ready to be rigged. I may continue on my way around the world or I may sell it since....

---

15   Kobek had an unprovable theory about this letter. Considering the text's rambling nature, its length compared against every other correspondence, and Zodiac's lapses into cursive, Kobek believed that the letter was composed whilst Zodiac was drunk. Probably.

I have bought acreage in northern California and am planting it in fruit, nut, and food trees. It is a beautiful place...

...I have my choice of two wonderful worlds. I have been heavily involved with both these words recently and havent been able to do much publishing. Also, in addition to my job 8 1/2 hours daily... and wasting about two hours daily in driving time, I have been attending college daily in another city several hours daily and on Saturday, in courses on machineshop technology and welding technology...

...I don't know if I'll have any future mailings. It depends on my workload and I dont *[sic]* feel such skimpy publishing justifies my holding a spot others could use. If this is my last shot....its *[sic]* been fun....I wish you all the best....you're great people.

Doerr's resignation was not an uncommon phenomenon. Fandom burned through people, Many sent in written resignations. It happened enough to earn its own acronym. **GAFIA**. Or: **G**et **A**way **F**rom **I**t **A**ll.

Doerr never sent FAPA another fanzine. By the November 1976 mailing, a new election had taken place. Doerr was no longer President. He remained on the membership rolls until August 1977, when he was dropped for a lack of activity and failing to pay annual dues.

Almost every thing in Doerr's resignation was either a misrepresentation or simply not true. Kobek started small. Doerr's claim of attending college courses. This was possibly true, but he'd also seen Doerr claim, in much earlier fanzines, that he'd graduated college. Kobek possessed a copy of Doerr's death certificate. It stated that Doerr was a high school graduate. No mention of college. And Kobek wasn't sure that Doerr had graduated high school. The writer found Doerr in the 1945 yearbook of Sharon High School in Sharon, Pennsylvania. A group photo. Doerr is 17 or 18-years old. And he is not pictured with seniors or juniors. He's in the back row with a gaggle of sophomores.

In March 1950, Doerr filed for financial compensation deriving from his service in World War Two. The application listed when Doerr entered the military. 13 April 1945. Twelve days after his eighteenth birthday. When he was still a sophomore. And well before the end of the school year.

Despite Doerr's claims of two available worlds, he never used his new boat. He admitted this the February 1984 issue of *Ocean Freedom Notes:* "I came here to Calif. from Lake Erie on an 18 foot sloop, then sold it & built a 25 foot sailboat. But I've never used it & now probably never will." In early 1975, Doerr tried to sell the boat, placing a classified advertisement in the February 1975 issue of *Rudder*.

Then there were claims about the new land and its impact on Doerr's publishing. Which made no sense. Upon buying his acreage, Doerr's first impulse was to start *Mendocino Husbandman*. He'd managed three issues across 1974 and 1975. Given the postmarks on *Pioneer* #13 and #14, it seemed likely that the former was a product of late 1974 while the latter was from early 1975. And, after buying the land, Doerr started appearing in other APAs. Throughout 1975, Doerr contributed to the Elanor-APA. Versions of *Patter* appeared in the January, May, and July mailings. And there was "Paul Doerr's Supplement" in REHUPA #15. There were two 1975 issues of *Patter* sent to FAPA. Kobek had seen a contents list for the September 1975 mailing of N'APA. Doerr contributed an issue of *Patter*. (The writer had no luck finding the fanzine.)

Doerr's **GAFIA** occurred at the moment of his greatest fandom triumph. He'd ascended to the Presidency. Upon election, he'd written a triumphant and joyful message. Perhaps the annoyances—the Vice Presidential chaos and a disappearing Official Editor—turned Doerr against fandom.

But Kobek doubted it. In that inaugural letter, Doerr didn't sound annoyed by the hassle. Just pleased by his own officiousness.

†

Starting with the month of June 1976 and going through October 1980, Kobek couldn't find a single letter or article published under from Doerr's full name. Even the classifieds did not say Paul Doerr. They said: P. Doerr, Doerr.

With two exceptions.

One was the *American Pigeon Journal*. As the title implied, it was a publication entirely about pigeons. In September 1978, Doerr began contributing a "Beginner's Column." This ran, intermittently, until June 1981. Kobek had no real way to judge the content of these columns. Were they unique in the field? Whatever the case, Doerr's most reoccurring theme was breeding pigeons to kill and eat their young. On at least one occasion, he described this as "adding utility" to pigeons. In his second to last column, Doerr claimed to have once worked at a post office. (Kobek found no evidence to support this assertion.)

Kobek thought about the *American Pigeon Journal*. It felt way off the beaten track. This was a long way from Neo-Paganism and Science Fiction.

And was in contrast to Doerr's singular stated idea.

Of getting away from it all.

Kobek came up with an interpretation.

He might very easily might be wrong.

Something happened.

Something drove Doerr from his normal circles.

Maybe Doerr's wife discovered that her husband was sending out material seeking sexual partners. But this didn't make sense. If Doerr was in the doghouse, why was he allowed to give FAPA his home address? Why was he allowed a gracious exit? What one tended to expect was the sudden departure rather than the slow disappearance.

The writer thought, again, of *Green Egg* and issue #66. Doerr confesses multiple murders and asks *Green Egg* not to run this confession. But they print it anyway. The issue dated to 1 November 1974. Its circulation was 1300 copies. Kobek couldn't estimate when the issues were mailed. Given the nature of small press publication, the writer doubted that it reached many readers before the middle of 1975. At the earliest.

Doerr's next letter was in *Green Egg* #67, dated 21 December 1974. Here, Doerr responds to issue #64 while ignoring #66, going out of his way to say that *Green Egg* can publish anything it wants from his letters. He never writes anything that he wouldn't say to someone's face.

He doesn't appear in issue #68, dated 1 February 1975. He appears again in #69, dated 21 March 1975, with a fairly lengthy response to issue #67.

There is never a response to issue #66. Or the appearance of his murder confession.

And then, in issue #70, dated 1 May 1975, Doerr has a very short letter about the *Gor* novels of John Norman. Followed by months of silence.

Doerr's final appearance comes over a year later in issue #79, dated 21 June 1976. His letter is unremarkable, the usual hodge-podge, interesting only for the final lines containing Doerr's return address. The text makes obvious that Doerr sent this missive after 20 March 1976, publication date of issue #77. He notes that he dug that issue's cover, a Frank Frazetta drawing. And asks why *Green Egg* isn't selling prints of its cover art.

By every available measure, March 1976 is after Doerr abandoned his Vallejo post office box. It's gone from every other letter and publication.

Yet, in issue #79, this is his return address:

Box 1444, Vallejo, CA 94590.

†

Kobek had a theory.

For which there was zero evidence.

The writer suspected that Doerr wrote his three *Green Egg* letters following issue #66 as a way of rounding out his tenure. To make sure that his last correspondence wasn't a confession. A slow drift and disappearance.

Kobek could not explain issue #79.

Or the return address's appearance after Doerr had, apparently, abandoned the post office box.

Kobek had another theory.

For which there was also no evidence.

1970s small press publication wasn't like the Internet. *Green Egg* circulated slowly, lingered on store shelves for months and years, traded and passed between interested parties. Nothing was instant. Knowledge and information took time to disseminate.

What if, later in 1975, someone came upon *Green Egg* #66?

What if they'd seen the confession and noticed the letter's return address?

Box 1444, Vallejo, Calif, 94590.

Vallejo.

Murders.

What if someone added two plus and two and come up with ZODIAC?

And what if this unknown person had reached out to Doerr, via his postal mail box, and asked the question.

Did you do it?

chapter ten

i have an erection!
i have no direction!

TOM MARSHALL A/K/A RAYO'S major chronicler was a man named Jim Stumm. Who'd published in *VONU LIFE/LINC*, once met Marshall in Oregon for something called VONU WEEK, and been a prodigious contributor to other Libertarian publications of the era.

Stumm'd also made several efforts at publishing. The most substantial was called *Living Free*. The first issue was dated March 1979.

Unlike almost everyone else from the 1970s Libertarian milieu, Stumm had neither stopped nor died. Never given up. As of 2021, *Living Free* was somewhere around issue #174. And still going. It was one of the most important publication efforts of the last half century—and it'd been done by a guy with a post office box in Buffalo, NY.[16]

And, of course, gone unstudied.

In early 1974, Marshall/Rayo disappeared. Never to be heard from again. As did his freemate Roberta. It was a mystery of the Libertarian world.

Ever since, Stumm'd spent a great deal of time thinking, and writing, about Rayo. Most of this appeared in *Living Free*. Some of the material making its way into his pseudonymously published book *Vonu: The Search for Personal Freedom*. And 2019's *The Life of Tom Marshall*.

---

16   PO Box 29, Hiler Branch, Buffalo, NY 14223.

Kobek discovered a Doerr appearance in the May 2002 issue of *Living Free*. Someone'd scanned the text and put it online. Doerr's letter was about the failures of the space program, then transitioned to the drug war, ending like this: "As President, I could pay off the national debt instantly without adding a single dollar to those in circulation. I could reduce crime by, probably, 80%. Want to eliminate illegal narcotics? Grab a few gutter pushers. Question them under torture. As they name names, grab these & do the same to them. You will move up the chain. Execute them as you finishing questioning. Follow the money. When you have reached the millionaires, politicians, bureaucrats, etc., you have just about eliminated illegal narcotics. Finally, why should non-citizens have American constitutional rights or financial help?"

Kobek wrote Stumm a letter, inquiring whether Stumm had copies of *Pioneer*. Stumm wrote back. Doerr'd sent copies but Stumm hadn't kept them. Stumm included a list of every *Living Free* issue with content written by Doerr. And added some new knowledge.

Doerr hadn't just published in *Living Free* under his own name.

He'd also used a pseudonym.

He'd called himself Tarl Cabot.

†

Tarl Cabot was the protagonist of John Norman's *Gor* novels, the books that Doerr mentioned in multiple letters and fanzines. Early novels in the series were a pastiche of Edgar Rice Burroughs. Rough sex edges were present. But they weren't predominant. 1968's *Priest-Kings of Gor*, for instance, is mostly about a war between a race of insectoid alien-gods.

Somewhere in the mid-1970s, the *Gor* novels took a turn.

They had become tedious, long, and overly concerned with rape.

To verify the narrative change, Kobek went to Los Angeles County's very best used bookstore. The Iliad in North Hollywood. The earlier *Gor* books were available in great numbers. But the store had only one copy of any *Gor* novel published after 1975. *Beasts of Gor.*

Ballantine Books issued the first six novels. In 1972, Norman moved to DAW Books. Ten years later, DAW advertised that over 3,000,000 of its *Gor* books were in print. And DAW hadn't republished the pre-rape material. Those 3,000,000 copies were chock-a-block with rape.

Looking at the shelves of The Iliad, stuffed with early novels but deficient on the rapey ones, Kobek assumed that the later *Gor* novels were too well-loved by their readers to make it to the secondary market.

Beasts of Gor's back cover sported the following catalogue copy:

BEASTS OF GOR

On Gor, the other world in Earth's orbit, the
term beast can mean any of three things:
First, there are the Kurii, the monsters
from space who are about invade the world.
Second, there are the Gorean warriors, men
whose fighting ferocity is incomparable.
Third, there are the slave girls, who are both
beasts of burden and objects of desire.

Kobek bought *Beasts of Gor*. Kobek read *Beasts of Gor*. It was the worst thing that he did while researching Zodiac.

The first fifty pages felt like an Oxford Union debate that ended with a unanimous vote carrying the same motion: this House believes that human biology, free from the restraints of a sick and weak civilization, demands the kidnapping and enslaving of quasi-feminists and teaching 'em womanhood through rape. The next thirty or so pages were about a Gorean chess match. Then it was back to rape. And on it went. Over the remaining 370 pages, Tarl Cabot sure did a lot of slave rape.

In countless letters and fanzines, Doerr identified 1969's *Nomads of Gor* as his to-die-for favorite. The novel is part of the original Burroughs-esque scheme, but its final pages hint at coming changes. There's a long and excruciating scene. An American quasi-feminist, enslaved in early chapters, enters into a mutual seduction with Tarl Cabot.

The quasi-feminist thinks that she's seducing Cabot. But then he convinces her that she'll be a true woman only when she licks her chains. There are long and near-endless paragraphs of the slave-girl's dialogue. She's imperious and flirtatious, thinks that Tarl Cabot really digs the exchange.

Unlike the reader, she's unaware of Tarl Cabot's thoughts. She has no idea that his inner monologue goes like this: "I considered raping her."

This wasn't quite the bonanza of the later books.

But *Nomads* was getting there.

In the Gorean social hierarchy, slave girls are distinguished from free women by two physical alterations. One is the presence of pierced ears.

The other is a brand, usually seared into the meaty flesh of their upper right thigh. The most common brand is the Gorean letter *kef,* which looks like an ornate K.

But there are other brands used by different peoples. Including the Tuchuk, one of four wagoneer tribes in *Nomads of Gor.* Most of the novel is about Tarl Cabot becoming a de facto Tuchuk. The book describes the Tuchuk brand like this:

> ...the brand of the Tuchuk slave, incidentally, is not the same as that generally used in the cities, which, for girls, is the first letter of the expression Kajira in cursive script, but the sign of the four bosk horns, that of the Tuchuk standard; the brand of the four bosk horns, set in such a manner as to somewhat resemble the letter H', is only about an inch high..

John Norman was not big on putting illustrations in his books. He never drew the brand.

There was no official image.

Kobek did a Google Image Search for "Tuchuk brand." The results were homemade interpretations of the above text.

They tended to look like this:

Months earlier, Kobek discovered a short entry for Doerr in the 1980 *California Brand Book*. This volume was published by the State of California's Bureau of Livestock Identification. It listed all brands registered by individuals and corporations, containing not only the name of the registeree, but also a visual depiction of their brand.

Doerr's brand looked like this:

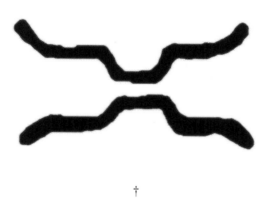

†

Kobek received copies of *Living Free*.

Doerr was in the inaugural issue, dated March 1979. The letter did not appear under his full name. Doerr was identified as "paul d."

The letter was in response to something called *Odd Man Out*. On the first page of *Living Free* #1, Stumm established an editorial policy. It was much like that of *Green Egg*. Stumm would print anything sent to him. Unless people told him that the letter was not for publication. Considering this policy, and given that the letter was composed before *Living Free* existed, Kobek suspected that Doerr had no idea his missive would be published.

Doerr's next appearance came with issue #3, dated July 1979. He had two letters in the issue. One from March 1979, presumably written after Doerr received *Living Free*'s inaugural issue, and another from May 1979.

Both appeared under the pseudonym Tarl Cabot.

In the March 1979 letter, Tarl Cabot wrote about speaking with many women in "multiple marriages" and discovering that they enjoyed the arrangement even more than the men. But needed a man to rule the roost. Otherwise, the letter was about living that vonu life.

In the May 1979 letter, Cabot explained his plans for the future:

> I have my land (10A) in N. Cal... I am still working in town, so I'm considering finding someone (women) to live on the place & work it until I can move in permanently. I am seriously considering having several wives & children. Give them all training in weaponry, scouting & evasion, karate, etc & having a small, self sufficient and self defendable little empire when the roof falls in...

Tarl Cabot's next appearance was in *Living Free* #6, dated February 1980. Doerr wrote the letter in November 1979. It contained the usual themes, with only one unique point. Tarl Cabot wanted a microform reader.

Throughout the mid-20th Century, microform was the preferred method of archival print reproduction and distribution. Months of a publication could be stored on an object no bigger than a snuff box. Tarl Cabot asked if anyone would sell him a micro reader, preferably one that worked on battery power. In the March 1972 issue of *VONU LIFE*, Doerr had inquired about microform, asking if it was really as good as Rayo said. But then the idea went away. It didn't resurface until this Tarl Cabot letter, the first discoverable instance of Doerr's hardcore interest in microfilming, an idea that would consume much of his latter days.

In all likelihood, Doerr cribbed this idea from John Zube, a German philosopher whose writings appeared in Stumm's publications. Zube'd come up with an amazing idea: reproducing every Libertarian publication on microfiche. This was the cheaper version of microform. Up to 144 pages of material could fit on a wafer thin film with the dimensions of an index card.

By the late 1990s, Zube'd gotten up to about 2000 fiches, with hundreds of thousands of filmed pages. These existed under the general name of *Peace Plans*. Zube published his own original material under the same title, interspersing them with reproduced documents. Doerr appears in *Peace Plans* #650, dated to 1986, answering Zube's questionnaire about how to achieve peace. As of late 2021, the German was still alive in Australia. In their short correspondence, Zube found Kobek both annoying and moronic.

Peace Plans microfiches looked like this:

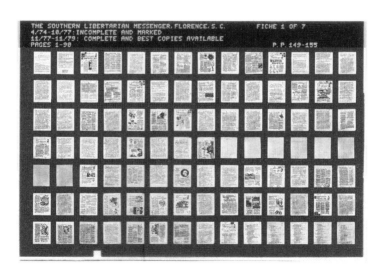

Somewhere in the 1970s, Doerr'd started calling his publishing outfit Paldor Publications. Around 1984, he renamed it. Luna Ventures. This coincided with the move towards microfiche.

In *Peace Plans* #724, Zube reproduced a one-page sheet that Doerr mailed in late 1984 or early 1985. Zube'd titled it "A HELP!"

Doerr lays out future plans for Luna Ventures. He's giving up his fanzines, which he calls his "littles." The new focus is upscale publishing. Doerr mentions three titles in the works: *SCIFANT,* a SF/Fantasy magazine, *Galactica,* dedicated to the exploration of space, and *Buckskinner's Life,* which is just *Pioneer* under a new name. He asks people to contribute art and writing, then puts forth a notion of envisioned distribution: thousands of copies sent to libraries and newsstands and magazine racks. He asks people to advertise in the new publications. Doerr also claims to have microfiched *Pioneer*s #202 through #319. He writes that each fiche contains 98 reproduced pages.

Kobek discovered only two of Doerr's publications issued after 1976. *Sanctuary News* #3, which Kobek dated to either 1981 or 1982, and *Filkin,* which Doerr created for the August 1985 mailing of APA-Filk. The writer spoke to someone who'd had a short story appear in *SCIFANT.* They reported holding a small, stapled chapbook. But could no longer find it. Otherwise, there was nothing. This was not for a lack of trying.

As for the implied plethora of *Pioneer,* Kobek could not see how this was possible. *Pioneer* #1 was published in 1968. By January 1975, Doerr was on #14. An average of two issues a year. Using January 1976 as a starting date, and assuming that the one-sheet was mailed in January 1985, Doerr would have had to produce another 305 issues of *Pioneer* in a ten year period. An average of 30 1/2 issues per annum. 1666 pages of material, at a rate of 3 1/2 pages a week. Or 186 pages per year. Which would include not only the writing but also the mimeographing. In Doerr's most prolific year—1975—he'd produced about 51 pages of new content. If Doerr had stuck to his FAPA vow of giving up publishing, if he'd done nothing between 1976 and 1980, it would mean the new issues of *Pioneer* were concentrated between 1981 and 1984. About 416 1/2 pages per year.

Peace Plans #811 contains a letter from Zube to Doerr, dated 5 July 1988 and sent in response to a Doerr letter of 14 June 1988. Most of Zube's letter is about the difficulties of microfiche production and also a response to microfiche that Doerr has sent Zube. Doerr in hero-worship mode: he's mailed Zube microfiche because Zube is the guy most associated with Libertarian microfiche. *Look at me. Here I am. I'm like you. Let's collaborate.*

The fiche contained *Skinner #1*, which sounds like a modified version of *Buckskinner's Life*. More than three years after the one-sheet announced its existence.

On the 5th page of his letter, Zube asks: "Will you attempt to produce some quality fiche editions of PIONEER?" Kobek thought this split both ways—either there's never been *Pioneer* on fiche, or Zube, a fiche snob, is suggesting that the previous efforts were garbage. On page 4, Zube notes that Doerr had produced good quality fiche of *L-5 News* issues from 1975 and 1976. *L-5 News* was a publication of the L-5 Society, an organization dedicated to the colonization of space.

Earlier, Kobek found evidence of Doerr addressing a 1985 open forum held by the Presidential National Commission on Space. The writer was in this sub-vonu mess because of a *Living Free* issue in which Doerr wrote about space colonization. And Doerr, in 1985, was about to publish *Galactica*. In 1988, he's bootlegging a space newsletter.

In 1970, Zodiac sent a card on 5 October and then the Halloween Card of 27 October. These mailings deviated from previous Zodiac letters. Both bore a special commemorative stamp.

It looked like this:

Apollo 8 launched in the early morning of 21 December 1968. Three days later, while the mission's astronauts were literally over the Moon, they read aloud the Biblical story of Genesis. Hence the stamp's inscription.

Adjusting for time zones, the launch was about six hours after Zodiac's first attack. The one out on Lake Herman Road.

IN THE BEGINNING, GOD...

By 5 October 1970, the Apollo 8 stamp was unavailable. It was a commemorative issue of 5 May 1969. Printed on sheets of 50. 153,743 impressions before the plates were decommissioned, meaning there were 7,687,150 individual stamps. On its day of its release, the Post Office sold through 908,634.

By 30 April 1970, the *Daily Chronicle* of De Kalb, Illinois was reporting: "The Apollo 8 stamp... has been a scarce one at local Post Offices, and has not been available at the Philatelic window in Chicago for some time."

In October 1970, Zodiac couldn't have gone and bought the stamps at his local Post Office. Which suggests a pre-existing desire for the stamp. It's possible that Zodiac couldn't get enough of the joke, of the overlap in timing.

IN THE BEGINNING, GOD...

But it was just as likely he was into space exploration.

And so was Doerr.

†

Cabot made three more major appearances in *Living Free*. Issues #7, #9, and #13. Dated, respectively, April 1980, October 1980, and June 1981. More farming, more Libertarianism. The only notable thing was the beginning of Cabot's issue #7 letter: "As a male chauvinist pig, I wish to here & now extend an invitation to any females who might wish to live on a mountain in No. Calif. with a dirty old man." A return to the idea that first surfaced in a 1968 *Berkeley Barb* classified, the one that Tom Marshall made real. Given the pen name, one could read this invitation as a wolf summoning sheep. Or an opportunity to be branded.

Doerr's next appearance in *Living Free* was issue #14, dated August 1981. A letter from "paul d." Followed by a "subsistence & survival" piece written by Paul Doerr. Standard fair. The first time that a letter appeared under his full name was in *Living Free* #16. Dated to November 1981. The usual content. Self-defense, farming, paranoia, and the desire to purchase a microform reader. There was no transition, no sense of the thing having changed, no explanation of why Tarl Cabot was abandoned.

Around the same time, Doerr re-emerged in other publications. The first appearance that Kobek found was a column in the October 1980 issue of *Which Way?/Witch Way,* a small pagan fanzine. Like the piece in *Living Free* #14, it was about survival and subsistence. Recycled *Pioneer.*

For four years, Doerr went into occlusion. It wasn't total. But it never is. That was the lesson learned by any political radical who went underground. One can never disappear. That's impossible. But no one needs to disappear. They just need to hide. And that is achieved by information management. Incoming and outgoing. For roughly four years, from the middle of 1976 through the end of 1980, Doerr was functionally invisible.

Presented with the first issue of *Living Free,* Doerr had the same impulse whenever he discovered a new venue. He had to write.

He had to send a letter to the editor.

But he was in hiding.

He needed a new name.

And chose the most fucked-up thing from Science Fiction.

†

In the August 1981 issue of *Pagana,* Doerr ran the following classified:

```
---------------------------------------------------------------------------
Advertisement by male chauvenist dirty ole mountaineer.  Ladies!  Do you want to get
out of the rutrace?  Do you want to live, primitive style, on a very secluded
mountain in northern california?  One or more, with or without kids, write me.
Paul Doerr,  225 e utah, fairfield, ca 94533...
---------------------------------------------------------------------------
```

Ladies!

The same theme was in May 1982 issue of *The Communicator,* edited by prisoners in the maximum security penitentiary at Springhill, Nova Scotia. Doerr's included letter read like the weirdest personal known to man:

Hi,

I notice that the *COMMUNICATOR* is giving more space to women and children. Those have been badly neglected subjects. Perhaps they have never made as much "noise" as the men? Maybe they have been considered sixth class citizens?

I have wondered what women do if/when released. Are they interested in small subsistence farms, mountain-living, survival, etc., as many men are. If you print a short notice in the *COMMUNICATOR,* perhaps some of them would like to write me. Since I've been into this sort of thing for many years, perhaps I could answer some of their questions. As you know, I have bought some land on a mountainside and am building my cabin, sheds, etc., so I have some practical experience at it.

The idea would reoccur in the Fall 1985 issue of *Green Revolution.* Another letter from Doerr. Its text read like this:

Women of all ages and in all societies are often mistreated, abandoned, battered, raped, thrown away, caused to just disappear every year, never to be heard of again... I want to produce a regular publication on these happenings...

I want articles on and by women themselves and what happens to them, what some have done, and what they can do, from self-defense to group living, from co-op companies to moving out onto land with a garden, chickens, a cow, and a little shack with a wood stove, oil lamps and bucket water. I want articles on conditions in prisons and public institutions...

A friend suggested that you might know some women who would like to live on a mountain in northern california. The nearest neighbor is about half mile away, no utilities,

200 miles north of san francisco. they could have horses, chickens, etc. I work near San Francisco and only get there on weekends. It is nice but "quiet."

Doerr was a man who called himself Tarl Cabot. He'd registered the Tuchuk slave brand with the state of California. He had written multiple letters about *Gor*.

"Women of all ages and in all societies are often mistreated, abandoned, battered, raped, thrown away, caused to just disappear every year, never to be heard of again...."

An exact description of *Gor*.

Kobek thought of several books from both of Doerr's WANT LISTs. *Venus School Mistress* by Anonymous. *An Excess of Love* by Jac Lenders. *Our Fair Flagellants* by Jerome Hornell. *Bondage Trash* by Jon Horn. *The Story of Seven Maidens: Slavery in West India* by Anonymous.

High-brow BDSM porn.

"I want articles on and by women themselves and what happens to them..." A request for real world *Gor*.

Material from the people who'd suffered it.

†

Doerr disappeared from *Living Free* for three years, reemerging in issue #45. Dated September 1988. In this letter, written in June 1988, Doerr returned to his usual themes. He complained about the government. And, yet again, extended his offer to women. *Girl, would you like to live on a mountain?*

In *Living Free* #47, dated February 1989, Stumm published a letter by a correspondent named Wally G: "In closing I should like to say that I admire the offer of the fellow who is willing to take several people (preferably females) and settle them on his place — but for some reason I seem to question his motives."

Doerr reiterated his offer in *Living Free* #49. In issue #50, Wally G responded again: "NOW — in regards to the 1st part of your letter - your offer to take some <u>women</u> into your cabin in northern Calif., etc., etc.. Care to expand on this noble gesture as to why only women ???"

In that same issue, Doerr responds to Wally G's first letter: "If Wally is commenting on me: there are boy's towns, boy's farms, boy's ranches, etc. but how many for girls or women? Females are more willing to stay & care for. Ever see many bachelor's pads? Also, I like women. As for <u>several</u> women: One woman, I could force to do whatever I wanted, perhaps. But several? Also, if several females are living together, they could take care of their children (& even some strays) easily by taking turns."

†

Kobek searched the public records of Mendocino County and discovered the parcel number of Doerr's property. 034-143-19. On a whim, the writer plugged the digits into Google Search.

What the hell? What's the worst that can happen?

The first result was for 29341 Eel River Ranch Rd, Covelo, CA 95428. Realtor.com.[17] The property had gone up for sale in 2018. Multiple photos included. Most depicted the land itself. But a few contained images of a cabin. Several photos depicted its interior, an uninsulated hovel that made Ted Kaczynski look like a practiced master of home décor.

One wall was lined with books on makeshift cinder-block shelving. Below the books, on the floor, was an old magazine, half of its cover torn away. Kobek determined that it was an issue of *Popular Mechanics*. August 1962. Which established one thing. Doerr kept old magazines for decades.

One photo depicted the cabin's toilet.

In his youth, Kobek had dreamed big dreams. Famous writer!

Now he was asking himself: *if Doerr were the killer, then am I not the first man to behold, burdened with intolerable secret knowledge, the commode into which Zodiac pinched his mountain turds?*

The cabin was impossibly small.

---

17   Archived at: https://web.archive.org/web/20211005162418/https://www.realtor. com/realestateandhomes-detail/Eel-River-Ranch-Rd_Covelo_CA_95428_M18439-01609

In issues of *Mendocino Husbandman*, Doerr wrote of his trouble with the local authorities. They didn't want to approve the cabin. Because of its size. Around 250 square feet. Realtor.com included old photos, presumably taken by Doerr. Black-and-white, depicting the cabin as it was being built. To Kobek's eye, these images originated from the mid-to-late 1970s.

It wasn't what the photos showed. It was what they didn't. The cabin and the land lacked amenities that would allow multiple people to survive.

One of Doerr's requests for mountain *ladies!* appeared in a magazine dedicated to prisoners, seeking women fresh from jail.

Individuals who would never be missed.

Repeated throughout the 1980s, the scheme was impossible. The photos proved that. If some unfortunate had taken Doerr up on his offer, they could not have survived on the land. Not without major upgrades and improvements. And the 2018 photographs proved that Doerr had never upgraded the cabin. The scheme could never have been true.

If the man'd been Zodiac, and if any woman had gone to the mountain, it could have only ended in the bloodiest of disasters.

†

Another dubious scheme appeared in 1982.

Kobek found mention in classifieds in *Soldier of Fortune* and multiple issues of *Circle Network News*, a Neo-Pagan circular.

The clearest statement was a half-page advert in the Samhain 1982 issue of *Pagana*, the newsletter of the Pagan/Witchcraft/Occult Special Interest Group of American Mensa.[18] The advert began like this: "Pagans move a <u>lot</u> and have a problem staying in contact. I always did, and do. I had a PO Box (1444, Vallejo, CA) and, having dropped it, still have people hunting for me."

---

18 Mensa membership is limited to individuals capable of achieving high scores on IQ tests. From comments in *Patter* and *Green Egg*, it would appear that Doerr was a member sometime in the 1970s. To his credit, he found the organization a bit shit. The most interesting and salacious comment on the subject comes from the May 1974 FAPA *Patter*: "… I have to fill my tank two or three times a week just to get to work, not to mention the Mensa orgies I like to go to in the Bay Area, and don't get to often enough…"

Three paragraphs followed. The first announced Doerr's decision to operate a postal service. He'd receive mail for any individual who paid $30 a year, holding and forwarding letters in bunches. This was the same as the classifieds.

The one in *Soldier of Fortune*'s May 1982 issue looked like this:

> **$30/YEAR — USE THIS HOME ADDRESS — Letters mailed/forwarded/held/other servies. Confidential. Info. 50¢. DOERR, 225 E. Utah, Fairfield, CA 94533.**

The second paragraph offered expanded service. For an extra $20, Doerr would pay people's bills and taxes, store sensitive documents, and keep a record of where, and with whom, his customers were traveling. If a customer didn't get in touch with some regularity, Doerr would contact the police.

In the third paragraph, Doerr established bonafides for this service by mentioning well known appearances in other print outlets, naming *Green Egg* and *The Acolyte*. The latter was a fanzine edited by Francis T. Laney and Samuel D. Russell. It ran between 1942 and 1946. Doerr's sole appearance was a short letter in issue #11. Dated June 1945.

Green Egg made sense. *Green Egg* was the template for every publication like *Pagana*. But *The Acolyte*? This publication was the first regular fanzine dedicated to the memory of Howard Phillips Lovecraft. And Doerr's appearance was 37-years old.

Kobek remembered something in *Pathan* #1, the first of Doerr's fanzines, the one sent through N'APA in June 1968. Discussing the Missing Link, Doerr wrote: "There is also the Migo of the Himalayas Mountains (I wrote of this in Meade Laynes old Acolyte), and closer to home, Bigfoot in Calif."

The Acolyte #11 letter wasn't much more than two paragraphs, taken from a reference book, about the Abominable Snowman. The September 1945 *Weird Tales* published a near identical letter quoting the same paragraphs, without attribution, making it seem as if Doerr wrote the reproduced words. The other major differences were two additional lines in *Weird Tales*: "If anyone knows about anything else about the Mi-go or the other things Lovecraft wrote about will he or she please write and tell me. I will answer any letter."

When he'd found this material, Kobek took it to mean that Doerr, back when he was 18-years old, believed in prehistoric survival. And believed that when Howard Phillips Lovecraft, a strict materialist and atheist, wrote about big stupid supernatural monsters, he was writing a secret truth.

Around the same time, Doerr made other print appearances in which he wrote about the Abominable Snowman. One of these occurred in *Flying Roll*, a UFO newsletter edited by Meade Layne, founder and director of the Borderlands Sciences Research Associates, a California-based esoterica and occult research organization. Kobek found references to Doerr's appearance in *Flying Roll*, knew that it occurred in a 1946 issue numbered "Gamma I." But the writer could not find a copy, which meant that he couldn't summarize its contents. Given the editorial names—Meade Layne running *Flying Roll* and Francis T. Laney putting together *The Acolyte*—one could understand Doerr's confusion in *Pagana* and *Pathan*.

This was the one instance where Kobek discovered Doerr making a factual mistake. Yes, the man often lied, and yes, he often recycled garbage information from esoterica paperbacks, but there was no other instance of Doerr being flat-out wrong about a factual detail in his own life.

Doerr might have mixed up the publications, but he was persistent in the error. He made it in 1968, when his *Acolyte* appearance was 23-years in the past, and made it again in 1982. Fourteen years later. In an advertisement for a mail forwarding service.

If Doerr were Zodiac, Kobek had a hard time believing that Doerr would receive other people's mail and not read it. That this was not the whole point.

Kobek showed *Pagana* to a friend, who suggested a different possible motive: that by taking on other people's mail, Doerr was creating plausible deniability. That, in the event Doerr received something objectionable through the post, something that he himself ordered, he would have an explanation for concerned authorities. Or that he could order objectionable material under the names of his customers. And deny all knowledge.

Doerr offered this service from his home in Fairfield.

225 East Utah Street.

Where he lived with his wife. Where despite his claims of moving a <u>lot</u>, he'd been stationed since the mid-1960s.

The mail service removed the possibility that Doerr's wife forced her husband to give up the Vallejo mailbox. If she had objected to his various print misadventures, existing solely through the auspices of his post office box, why would she, six years later, be amenable to a massive influx at the home address?

Kobek's bias wouldn't let him see this as anything other than confirmation. An external pressure forced Doerr to abandon the mailbox. It brought the writer back to the *Pagana*'s second sentence: "I had a PO Box (1444, Vallejo, CA) and, having dropped it, still have people hunting for me."

Kobek didn't want to read too much into this. One of Doerr's favorite verbs was hunting. He was always hunting things. He was hunting books, boats, weapons, animals.

But.

This was the only time that Doerr wrote of other people hunting Doerr.

†

Kobek continued corresponding with Jim Stumm. The writer wondered about Doerr's letter in *Living Free* #1, the text making it clear that it was mailed in response to something called *Odd Man Out*.

A publication for which Kobek could find no reference or explanation. He sent an inquiry to Stumm, who responded by sending Kobek copies of the four published issues.

In essence, *Odd Man Out* was the *Living Free* alpha test. Its issues arrived throughout 1978, and there, in #2, was a letter from Doerr. It wasn't particularly interesting, only Doerr being Doerr, going on about farming and how he liked war because it reduced population numbers. In the table of contents, Stumm noted that Doerr mailed the letter 3 March 1978.

Square in the middle of Doerr's disappearance, of his **GAFIA**. Which began around May 1976. Less than two years after sending his FAPA resignation and he's receiving a small publication and sending letters.

Along with the *American Pigeon Journal*, this was one of the two exceptions to what Kobek thought of as Doerr's Dark Period. 1976 to 1980. A time of occlusion, of almost no writing or letters.

Hardly even a classified, and even then, not under the full name.

The first and second pages of *Odd Man Out #1*, dated February 1978, made reference to something called *Ego Trip* while also explaining the circulation of the new publication:

> EGO TRIP NEWS: Both ET numbers are alive & well. ET 7 has been returned to me twice since I sent it out. 1st becus the forwarding address was lost, & the 2nd time because one ET'er has apparently moved. So I've mailed this thing 3 times, which is Too Much. Please, if you have any problem with ET, write me a note about it. DO NOT sent me ET itself...

> For some time I've been thinking about doing a publication something like VONU LIFE. EGO TRIP was a step in that direction, altho not enuf of the writing in there has been self lib oriented... ODD will be done on carbon sets... Circulation will be 20 copies, which I will send out free to whoever I like, mostly people who get ET, plus a few others...

Kobek guessed that *Ego Trip* was a round robin. Stumm would prepare material, send it to another samizdat Libertarian, the latter would add their own material to the issue and pass it on to the next. Kobek sent Stumm another letter. Inquiring about *Ego Trip*. Stumm responded by sending, under separate cover, a letter and a package.

The letter confirmed Kobek's thesis.

Ego Trip was, indeed, a round robin. Paul Doerr had been a contributor. Its issues could not be reproduced because the archives were over two thousand pages of loosely organized content.

The package contained a variety of material, including xeroxes of each issue of *Ego Trip*'s first page, and a page from *Ego Trip #7* that mapped the publication's distribution network.

It also included a handwritten list of the dates when Stumm mailed issues of *Ego Trip:*

Jim Stumm mailed EGO TRIP on these dates:

even numbers	*star series*
ET1 — 2/17/76	ET3 — 8/1/76
ET2 — 6/2/76	ET5 — 1/26/77
ET4 — 10/4/76	ET7 — 2/7/78
ET6 — 7/6/77	
ET8 — 5/19/78	

The map looked like this:

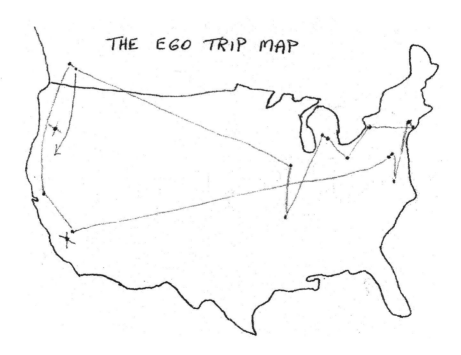

As of 7 February 1978, one of the map's points, the one farthest to the west, was Fairfield, California.

The package also contained Doerr's contributions to *Ego Trip*. The first item was a handwritten letter, the same script used in *REHUPA* #15 and Doerr's Presidential note in the May 1976 FAPA. Kobek made an observation: while the cover of *Unknown* #19 (page 99 of this book) demonstrated that Doerr could write in multiple scripts, for whatever reason, it did not employ Doerr's default handwriting.

Doerr mailed the letter on 16 January 1976, postmarked Oakland, California. In it, he asked if he could join the round robin. Doerr'd folded the paper in on itself and used its exterior as the envelope.

Another item in the package was another of Doerr's handwritten letters, part of an unknown issue of *Ego Trip*. Its first two pages were xeroxes, while its third page was handwritten on the reverse of someone else's contribution to *Ego Trip*.

Beneath this letter was a copy of a Doerr fanzine.
The Shangrila Pioneer.

†

Kobek'd seen *Shangrila* listed in Allan Beatty's *Fanzine Directory 2*, which attempted to catalogue every SF/Fantasy fanzine published in 1976.

Given the rarity of Doerr's fanzines—particularly those not circulated via Amateur Press Associations—Kobek imagined that *Shangrila Pioneer* was lost in time. He'd questioned whether it even existed. And now somehow, in his own hands, he held what must be the only extant copy.

Despite the title, the fanzine was only another issue of *Pioneer*. The usual mix of eschatology and alternative housing. Doerr explained the new title as a response to the founding of "the Kingdom of Dwarf." The idea, basically, was that Doerr was establishing his own dominion in the Kingdom. And calling it Shangrila. *Pioneer* was now its official organ.

Doerr'd provided a mailing address for the Kingdom of Dwarf: Box 2073, Salem, MA, 01970. A search on the box returned a few classifieds scattered throughout 1975 and 1976, hinting that someone named David the Dwarft had started his own monetary system. No mention of the Kingdom. One ad, in the 5 June 1975 *Great Speckled Bird*, offered a different address and the only hint at what it might all be about: "WHY NOT rox and pebbles, instead of dollars and cents. Build trust stop illuminati. Refer you to: David, the Dwarft, P.O. Box 233, Melrose Park, Ill. 60160."[19]

Kobek recognized this.

The *VONU LIFE/Green Egg* impulse.

Find a thing, get enthusiastic, imitate that thing, make a fool of yourself.

Try not to confess to murder.

†

The second letter, the one Doerr contributed to *Ego Trip*, was dated in a unique fashion: "Today is Earth 270 - 1976." Kobek'd read enough Science Fiction to *grok* Doerr's date. 1976 was obvious. 270 was the calendar day, shorn of its month.

Sunday 26 September 1976.

Well after the **GAFIA**. And well after Doerr was supposed to be busy with his cabin and his boat. Confirming the presence of Fairfield on the map in *EGO TRIP #7*.

Which meant: the resignation letter was not true.

Which meant: that Doerr never went anywhere.

Which meant: that Kobek's specious theory about Doerr's **GAFIA** was feeling a <u>lot</u> more likely.

There was something in Doerr's January 1976 letter to Stumm, which predated *Shangrila Pioneer*: "There is no way I can hide so long as I publish Pioneer."

It asked its own question: why was Doerr trying to hide?

There was a dead zone between *Shangrila* in 1976 and 1981, the year when discussion of *Pioneer* erupted again in multiple publications. Kobek scoured every possible place where *Pioneer* might be mentioned. The best

---

19   In Gordon J. Melton's 1977 book *A Directory of Religious Bodies in the United States*, this address corresponds to that of God's Kingdom on Earth, C/O Bishop David Zenor. Melton specifies that this is a mail-order church.

that he came up with was directories of irregular periodicals that listed Paldor Publications. But this could be old knowledge, stuff cataloged in 1975 or 1976 that never stopped being listed. If Doerr was, indeed, publishing those 1666 pages, there was zero available evidence that anyone had seen them.

For instance: issue #1 of Beatty's *Fanzine Directory* attempted to catalogue every fanzine published in 1975, working off Beatty's personal encounters and using multiple third-party sources. This issue includes entries for *Mendocino Husbandman*, *Pioneer*, and, weirdly, either *Hobbitalia* #2 or #3. Kobek knew from where Beatty'd cribbed most of the 1975 information about Doerr: issues #14 and #17 of Ned Brooks's *It Comes in the Mail*. This was a fanzine, published for several years, in which Brooks made a running list of the nonsense mailed to him by Science Fiction people.

As mentioned earlier, *Fanzine Directory* #2 covers 1976. And includes *Shangrila Pioneer*. Beatty notes that he's seen a copy with his own eyes.

Fanzine Directory #3, which documented 1977, has zero entries for Doerr. No *Pioneer*, no nothing.

Given that *Fanzine Directory* #3 was published in January 1981, which allowed four years for cataloging, the best possible inference is that Doerr wasn't publishing.

But this didn't mean that it didn't happen.

Only that Kobek could not find any evidence.

Shangrila stated the following: "To subscribe ti [sic] The Shangrila Pioneer you must be a member of the Dwarf Kingdom and Shangrila."

Kobek remembered, yet again, that "Paul Doerr" was a character on the page. If you read the statement on its surface, it sounded like the utterance of a hopeless and clueless guy.

But assuming that the Shangrila idea wasn't abandoned with the next issue, it would whittle a readership to nothing. No one was going to follow through on the requirements.

"Paul Doerr," character of the page, might be dumb.

But Paul Doerr, the living man, was not.

If you can't hide while you publish *Pioneer*, you could always find a pretext to cease publication.

†

If Doerr were Zodiac, if he'd fucked up with *Green Egg,* if someone had called his number, if he felt that he had to disappear but couldn't give it up, then *Ego Trip* or *Odd Man Out* was where he'd go.

A publication with extremely limited circulation, a place where you know every one who's reading your writing.

Kobek saw this theory in practice. In the final issue of *Odd Man Out,* dated December 1978, Stumm explained a coming change:

> DEATH & REBIRTH: This will be the last issue of ODD MAN OUT. But soon I will publish the 1st issue of a successor mag, a "son of OMO," which will be named LIVING FREE... It will be printed by photo offset with 33% reduction... LF will be offered for sale, rather than given away. But those who regularly send info that I can use in it will receive a free subscription.

The operative word is *offset.* It's different than mimeography or carbons. It's printing that requires setup and special equipment. Offset can't be done at home and is pointless for small editions. It's almost impossible to find a printer who'll do an offset run below a thousand copies. This is something that Doerr knew. Demonstrably. It's in a letter on page 3 of *VONU LIFE* #6: "I found offset printer $5.50/3,25 per 1000, reduction, etc free."

Anyone who read *Odd Man Out* #4 and knew about offset would understand the coming change. *Living Free* wasn't for a small circle of associates. It was for public dissemination.

In the first issue, Stumm relied upon letters that'd came in response to the final *Odd Man Out.* But he'd paid the writers a courtesy: no one's last name is used. Doerr's initial *Living Free* appearance is as "paul d."

On the front page, Stumm lays out his editorial policy. He asks correspondents to inform him if they want their letters published. And under what name.

Which means: the Paul Doerr who's fine appearing as "Paul Doerr" in *Ego Trip* and *Odd Man Out* readers is not comfortable appearing as "Paul Doerr" in *Living Free*'s wider and uncontrolled distribution.

So he becomes Tarl Cabot.

†

In the *Ego Trip* letter, Doerr wrote the following: "I'd like to buy a bunch of old Sunday color comics with the Prince Valiant strip."

Kobek remained convinced that *Tim Holt* #30 was the sole determinant of the Zodiac era.

And here was Doerr.

Looking for old comics.

There'd been the inquiry to reach comic collectors in the August 1968 *National Fantasy Fan*. In the February 1975 FAPA *Patter*, he'd written about hunting *Vampirella* comix. He'd mentioned liking comics in *REHUPA* #15.

And now there was this.

Doerr was a collector.

†

Doerr appeared in *Living Free* throughout 1989 and 1990, writing about how lax immigration policy allowed immigrants to bring disease into the United States, and how he believed political and social leaders should be executed at the first sign of dereliction. In his last letter of 1990, running in *Living Free* #59, Doerr proposed a system in which computers chose who should be executed. And when.

Then he disappeared from the publication for eleven years.

The 1990s were a period of relative inactivity. As Kobek moved closer to his own time, the record became increasingly opaque. But he knew that the 1990s weren't a disappearance like the six years between 1976 and 1982. Doerr still sent letters and placed classifieds. They were less frequent.

In 1994, Doerr registered Luna Ventures as a corporation. In that same year's edition of the *Poet's Market*, a pre-Internet guide for writers looking for venues accepting work, the following text appeared: "**LUNA VENTURES; POLY; SCIFANT; UNKNOWN; BACKWOODS; OWLHOOTERS (IV-Themes, Science Fiction)**, P.O. Box 398, Suisun City, CA 94585-0398, founded in the 1930s, editor Paul Doerr. This publisher puts out a number of monthly newsletters, all of which use poetry on appropriate subjects. *Poly* is about life-styles such as polygamy and group marriage. *SCIFANT* focuses on science fiction, fantasy and horror and is published in microfiche only. *Unknown* is about 'anomalies, the mysterious, the unusual, such as witchcraft, appearances and disappearances, Bigfoot, UFOS.' *Swashbuckler* is about Renaissance Faires, fencing, swashbuckling, and related topics. *Backwoods* deals with subsistence farming, animals and survival. *Owlhooters* is about treasure, prospecting, bounty hunting, collecting, etc. All use poetry relevant to their themes. All are 12 pgs. condensed type except *SCIFANT*, which is 98 pages."

Some of these publications had existed. But hadn't survived. Part of this was due to Doerr abandoning, mostly, Science Fiction fandom, and the collector mentality of its denizens. But. Doerr also lied. The evidence was in things like *Poet's Market*. There were multiple instances, in multiple guides, where Doerr claimed to have started publishing in the late 1930s. When he was ten years old. In *The Catalog of UFO Periodicals*, a 1982 book by Tom Lind, Doerr claimed he began publishing *Unknown* in 1960. This was demonstrably untrue. The first version of *Pioneer* #1, dated to 1968, made no mention of *Unknown*. The second version, provisionally dated to somewhere around 1971, contained an advertisement for the publication. And Kobek couldn't forget the supposed 1666 pages of *Pioneer*.

Other titles for which Kobek found listings, but no extant texts, were *Intentional Families, The Keep, Enhanced Reality, Skinner, Simple Living,* and *The ConCom guide, or, How to sin more and suffer less.* In its catalog, the Library of Congress contained entries for microfiche copies of *Owlhooters* and *Swashbuckler.* Kobek sent in a duplication order. The Library wrote back. They did not possess either publication.

Kobek discovered which company Doerr used to produce microfiche. Kobek wrote to the company. Their records did not go back to the 1980s or 1990s.

Near the end of the 1990s, Doerr consolidated his publications into a single title. He called this *DOE.* And he got an email address: doee@netzero.net.

†

Doerr returned, properly, to *Living Free* in issue #119. Dated April 2001.

Part of a late renaissance. The lion in winter. Doerr in his seventies and sending out a great deal of material. Tips on farming, on raising chickens, on seeds, on cooking, on bee keeping. And he was, once more, looking for land. There were letters in *Country Conversation & Feedback,* in *Rural Heritage,* in *Backwoods Home Magazine,* in *Countryside and Small Stock Journal,* and *Bee Culture.*

With the exception of an entry in the September 2001 *Bee Culture,* its text about making war on the enemies of the hive, the letters in these publications were gentle. Almost pastoral. A letter in the November-December 2001 issue of *Backwoods Home* contained a curiosity. In the 1960s and 1970s, Doerr often bragged about killing a "tigre" with a "sword + spear". In this late effort, the tigre has become a jaguar.

Throughout the 1980s and 1990s and 2000s, Doerr appeared in a small fanzine called *Message Post.* Later retitled to *Dwelling Portably.* Most of these appearances were short, one paragraph subsistence and survival tips. The April 2005 *Dwelling Portably* contained a condensed excerpt from *DOE* #49. Which would indicate, at least, that one issue existed.

From what Kobek could tell, Doerr began publishing *DOE* no earlier than 1995. Had he managed 49 issues in seven years? Or was the numbering arbitrary? 1666 pages. *Pioneer* territory.

The *DOE* #49 excerpt was about shanty boats on the Mississippi River. Kobek realized that he'd read the piece before.

It had appeared in *Pioneer* #1. Both versions. It had been rewritten for *DOE* #49, but in its content, progression, and form, it was almost identical to the material in a fanzine from 1968.

Here, at the end, Doerr went back to the beginning.

†

Doerr's Twenty-First Century *Living Free* letters had the old crazy. He wrote about torturing drug dealers, about the failure of the space program. He contributed short stories about surviving the nuclear holocaust through subsistence farming, one of which ended with the following: "Shooting from behind is safest. You are only issued one of you."

Doerr's last appearance was in #134, dated to September 2006. The letter took up half a page. Bio-warfare, nuclear holocaust, terrorism, ecological ruin, pandemics. The letter read like a map of the new millennium. The cartographer drew it forty years earlier. Back then, Doerr saw a fallen and doomed world. And now his prophecy had come true. In the grotesque Hell of 2021, the map was more accurate than ever.

Say this for the old man: he was consistent in his concerns. And prescient.

In this final letter, Doerr wrote about living on a 1800s style farm house as a child. Almost certainly another lie. Kobek knew where Doerr lived for most of his early life. A series of sad apartments in Sharon, Pennsylvania.

At the letter's end, Doerr mentioned that health reasons prevented him from returning to his cabin in Covelo. He wanted to trade the land where he'd hoped to bring women parolees. He wanted something along the coast, where he would have easy hospital access.

In less than a year, the old man was dead. Cardiac arrest. Secondary complicating factors: hypercalcemia and cancer of the head and neck.

The old man was gone.

chapter eleven

bathing in the sick grey gloom of a sick grey room

KOBEK SPENT MONTHS poring through Doerr's remains. Nothing excluded the man. There was neither a hint nor a scrap of information that would prevent Doerr from being Zodiac. Each time that Kobek found something of note, Doerr was only brought closer. It could have been confirmation bias. But. Kobek hadn't taken a single piece of information and bent it out of shape. All he'd done is order fanzines from libraries. All he'd done was find ANFO and books and mimeographed publications that solved long standing questions about Zodiac. Whatever else this was, it wasn't fantasy. Nothing was being made up.

And yet the writer could not escape the feeling that he had failed.

Kobek predicated his hunt on a theory: someone could take hyperspecific references within Zodiac letters and then, parsing that data, find an individual with direct connections to these references. Establish enough specificity and you find Zodiac.

Kobek looked over what he'd written and researched. He only saw the flaw. He'd found what he considered very good evidence for Doerr's potential inclusion as Zodiac but little that the writer believed definitive.

Consider the identification of *The Strange Ways of Man* as the source material for slaves in the afterlife. Kobek was certain that this text was used by Zodiac. Kobek knew that Doerr had owned the book.

But Kobek couldn't prove which edition. And even if he could prove that Doerr was selling the paperback, this would not preclude the possibility of Doerr's owning the hardcover.

Another example was *Tim Holt* #30. Kobek could prove that Doerr was looking for comic books in the late 1960s. The writer could prove Doerr's interest in publications about the Old West.

From a paragraph in Doerr's contribution to the 27 January 1975 mailing of the Elanor-APA: "I have some old E.R. Burroughs fanzines to sell or trade. Also, some hardcover (I think) Doc Savage books...maybe firsts...I haven't cracked them to see. Also a few OLD Western pulps."

Kobek could establish, in theory, a low number of people collecting back issue comic books in the North Bay. No more than five. Arguably one. But he couldn't prove that Doerr owned the comic. If the writer was being fair to himself, he never thought that this was possible. Even in the informational dystopia of 2021, it was impossible to establish which back issues were owned by a specific collector.

The most hyperspecific proven reference—the shared usage of ANFO by both Doerr and Zodiac—posed its own problems. The writer could prove that the Minutemen were circulating the recipe for ANFO. And, prior to Zodiac, the Minutemen were the only people sending anonymous letters with the cross-hair logo. And that Doerr was a Minuteman.

But there was still a leap of inference.

The writer decided to review everything.

†

He started with the data that didn't come from the publications, the material that didn't fit anywhere else.

For years, Zodiac researchers had speculated that the killer worked on Mare Island and was former military. A description of Doerr. What Kobek hadn't seen was much emphasis placed upon the *Examiner* of 4 July 1969, the day that Zodiac shot Darlene Ferrin and Michael Mageau. A headline on the paper's front page: MARE ISLAND SUB BLAME ON WORKERS. The story described an investigation of the House Armed Services subcommittee.

On 15 May 1969, a submarine sank at the Naval Base. The subcommittee's report blamed the workers. This is exactly where, and on what, Doerr worked.

Kobek found the subcommittee's report. Doerr was not named.

But Kobek could guess one thing. Given that Doerr was a reader of the *Examiner*, he would have seen the headline. Or heard the news on the radio. And spent Independence Day in a fit of worry.

In 2004, a paper appeared in *Behavioral Sciences and the Law* 22(3). It was titled "A comparative analysis of North American adolescent and adult mass murderers." Its six authors had written the following:

> Fifty-nine per cent of the adolescents and 90% of the adults had a precipitating or triggering event before the mass murder. We defined such an event as "significantly mentally or emotionally disturbing to him, or ...obvious from scrutiny of the perpetrator's history" (Meloy et al., 2001a, p. 722).... Adult triggers included termination from a job or envy over another's promotion, bankruptcy, confrontation by an employer, actual or perceived abandonment by a sexual intimate, jealousy, erotomanic beliefs, child support issues, or property damage or trespass. Most precipitants occurred within hours or days of the mass murder, although direct causality could not be established.

Speaking of holidays.

On 13 October 1969, Zodiac mailed the letter claiming Paul Stine. Its text contained a temporal reference to its date of composition. Other letters had dates that could be inferred, but this was the sole letter stating the day that it was written. "This is the Zodiac speaking. I am the murderer of the taxi driver over by Washington St + Maple St last night, to prove this here is a blood stained piece of his shirt."

Last night.

Stine was shot 11 October 1969. The letter was written 12 October. It had not been mailed until 13 October 1969. The delay couldn't have been because 12 October was a Sunday.

Zodiac mailed multiple letters on Sundays. The 4 August 1969 letter, the one that debuted the Zodiac tradename, might have been hand delivered on 3 August. Which was a Sunday. And Zodiac had mailed correspondences on 9 November 1969 and 26 July 1970. Both were Sundays. The killer knew how to bring a letter to the post office.

Kobek had a theory, one that he'd developed long before Googling FANZINES VALLEJO. The attack at Blue Rock Springs occurred on 4 July 1969. A federal holiday. No one was working. Zodiac had all day to kill. But Zodiac killed at night. After the Independence Day celebrations were over. Kobek suspected that Zodiac was a man with obligations. That he'd spent 4 July with family. A party, a meal, see the fireworks. And then, when it's over, go out and shoot two kids in a 1963 Corvair.

12 October 1969 was also a holiday. Columbus Day. It was the second Columbus Day after the federal government had established the celebration as a holiday falling on the second Monday of every October. That law would not go into effect until 1971. In 1969, the holiday was celebrated on a Sunday.

It's hard to remember, now, when Christopher Columbus is seen as the inauguration of genocide, but in the 1960s, establishing Columbus Day was a way of weaving Italian-Americans into the county's fabric. It wasn't about genocide. It was ethnic pride. An Italian had discovered America. There'd been a hard fight to get Columbus Day recognized as a federal holiday. The victory mattered. The celebrations leading up to 1971 were intense.

Kobek suspected that the delay of the 13 October letter meant that Zodiac was Italian. Or had an Italian family.

The writer looked at available census data. Kobek found Doerr, traced his ancestry. The man's stock was the old American polyglot, the bastard offspring of the Nineteenth Century. The English/German/Scottish/Whatever.

In the 1940 census, Kobek found Doerr's wife and her family. She was 15 years old. She lived with her parents. The census table listed each individual's place of birth. Paul Doerr's wife and her siblings were born in PENNSYLVANIA, the word written out in block caps. But her parents?

ITALY.

Doerr wasn't getting away from his family on 12 October 1969.

Speaking of that home.

In the early minutes of 5 July 1969, fresh from Blue Rock Springs, Zodiac went to a payphone in Vallejo and called the police. He'd told them what he'd done. The call occurred around 12:40AM. Zodiac shot Darlene Ferrin and Michael Mageau somewhere between 11:50PM and Midnight.

Exact timing was impossible.

Mageau only gave estimates. Of when the Corvair arrived at the parking lot, of the shooting, of the arrival of Jerry, Debbie, Roger. Three hippie types in a brown Rambler, the ones who would get in touch with the cops. Mageau said that the hippie types arrived eight-to-ten minutes after Zodiac departed. But Mageau was in California dirt, approaching death. In the same interview, he couldn't remember if it were he or Darlene in the front seat of the car, flashing the headlights, trying to summon help. When he'd never left the ground. His sense of time can not be trusted.

Debbie, Jerry, Rodger find Michael Mageau. He asks them to get help. They drive to Jerry's house and call the police. A dispatch report says that their call comes in at 12:10AM. At normal speeds, the distance from Blue Rock Springs to Jerry's house was about seven minutes. But there's no way that the three hippie types didn't race home. They'd just seen a bleeding boy and a dying girl.

Assume that it took about five minutes from their arrival until their departure. Further assume that it takes five minutes to get to Jerry's house. Assume that Mageau's estimate of ten minutes is roughly correct. It puts the shooting closer to 11:50PM than Midnight.

11:50PM is fifty minutes from 12:40AM.

From when Zodiac makes the call.

Vallejo is small. It's eight miles across.

It's a ten minute drive from Blue Rock Springs to the phonebooth used by Zodiac. So why is there a 50 minute delay before Zodiac calls the police?

Many theories have been offered.

Maybe Zodiac drove around town. Maybe he lived in Vallejo and went home and changed his clothes and then walked to the phone booth.

Mageau told the police that Zodiac left the parking lot and headed south. The cops assumed that he was driving towards Springs Road. Before the intersection with Springs Road, there's a turn off to Lake Herman Road. David Faraday and Betty Lou Jensen. Lake Herman Road connected to the I-680. Which connected to the I-80. Which went to Fairfield.

The phone booth was at Tuolumne & Spring Road. Google Maps estimates that travel from Blue Rock Springs down Lake Herman Road to the I-680 to the I-80 to Paul Doerr's house and then to the phone booth would take approximately fifty minutes.

But this theoretical action is happening late at night. No one's on the road. It's going to be faster.

Kobek could see how it might happen. Shoot the victims, hit the streets. The car has been seen. But a phonecall must be made. It wasn't the only time that the killer made a phonecall. Another happened after Lake Berryessa. Zodiac drove to the city of Napa and called the police. Zodiac could have called from anywhere. But he called from Napa. The best guess is that the killer didn't realize Napa PD lacked jurisdiction over Lake Berryessa. When he called the Napa PD, he first talked to the operator. He asked to be connected to the police. He calls what he believes to be the relevant jurisdiction.

Imagine that Doerr is Zodiac. He's just shot two kids. He knows that he's going to make the phonecall from Vallejo. But maybe people can identify his car. Does he risk driving in the death machine? Or does he do the most logical thing? Does he go home and switch cars? Then drive back to Vallejo. Go to the phone booth. Make the call. Connect to the relevant jurisdiction.

Approximately fifty minutes.

The timing was perfect.

And that's only if Mageau's recollection were accurate. If Zodiac drove north out of the Blue Rock Spring, he'd be on Columbus Parkway. This road connects, directly, to the I-80. It shaves ten minutes off the journey.

If Doerr were Zodiac.

†

Kobek returned to the fanzines and the letters. He'd done this before. Doerr had written so much, and in so many places, that it was impossible for the writer to comprehend every nuance of content. And new information rewrote the old. Previous references cast in a different light.

But now he was going back after he'd uncovered every scrap of available data.

†

Here are some minor things that the writer found:

1) Somewhere after issue #1 of *Pioneer*, Doerr established a unique numbering scheme. Each issue's pagination was a continuation of the previous issue's page count. The first page of the hypothetical *Pioneer* #6 would be numbered 111 and continue through to page 131.

This might explain the *Pioneer* microfiche. Could Doerr have misrepresented page numbers as issues?

2) When Kobek first read *Pioneer* #10, he could not shake the feeling that the issue predated #9. The former lacked any references past 1971. *Pioneer* #9 was from late 1972. Looking at the pagination, Kobek discovered that *Pioneer* #9 started with page 156 and ended with page 173. *Pioneer* #10 began with page 159 and ended with page 174. This suggested an unreliability. Issues might have been sent out of order. Certain issues might have been sent to different audiences. Or never appeared at all.

3) About half of *Hobbitalia* #3, ten pages long, was recycled from *Pioneer*. Its second page was an essay about Doerr creating a new language, using Cirth as its basis. Doerr had used this alphabet for his cipher in *Hobbitalia* #1. He called his new language Dorian Cirth. This page was numbered

223, which meant that it was from an issue of *Pioneer*. The next three pages were about building smials. These were not numbered with the *Pioneer* scheme. But the same text was reproduced in the January 1972 issue of *VONU LIFE*, which notes that the material came from *Pioneer* #8.

4) Re-reading *Pioneer* #10, Kobek realized that most of its first eleven pages were recycled from *Pathan* #1 and *Panthan* #2. Doerr had copied, completely, *Pathan* #1's material about prehistoric survivals. And then reproduced a section from *Panthan* #2 about Doerr's visit to Canada's Headless Valley on the Nahanni River.

5) *Pioneer* #13 opened with a poem:

> *Where Sirens*
> *Still breathe the sea spray,*
> *And sing*
> *In the enchanted moonlight,*
> *On a beach of gold and topaz,*
> *That was made for ....and me*

The initial four lines came from the July 1894 issue of *The Century Magazine*, taken from an article about the Amalfi Coast by F. Marion Crawford. The passage in question read: "Here the sirens still breathe the sea spray, and sing in the enchanted moonlight as Ulysses, lashed to the mast, sweeps by in his dark ship." The final two lines were adapted from the poem "Dream Island" by Don Blanding. Kobek found no evidence of Crawford's article being reprinted after 1894. This seemed of some importance. It established that Doerr was like Zodiac: someone who quoted from books of the Nineteenth Century.

6) *Green Egg* #49, dated to 11 August 1972, contained a very long letter from Doerr. It included the following: "I am hoping to have my new boat finished in a very few months now... I hope to eventually quit and move out somewhere in the Delta Country where peace reigns." Kobek assumed that the Delta Country in question was the Sacramento–San Joaquin River Delta. This impression was reinforced by a line in *Pioneer* #13: "I imagine, like anywhere, it depends on who you are whether authorities hassle [unreadable]. Doubt Erle Stanley Gardner would be bothered in his houseboats on the Delta. Not knocking Gardner, just that he has more weight than the common peon."

Gardner was the writer who created Perry Mason. In 1965, he'd published *The World of Water*. A book about living on houseboats in the Delta Country. In the July 1969 issue of *Popular Science,* he'd contributed an article entitled "The Case of the Hospitable Houseboat." It was about living on houseboats in the Delta Country.

In December 1967, Gardner contributed a four page article to *Popular Science.* It was about the development of anti-riot technology. Zodiac had lifted material from this article for his letter of 4 August 1969.

7) The cover illustration of *Hobbitalia* #3 was the drawing of a princess. Standard issue for the hippie era.

Kobek first examined *Hobbitalia* #3 before he'd perused the Society for Creative Anachronism's publications. Looking again, now, imbued with unholy knowledge, he recognized Doerr's illustration.

Doerr had stolen it, wholesale, from an one-page SCA mailing announcing a tournament. This event took place on 23 March 1969 at the Douglass Street playground in San Francisco's Noe Valley.

The original illustration bore the signature "Janet." Doerr removed this and replaced it with "thanx to janet."

From Kobek's provisional dating, *Hobbitalia* #3 was published in late 1972. Which meant: for at least three years, Doerr held on to the most meaningless ephemera, a one-page SCA announcement of a long distant tournament. This was not a man who threw things away.

It also meant, that in 1969, Doerr was on the Bay Area SCA's mailing list. He would have received the August 1969 issue of *The Page* newsletter. What he would have seen, upon receipt, was a front page announcement. About the SCA's involvement with the Third Annual Renaissance Pleasure Faire & Ha'penny Market.

Which happened every weekend day in September 1969.

Including 27 September 1969.

The day that Zodiac dressed as a medieval executioner and stabbed college kids at Lake Berryessa.

8) Considering this previous point, Kobek noted a sentence in a Doerr letter present in the Winter 1992 issue of *First Fandom*: "I work at renaissance faires and SCA, but may move more to other pursuits."

And the writer also recalled that, in February 1995, Doerr established a California non-profit corporation (#C1928585) called the Day After Faire.

†

By now, Kobek had read well over a hundred thousand of Doerr's words. Very possibly more than two hundred thousand. He'd noticed something. Doerr repeated himself. He repeated himself in the same year and he repeated himself over the decades.

In May 1975 FAPA *Patter*, responding to a fanzine by Walter Breen in the February 1975 mailing, Doerr wrote:

> Sadism/sex in the prozines? You have never read the pulpsize Marvels of the late 30/early 40s. There were 6 or 7 issues... not the Crawford Marvels, the next ones.,, Planetsize ones. They were full of such stories as a bunch of naked women loosed in a highwalled estate...men hunting them with spring guns loaded with acid marking dyes. The woman found with the most acid burns on her body at the end of the hunt was killed painfully.

Kobek hunted the pulpsized *Marvels*.

He found the story. "Fresh Fiances for the Devil's Daughter." Appearing in the May 1940 issue. The author was Bruno Fischer, writing under the pseudonym Russell Gray. The story's most obvious literary antecedent is "The Most Dangerous Game." This wasn't confirmation bias. The story had been reviewed by multiple online commentators, their minds uninfected by Zodiac. Almost all of them made the connection.

"Fresh Fiances" opens with a New York literary agent at a publishing people party. He meets a woman who attempts to seduce him. The literary agent is at the party with his wife and digs being married. He rejects the seductress's advances. The agent and his wife go out into the street. They laugh about the would-be seductress. Unfortunately, she's also on the street and she hears their ridicule, the mockery and the laughter. The agent and his wife go home. Days later, the literary agent gets a letter from his best client, asking him to go to the seductress's apartment and examine her fiction. He doesn't want to do this. But his best client, his moneymaker, has asked for a favor. He goes to the apartment. The seductress's fiction is a pretext.

There's another attempt at seduction. The literary agent resists. The seductress has a giant servant. The literary agent is assaulted by the giant. The literary agent blacks out. He wakes up in a torture chamber. He's whipped. Sex is demanded. He resists. He's set free and goes back to his apartment on Washington Square. The next day, the literary agent gets a gun. He's going to shoot the woman and her servant. When he gets to her apartment, it's empty. The building superintendent says that she's moved. An unspecified amount of time later, the literary agent receives a note from another writer, inviting the agent and his wife to a party in an upstate estate.

The agent and his wife go to the party. Upon arrival, they discover that the writer who invited them, and that writer's wife, are tortured slaves of the seductresses. As is the agent's best client and her husband. Everyone's beaten and whipped and brought into a dungeon. At which point the story plays out as Doerr described it. The men are forced to hunt each other's naked wives. The men shoot the women with acid darts.

At the end of the evening, the woman with the most acid burns will be murdered. The rest will be freed. There's a long extended hunt followed by a crap ending in which the literary agent and his wife bring down vengeance and escape the estate.

In *Inside* #17, dated to March 1957, Doerr placed a classified:

```
          WANTED, CHEAP
SF SETS LIKE WEIRD TALES, MARVEL, ETC.
—MAGS IN LOTS OF 100 OR 1000, DIFFER-
ENT—FANZINES BY THE POUND—BOOKS BY
BURROUGHS, LOVECRAFT, DERLETH, SMITH,
HOWARD—HAVE STAPS, METERS, OLD NON-SF
MAGS FOR SALE OR TRADE—P. DOERR, 689
PRINDLE, SHARON, PA.
```

The Winter 1992 issue of *First Fandom Report* printed one of Doerr's letters. A paragraph read like this: "SF prozines could be quite pornographic. Remember *Marvel* pulps -- about 8 of them? If I could get copies of those I'd reprint them on microfiche and then sell them."

The letter was published seventeen years after the May 1975 *Patter*. Thirty-five years after *Inside* #17.

Across decades and more times than he could count, Kobek read about Doerr sailing to California in a sloop that navigated from Lake Erie. Kobek read so much about Doerr's new boat that the writer wanted to scream. Kobek read, so many times, about *Gor.*

While the writer hadn't found all of Doerr's output, he was certain that he'd missed none of the consistent themes. Doerr repeated himself. *I wrote for The Acolyte.* Seventeen years of distance from *Patter* and he's still talking about *Marvel* pulps. "Fresh Fiances for the Devil's Daughter." A story that no one else remembers. *Panthan* turns into *Pioneer* #10. *DOE* #49 recycles *Pioneer* #1. Kobek might have missed some detail, even something that could exclude Doerr as Zodiac, but he had not missed any major topic.

Doerr was the one individual in the San Francisco Bay Area who shared a near identical body of knowledge with Zodiac. These things happen. It was not impossible that two individuals in the same region of the same rough age had the same hobbies and tastes. God is a hack screenwriter.

Doerr repeated himself. And Doerr liked to be the smartest person in the room. He was an autodidact with a library card. He lived with an intolerable knowledge. Doerr knew, correctly, that he was much smarter than the fancy lads from Harvard and Yale. But he also knew that something kept the world from acknowledging his intelligence.

There is a presumption in being the man who offers unsolicited information. *I know something that you do not.* It's there in a letter to *Tournaments Illuminated,* a lecture about baskethilts to people who've spent four years researching and dissecting medieval weaponry. He'd thrown in a factoid about Ancient Rome and the steam engine. *I know something that you do not.* In all of Doerr's writing, there was a constant and burning desire for recognition. Kobek suspected that this yearning motivated most writers. A long time ago, Kobek suffered the affliction. Now he could see it in others. The writer was like a dope-sick junky rolling into a new town, walking down Main Street and discovering, in less than five minutes, who's holding.

Look at me. Here I am. I am gifted. Why won't you see that I am gifted?

Kobek had read all the major contemporary reporting about Zodiac. He'd watched the Cipher Killer transform into a Satanic menace threatening the lives of school children. An occult god come to strike the unwitting and unwary. Doerr had read these reports. They couldn't be missed. Not when you work in Vallejo, not when you read the *Examiner* every single day.

Zodiac wasn't just a killer. Zodiac wasn't just a writer. Zodiac was a place. Zodiac was where individuals went when they wanted to prove that they were smarter than everyone else.

Doerr placed a classified in a 1980 issue of *Shavertron*. A fanzine dedicated to Richard Shaver. The factory worker from Detroit who'd heard voices and convinced one-third of Science Fiction that subterranean survivals lived beneath the planet's surface. The classified looked like this:

```
Wanted: books/mags on witch-
craft, satanism, voodoo, sac-
rific, multi-marriage...
P. Doerr, 225 E. Utah,
Fairfield, CA. 94533.
```

Witchcraft. Voodoo. Satanism. Sacrifice. How everyone thought about The Zodiac. For decades, these topics obsessed Doerr. One need only look at WANT LIST in *Patter* #1, read the titles that Doerr was trying to unload.

Paul Huson, *Mastering Witchcraft*. Milo Riguard, *Secrets of Voodoo*. Sybil Leek, *Diary of a Witch*. Louise Huebner, *Power Through Witchcraft*. Anton LaVey, *The Satanic Bible*. Leo Louis Martello, *Weird Ways of Witchcraft*. Douglas Hunt, *Exploring the Occult*. Martin Ebon, *Witchcraft Today*. Brad Steiger, *Sex and Satanism*. Charles Lefebure, *Witness to Witchcraft*. Sax Rohmer, *The Romance of Sorcery*. Richard Cavendish, *The Black Arts*.

In March 1985, Doerr established a non-profit called Investigator. California entity #C1270133. These were the first three items in Investigator's articles of incorporation:

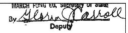

```
                              I                    MARCH FONG EU, Secretary of State
The name of this corporation is Investigator.      By Gloria Carroll
                                                              Deputy
                             II
A. This corporation is a nonprofit public benefit corporation and is not organized
for the private gain of any person. It is organized under the Nonprofit Public
Benefit Corporation Law for charitable purposes.
B. The specific purpose of this corporation is to investigate the increasing number
of mass murders, cults and other unusual happenings.
                             III
The name and address in the State of California of this corporation's initial agent
for service of process is: Paul Doerr, 225 E. Utah, Fairfield, Ca. 94533
```

The idea was to produce a publication called *Investigator*. In the 1995 edition of the *Standard Periodical Directory*, this publication's contents are described like this: "Covers investigations of serial killings, missing children, conspiracy, etc."

For most of his 1980s publications, Doerr applied for ISSNs from the Library of Congress. These eight digit numbers were identifiers assigned to publications. The publisher applied for the number. The Library of Congress issued a provisional ISSN. The publisher sent the Library a copy of the publication, at which point the ISSN was confirmed and made permanent.

The Library had confirmed ISSNs for *Poly, Backwoods, Swashbuckler, Unknown, Owlhooters, Scifant, Owlhooter's Gazette, Pioneer, Luna City Press,* and *The ConCom Guide*.[20]

And while Doerr had been assigned a provisional number (0882-1356) for *Investigator*, the Library never confirmed its existence.

Doerr shared the same body of knowledge as Zodiac. He was obsessed with witchcraft and Satanism and sacrifice. He wanted to people to know that he was the smartest person in the room. The first four victims were from the city where Doerr worked.

He was a man who loved having secret knowledge that other people did not, knowledge that could be distilled into a letter and shared with a publication. He'd established a business entity to investigate the occult and mass murder.

And he was a person who could, with a letter or a fanzine, solve multiple Zodiac mysteries.

But it never happened.

Not in any of the letters, not in any of the fanzines. There was no mention of Zodiac. Kobek might have missed a stray reference but had missed no major obsession. Across years and decades, Doerr repeated himself.

Absence of evidence is not evidence.

But there was another absence. One for which there was evidence. One that was definitive.

---

20 To confirm a copy requires only a copy of the cover, the title page, and an editorial page. And there are no standards of quality. It's possible that few, if any, of these publications existed beyond their ISSN confirmation.

In his letters and fanzines, Doerr portrayed himself as a man on the make. He was looking for girls. He was trying to start free love communes. He wanted women to live on his mountain. This sexual yearning and availability were constant running themes in the character of "Paul Doerr," the faceless voiceless creature of the typed page.

The real Paul Doerr, the man, lived at home with a wife.

A woman whom he married in the 1949.

To whom he would be married until death.

They lived in a tract house in Fairfield. Doerr had a daughter. She'd been in Fairfield for the early fanzine period and the Zodiac years. For the hunting of girls for sailboats and partners for sex communes.

These people were the most definitive fact of Paul Doerr's life.

His real life.

And this definitive fact never made an appearance in his writing.

So Kobek had a question.

Where in all of Doerr was Zodiac?

There was an answer of economy. Doerr didn't attempt to solve the mystery because for Doerr there was no mystery and the solution could not be named.

And that solution was himself.

†

But perhaps this devotee of media and print publications had missed Zodiac. Maybe, despite working in Vallejo, the story somehow escaped notice. The problem with this idea was that Kobek had proof of Doerr paying closer attention than anyone else.

The evidence was in *Living Free* #3, which ran two letters from Tarl Cabot. The second letter was dated May 1979.

One of its paragraphs read like this:

> I wd expect cannibalism to become quite common in real
> troubles. It always has. It was a $ business in the Stalingrad

siege. The Catholic Church approved it in the Andes crash recently. Some people were arrested in Calif. a couple of years ago with half eaten fingers in their pockets.

The last sentence referenced the 13 July 1970 arrest of two men.

Stanley Dean Baker, 22, and Harry Allen Stroup, 20. Picked up by the California Highway Patrol. They'd been driving a stolen car that belonged to a social worker from Montana. A week or so earlier, the social worker was dismembered in Yellowstone National Park. His body split into six pieces. His heart hacked out of his chest and missing.

When the Highway Patrol searched Baker and Stroup, they discovered that each man carried a bone in their respective pockets. Meat still attached. Stroup claimed that they were chicken bones carried for good luck. Baker contradicted him. He said: "I have a problem. I am a cannibal."

Then he said that he'd killed the social worker. There'd been LSD and, presumably, gay sex followed by gay shame. Baker hacked the social worker apart. Split the body in six pieces. Ate the heart. And cut off the fingers, gnawing the flesh away with his own mouth.

In October 1970, Baker pleaded guilty to first degree murder. He admitted killing the social worker. And eating him. He then became the star witness at Stroup's trial. The prosecution theory was this: working together, the two men killed and ate the social worker. Baker denied the story, claimed that he'd worked alone. On the stand, Baker's testimony was acid bizarro, filled with stories of controlling the weather, magical wars against Jimi Hendrix, and Church of Satan membership.

But then something happened.

The prosecution asked Baker if he knew anything about the murder of Robert Michael Salem. Baker refused to answer, citing his Fifth Amendment right to avoid self-incrimination.

Robert Michael Salem was a San Francisco lamp designer. He lived near City Hall. On 19 April 1970, after a few days of silence, Salem's friends worried that something was wrong. They forced their way into Salem's apartment. Inside, they discovered their friend. Dead. His throat slashed open, part of his ear cut away and missing. His killer had walked through the apartment, dripping gore, and used Salem's blood to write on the apartment walls. The killer drew an Egyptian Ankh and then, beside it, wrote the following words:

SATAN SAVES ZODIAC

The scene looked like this:

The story broke on 20 April 1970.

The morning edition of the *San Francisco Chronicle* published a front page story: BIZARRE 'ZODIAC' MURDER.

And then, that same morning, Zodiac mailed a new letter. It was part of a pattern that characterized most correspondences after 15 October 1969. Whenever the media mentioned Zodiac—either the killer himself in a new context or some other criminal who'd invoked the name—the genuine issue original mailed a response. These operated on inference, never mentioning the provoking articles. But Kobek saw it in the newspapers of the era. On 7 November 1969, the *Examiner* reported about a school teacher in Martinez poisoned with arsenic by someone claiming to be Zodiac. Zodiac sent two correspondences across the next two days. On 18 December 1969, the *Chronicle* gossip columnist Herb Caen mentions Zodiac two lines away from Melvin Belli. Two days later, Zodiac mailed a letter to Belli. Somewhere around 4 or 5 October 1970, the international newswire Reuters issued a report on Zodiac. On 5 October, Zodiac mailed an index card on which he'd cut-and-pasted clippings from local newspapers, the texts arranged to respond, directly, to the Reuters report. On 27 October 1970, the *Chronicle*'s Paul Avery runs A 'JACK THE RIPPER' THEORY ON SLAYINGS. The story ends with Avery describing Zodiac in everything but name. That evening, Zodiac sends the Halloween Card.

And on the morning of 20 April, when the *Chronicle* reports on the death of Robert Michael Salem, Zodiac sent in a letter.

What the *Chronicle* didn't report was this: a bloody fingerprint had been left in Robert Michael Salem's apartment. And, by all accounts, this fingerprint matched one belonging to Stanley Dean Baker. The lead cannibal. Who presumably ate Salem's missing ear.

When Doerr sends the Tarl Cabot letter of May 1979, the story of Stanley Dean Baker is almost nine years old.

It's worth noting how little coverage this received in Bay Area newspapers. Four articles in the *San Francisco Chronicle*, all dating to 1970. Five in the *Examiner*. All dating to 1970. When Stroup is convicted of manslaughter in November 1970, the killers are never mentioned again.

In all of Kobek's reading—Doerr's hundreds of letters and over two dozen fanzines—Tarl Cabot's letter in *Living Free* #3 was the only appearance of anything Zodiac.

It opened up two possibilities.

Either: Doerr possessed an encyclopedic knowledge of California crime. He was the person who remembered old stories from a decade earlier. And this knowledge existed in a mind with all of his other obsessions. And Doerr worked in Vallejo. And wanted credit for secret knowledge. And could, by virtue of his independent interests, solve multiple Zodiac mysteries with a letter.

And somehow was disinterested in Zodiac.

Or: Tarl Cabot was the one time when Doerr let the mask slip.

No surprise that it occurred under a pseudonym.

chapter twelve

MANAC ES CEM, J.K.

HAVING RE-READ every one of Doerr's major letters and classifieds and fanzines, Kobek did something that he had avoided.

He returned to *Hobbitalia* #1.

Here, at the end, Kobek went back to the beginning.

The final two pages included Doerr's cipher in Tolkien's Cirth alphabet and identified it as both a "cypher" and a "code." The other pages were reprints from prior material and an interminable article entitled "Jewelry."

The latter was single-spaced. Eight pages long. It was about jewelry.

Hence the avoidance.

During his first and only read, "Jewelry" convinced Kobek that Doerr was smart. Extremely smart. He was not a good writer but his article demonstrated mastery of the subject and his reference material. Some things can be faked. But some things can't. Like eight cogent pages of organized historical and chemical detail.

In his first encounter, when Kobek was not especially suspicious of Doerr, the writer missed a major aspect. Now, re-reading "Jewelry," Kobek noticed that as Doerr made his way through gems and stones used in adornment, he'd gone out of his way to establish their relationships to astrological signs.

A paragraph stood out: "Beryl is the stone of the Zodiac twins. It is also one of the stones of the noon in astrological theory."

The article ended halfway down the eighth page. To fill the remaining space, Doerr appended quotes from two different sources. One source was *Amulets and Talismans* by E A W Budge. The other was *Antique Jewelry* by Fred W. Burgess. The quote from *Antique Jewelry* was about small arrow heads discovered in England and Ireland, with Burgess playfully hinting that they were the weapons of fairies and pixies. Doerr used the quote as part of a general idea in *Hobbitalia,* something only hinted at by #1 and subsequent issues. Doerr appeared to believe that Tolkien's books were lightly fictionalized chronicles of historical events. That hobbits were real.

He'd thought the same thing about Edgar Rice Burroughs.

Why not Tolkien?

Kobek found an online copy of *Antique Jewelry.* He searched for the word "zodiac," found nothing of note, and then performed an action that had become obligatory. The writer went through each page, looking to see if there were any illustrations that might have inspired Zodiac's cipher alphabets.

No luck.

Next, Kobek went to *Amulets and Talismans.* Again, Kobek flipped through the pages, looking for anything that resembled the cipher characters. On the 312th page, something caught his eye. It was an ancient Greek inscription. It looked like this:

ΔBΛΔNΔΘΔNΔΛBΔ

Kobek had thought about Zodiac for so long. Certain things were seared into his brain. The killer's letters were imprinted inside his head. It was no longer conscious.

When Kobek saw page 312 of *Amulets and Talismans,* he felt the jerk of recognition.

He couldn't say why, exactly, but the Greek inscription reminded him of something. Z13. The 13-character cipher that Zodiac included in his letter of 20 April 1970. SATAN SAVES ZODIAC.

The letter looked like this:

This is the Zodiac speaking
By the way have you cracked
the last cipher I sent you?
My name is ——

A E N ⊕ ⊗ K ⊙ M ⊙ ⅃ N A M

I am mildly cerous as to how
much money you have on my
head now. I hope you do not
think that I was the one
who wiped out that blue
meannie with a bomb at the
cop station. Even though I talked
about killing school children with
one. It just wouldnt doo to
move in on someone elses toritory.
But there is more glory in killing
a cop then a cid because a cop
can shoot back. I have killed
ten people to date. It would
have been a lot more except
that my bes bomb was a dud.
I was swamped out by the
rain we had a while back.

(20 April 1970, first page)

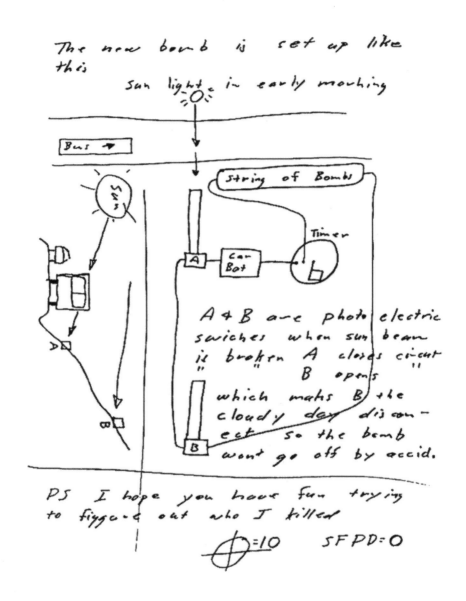

The new bomb is set up like this

Sun light in early morning

Bus →

Sun

String of Bombs

Timer

A

Car Bot

A & B are photo electric swiches when sun beam is broken A closes circut " " B opens " which maks B the cloudy day discon- ect so the bomb B wont go off by accid.

D

∞

PS I hope you have fun trying to figgure out who I killed

⊕=10   SFPD=0

(20 April 1970, second page)

Kobek looked again at the inscription in *Amulets and Talismans.* He counted its letters. 13 characters. And then Kobek read the rest of page 312. Only now did the writer realize that this was the page from which Doerr quoted in *Hobbitalia* #1.

The relevant passage looked like this:

a child. Little balls of crystal, set in metal bands, are found all over EUROPE, and in ENGLAND and IRELAND ; where and why these were made is not known, but they were probably used as amulets. Crystal was held in high esteem by the early Christians who regarded it as a symbol of the Immaculate Conception. And KING, in his *History of Gems* (pp. 104–8), describes a ball of crystal on which was engraved the Gnostic formula ΔΒΛΔΝΔΘΔΝΔΛΒΔ. Crystal has always been greatly prized in Scotland. Several of the Clans possessed crystal balls which were regarded as " stones of victory," and water in which they were washed was given as medicine to sick men and cattle. Crystal amulets protected their wearers against the Evil Eye, and saved them from bad dreams ; he who drinks from a crystal vessel will never suffer from dropsy, and a piece of crystal laid on the cheek will drive away toothache and will give relief, in any case, to the sufferer. Some of the Mexican Indians believe that the souls of both living and dead people dwell in crystal. And among some of the tribes in AUSTRALIA and GUINEA the magicians by means of it produce rain, for crystal is the rain-maker *par excellence.*

In *Hobbitalia* #1, Doerr condensed the page.
It looked like this:

> Little balls of rock crystal, set in metal bands, are found all over Europe, Britain and Ireland. Where, when, why or by whom made is not known. Some Scottish clans possessed crystal balls regarded as "stones of victory". Rock crystal (quartz) was believed to protect from evil eye, disease and pain. It was used as a burning glass in medicene, and to produce rain in ceremonies. It was powdered and taken for disease, Mixed with honey, it was thought to increase mother's milk. Some thought it fell from heaven or was petrified ice which would never melt. Some believed souls of the living and dead dwelt in the crystal.
>   AMULETS AND TALISMANS...E A W BUDGE

Doerr'd left out the inscription.

Kobek'd seen three unique copies of *Hobbitalia* #1. Two were post-marked 23 April 1970. Inverted for contrast, the postmark on the Marquette University copy looked like this:

Another copy bore a more legible postmark. It looked like this:

The Marquette University copy had a hand stamp. The other copy was machine processed. Kobek couldn't fathom why two fanzines mailed on the same day from the same post office would have different postmarks. The mysteries of the Postal System.

The third copy was mailed with a 6¢ Christmas stamp. It depicted *The Nativity,* dated 1523, by Lorenzo Lotto. Renaissance-Jesus kitsch collecting dust in the National Gallery of Art in Washington, DC.

This copy had one page more than the 23 April *Hobbitalia* #1s, including the first page of the WANT LIST that Doerr mailed with the June 1971 N'APA *Patter.* There was no date on the postmark but the stamp itself narrowed the possibilities. It was issued 5 November 1970.

On *Hobbitalia* #1's final page—the one with the Cirth cipher—Doerr left a space to write mailing addresses. When the issue was mimeographed, he would fold the fanzine three times, leaving this section facing upwards. Then he'd staple the pages together and write an address and place a stamp.

By including WANT LIST as the new final page in post-April 1970 issues, Doerr removed the address/stamp function of the cipher page. For the *Nativity* copy, Doerr folded *Hobbitalia* in the original fashion, now leaving the top third of the fanzine's first page facing upwards. He then stapled the pages together and scribbled an address and placed a stamp at the very top of the first page.

Kobek'd seen a very low resolution image of a fourth copy. As with the *Nativity* copy, the stamp and postmark were the first page. Meaning that it wasn't sent in April 1970. Kobek had a theory about the post-November 1970 *Hobbitalia* #1s: they'd been mailed out after an announcement appeared in *Green Dragon* #11, dated to December 1970, which read: "HOBBITALIA is available free for postage (an 8c stamp) from Box 1444, Vallejo CA 94590."

The 23 April copies were something else. Like the Zodiac letters, they were addressed in what looked like blue felt-tip pen, and both were mailed to pre-existing Tolkien oriented addresses. This was the M.O. demonstrated by *Pathan* #1. Publishing 101. Make a publication about a topic, like, say, Edgar Rice Burroughs. Then send it to places and people with a demonstrated interest. Doerr wrote about this in *Hobbitalia* #2: "Would the lotrs in the San Francisco/Sacramento area be interested in getting together? I have written several of the local smials in Green Dragon but never received an answer. Are they still with us?"

†

Kobek had a problem. How to establish that Doerr finished *Hobbitalia* #1 in the lead up to 20 – 23 April?

The answer was there in the 23 April copies. The first that Kobek saw, the Marquette University copy, was addressed as follows:

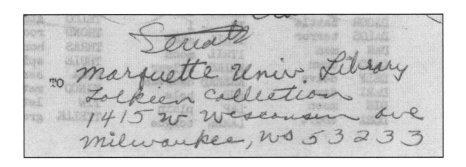

As far as Kobek could tell, this address appeared twice in pre-April 1970 Tolkien fandom. One occurrence was *Green Dragon* #6, dated March 1969. *Green Dragon* was an irregularly newsletter published by the Tolkien Society of America. The relevant passage looked like this:

> As said last time, ORCRIST is sort-of merging with TJ. If you have a sub to ORCRIST, let me know when you renew & I will extend your TSA membership by an appropriate #. (Incidentally, if you publish a Tolkien fanzine, please send me copies. I will trade for TJ one for one, and will credit you when your current membership expires. Also, please send one copy of each issue to the Marquette University Library, Tolkien Collection, Milwaukee WI 53   )

This seemed an unlikely source. How had Doerr gotten the full address and zipcode? The other publication that printed Marquette's address was *Tolkien Journal,* Volume 3 Number 3, dated to Summer 1968. *Tolkien Journal* was also published by the Tolkien Society of America, had editorial overlap with *Green Dragon*. Its relevant passage read like this:

> Countless items about Tolkien are published in fanzines and researchers will have a hard time finding these. Since the Marquette University library already has the manuscripts I think they would make a good depository for all related fanzines. If you publish anything about Tolkien please send a copy to the Marquette University Library, Tolkien Collection, 1415 W Wisconsin Av, Milwaukee WS 53233.

The second 23 April *Hobbitalia* #1 was addressed like this:

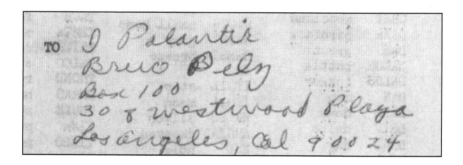

I Palantir was first published in 1960. The final issue, #4, was released in August 1966. So why was Doerr sending *Hobbitalia* to a fanzine defunct for three years and eight months?

The answer was in an earlier issue of the *Tolkien Journal*.

Volume 3, Number 1. Published in 1967.

Its title page offered the addresses of three major Tolkien fanzines. Including *I Palantir*. Exactly as addressed by Doerr. (Weirdly, all three addresses were repeated verbatim in another article in the same issue.)

This indicated—Kobek couldn't read it any other way—an individual who'd made a Tolkien fanzine while not being part of Tolkien fandom. If Doerr were networked into Tolkien fanzines, he would have known that *I Palantir* was almost four years out of commission. By 1969, no one was offering its address. But if Doerr had old copies of the *Tolkien Journal*, and wanted to get in on the action, then what would he do? Send copies to the addresses that you have at hand. Publishing 101.

There was another indicator that Doerr was not part of Tolkien fandom. In the *Hobbitalia* #1 cipher, Doerr makes two inquiries but comes up against a problem: Tolkien did not create a question mark for Cirth. Doerr invents his own solution: he borrows a character from Tengwar, another of Tolkien's scripts, and uses it as a punctuation mark.

By 1970, Tolkien fandom had published enough guides to Tolkien's languages in English that there were several competing and accepted orthographies. And none of them employ this character as a question mark.

If Doerr weren't part of Tolkien fandom, then how did he end up with the *Tolkien Journal*? An economic answer was Baycon '68.

At 8:30AM on 2 September, the same day as the Society for Creative Anachronism's tournament, the Tolkien Society for America held a panel.

An announcement of the forthcoming event appears in *Tolkien Journal* Volume 3, Number 3. Paragraphs above the address for Marquette University. Same editorial. The TSA would've brought copies of their publications. For sale after the panel. It would explain why the two extant copies of 23 April *Hobbitalia* #1s were mailed to addresses found in issues pre-dating Baycon.

There was another way to date the fanzine.

Green Dragon #13, dated February 1972, contained a short note at its end: "We recently received the following Tolkien or fantasy oriented fanzines which might be of interest to you: AMRA #55 from box 8243 Phil PA 19101. PALDOR from box 1444 Vallejo CA 94590."

PALDOR was, in fact, *Hobbitalia* #2.

Doerr, being Doerr, did something odd. The first page didn't identify *Hobbitalia* #2 by name. Instead, Doerr ran this at the top:

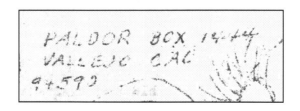

February 1972 was a few months after Doerr mailed *Hobbitalia #2* as his contribution to the September 1971 N'APA.

Green Dragon didn't mention *Hobbitalia #1* until issue #11, dated December 1970. And it couldn't have arrived before June 1970, the date of *Green Dragon #10.*

All of which meant: *Hobbitalia #1* was not circulating before April 1970.

Doerr worked on and finished *Hobbitalia #1* in the exact same moment that Zodiac mailed the Z13.

The 23 April copies were sent, essentially, fresh from the mimeograph machine. Presumably as soon as they'd been completed. Which meant that, in the days before 23 April, Doerr was interacting with, and condensing, *Amulets and Talismans.*

†

In *Amulets and Talismans,* Budge cites *The Natural History of Gems* by C.W. King. Kobek tracked down King's book. Budge gave page numbers that did not accord with Kobek's copy of King. The writer could not find the reference. But he did, later in the book, discover the same inscription. The passage read like this: "P. 302. Sol, Lord of the universe, in his four-horse car. Around the field the Gnostic invocation ABΛANAΘANAΛBA, 'Thou art our Father!'"

If Budge's inscription looked like Z13, then this one, identical to Budge but employing uppercase Greek characters, was even closer. Kobek looked again at Budge's book and noted that there was an entire chapter about Gnostic amulets.

The inscription appeared again on pages 207 and 209. In the former, Budge, like King, presents the palindrome in full upper case letters. The latter provides the Latin transliteration and cast doubt upon King's translation. The passages looked like this:

> On gems of this class we find figures of Priapus.
> He is represented as an ithyphallic man, four-
> headed, four-winged, and four-handed, holding four
> sceptres, and he has the tail of a bird of prey ;
> an inscription found on the reverse of such figures
> is the palindrome **ABΛANAΘANAΛBA.**

> and Ṣabaôth. The palindrome Ablanathanalba
> is said to mean " Thou art our father," but this
> can hardly be a correct translation.

Kobek typed out the inscription and placed it atop Z13.
It looked like this:

ΑΒΛΑΝΑΘΑΝΑΛΒΑ

$$A\ E\ N\ \phi\ \otimes\ K\ \circledast\ M\ \circledast\ \downarrow\ N\ A\ M$$

What was apparent, immediately, was repetition overlap between the two strings. Both began with the letter A, both had remarkably similar characters in their central 7th position, and both repeated their respective internal characters across sets on the 3rd/11th and 5th/9th positions.

This observation sent Kobek down a rabbit hole, culminating in his writing an academic paper. "An Internally Verifiable Possible Solution to Z13 and Z32 Produced by Multi-Stage Replicable Blind Data Test."[21]

The paper didn't prove a definitive solution to Z13 and Z32, a cipher mailed by Zodiac on 26 June 1970, but rather that a blind and procedurally generated computer simulation written by Kobek started with 371,651,680

---

21   Reader, nothing on this green Earth is more boring than Zodiac's ciphers. You have been spared a headache in the main text of this book. Accept the author's assertions *prima facie* or turn to Appendix C. And, yes, it is a shame that it's fallen to this.

potential outcomes to Z13 and ended up with two. One of which was the Greek palindrome.

The paper further proved that the palindrome could be resolved, using the same rotational technique, in both Z13 and Z32, and that the Z32 solution incorporated the Z13 ciphertext.

These resolutions required no anagramming, no secret names, nothing but what was indicated by the ciphers. The Z13 solution was flawed. But mirrored, exactly, the ON/OFF scheme of the bus bomb. And Z32 corrected the error.

There was a path to madness in all Zodiac studies.

Certitude.

For Kobek, the palindrome solution didn't need to be empirical truth, it need only be conditional truth.

A palindrome in a text quoted by Doerr in a fanzine first mailed 23 April 1970 resolved into a cipher sent by Zodiac three days earlier. And resolved another Zodiac cipher sent two months later.

It might not be *the* solution. But it was *a* solution. And was far better than any other attempt. And was the only one that could be dated.

†

There were two places where Kobek could place Doerr in time and physical presence. First: a 1985 public forum. It was part of the National Commission on Space. Members of the public offered opinions on the future of space travel.

The Commission's final report mentioned that Doerr spoke at the forum. Kobek located tapes in the National Archives. A way to hear Doerr's voice.

The writer put in a reproduction order. The Archives wrote back. They approved the reproduction but couldn't duplicate the audio due to COVID-19. The bureaucracy that fueled the vonu impulse.

The second place was the Society for Creative Anachronism's tournament at Baycon in 1968. There were about thirty photos of the event held in the archives of the University of California, Riverside. Putting the photos together allowed for a full 360° panorama.

Kobek had seen Doerr's high school year book photo and Doerr's photo in the June 1972 *Explorer's Journal*. The photos weren't particularly useful, each had their problems, but together they demonstrated something. Doerr had a unusually large chin. Which narrowed it down. A middle aged man with a large chin. Kobek guessed something else. Doerr would be carrying a camera. The June 1968 issue of *Modern Photography* published a letter from Doerr about SLR photography. Two months before Baycon.

Kobek scanned every face. Came up with plausible candidates. Then the writer found his man. Doerr was in several photographs. One captured him in profile.

Doerr looked like this:

Monday, 2 Sept 1968. Photos by Jay Kay Klein.
(Courtesy of the University of California, Riverside)

Other photos captured Doerr from a distance.
He looked like this:

After the murder of Paul Stine, on 14 October 1969, the SFPD released a sketch of Zodiac. On an unknown basis, the sketch had been refined. The second version was dated on 17 October 1969.

The drawings looked like this:

As Doerr had a mustache and no glasses at Baycon, why not draw a mustache on the sketches and remove the glasses?

Based on evidence in previous books, Zodiology genre convention almost demanded a modified police sketch. The writer adhered to form.

He modified the first sketch.

It looked like nothing, a comic ghost.

Kobek performed the same actions on the second sketch. As he removed the glasses, he realized that, for fifty-two years, the spectacles had distorted the image.

Take away the glasses and it's the drawing of an actual person. What one sees is someone with an extremely large chin and a very long nose.

It looked like this:

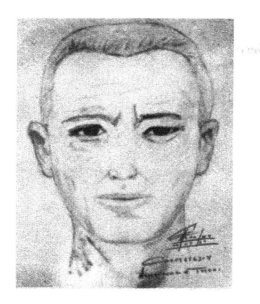

Kobek drew on a mustache. He compared the sketch against the photograph of Doerr in profile. Together, they looked like this:

Kobek thought of something that he saw in the beginning. A classified placed by Doerr. It appeared in the 23-29 January 1970 *Berkeley Barb*. After the Belli letter, before the 20 April 1970 letter that contained the Z13.

It looked like this:

> WANTED - CHEAP - BOOKS -
> Botony, Anthropology, Archaeolo-
> gy, Old Greek and Medit Civili-
> zation. Lowrainfall Flora Fauua
> Living Methods. SHELL ZEN
> YOGA OCCULT HEALTH. List,
> title, date, price, cond. Doerr.
> Box 1444 Vallejo.

Prior to 1970, the only evidence of Doerr's interest in the occult is a sentence in the first *Patter*, dated September 1968: "Witchcraft is returning. In some force, I might add. There are thousands of covens in England and it is rapidly spreading here. I would like to know of one here. I think there is one in San Francisco..."

This does not suggest mastery of the topic.

By the time that Doerr finds *Green Egg* in early 1971, he can write long, cogent letters about the occult.

Despite many claims as to when Doerr's *Unknown* first appeared, it was possible, just, for Kobek to give its inaugural issue a rough date.

In *Topside* #34, a Canadian UFOlogy magazine, the following appears:

> Interested in the fantastic? Then read UNKNOWN, a new letterzine devoted to the mysteri-
> ous - UFOs, psychic phenomena, pre-historic survival, ghosts, monsters, oddities, etc. jam-
> packed with the Unusual. Topside review: Fabulous, fantastic & fascinating! Exchange mags.
> welcomed. Subscription: 30¢ per issue. Send for your trip into the UNKNOWN to: Paul Doerr,
> Box 1444, Vallejo, California 94590, U.S.a.

Topside #34 is dated the Summer-Fall 1970. The previous installment is dated Winter and Spring 1970. #35 is dated Winter 1971, and contains another ad for *Unknown*. The fanzine is not referred to as new.

Publishing 101. Make a publication about a topic. Send it out to the people interested in that topic.

Which means: Doerr started publishing *Unknown* somewhere around the Spring of 1970.

†

Imagine that you've gone on a kill spree. Imagine that it has no ideological justification or obvious motive.

It's... just. this... thing... that. happened.

You've created a mystery in your own life. Imagine that your kill spree was reported upon in the Masonite fog. Everyone thinks that it's an occult crime wave. Imagine that you are as susceptible as anyone to the voices coming from the newspapers and radio and television. If not more so.

The kill spree is the most important thing in your life.

And you have no idea why it happened.

What do you do?

You look for an explanation.

Thou art our father.

†

Kobek now must believe one of two things.

That in the third week of April 1970, a person in the Bay Area was interacting with a 13 character Ancient Greek palindrome that resolved into Z13 and Z32, and that this resolution could be simulated with a blind, procedurally generated data test. And that this person in the Bay Area interacting with the Greek palindrome also looked like the Zodiac sketch, owned the right car, knew about cryptography, had knowledge of navigation, addressed letters to local newspapers in the same fashion as Zodiac, was into treasure hunting, knew the ANFO formula, collected comic books, was into space colonization, wrote in multiple fanzines about his desire to kill young people, had almost a decade later remembered the incident that provoked Z13, once had membership in a group that sent out anonymous letters using the crosshairs symbol, and had written a confession to multiple murders.

And was not Zodiac.

Or.

Doerr was Zodiac.

APPENDIX A

known extant doerr fanzines

Title	Date	APA Distribution
CHAMPAGNE NEWS	June 1968	N'APA June 1968
Pathan #1	June 1968	N'APA June 1968
Patter #1	September 1968	N'APA September 1968
Pioneer #1	November (?) 1968	N'APA June 1970
Patter #2	March 1969	N'APA March 1969
Panthan #2	September 1969	N'APA September 1969
Patter	March 1970	N'APA March 1970
Hobbitalia #1	April 1970	n/a
Patter	June 1971	N'APA June 1971
Trove #1	September 1971 (?)	FAPA February 1973
Hobbitalia #2	September 1971	N'APA September 1971
Pioneer #10	Late 1971 (?)	n/a
Unknown #19	October (?) 1972	n/a
Hobbitalia #3	October (?) 1972	FAPA May 1973
Pioneer #9	1972	FAPA November 1972
Patter	May 1974	FAPA May 1974
Pioneer #13/Livaboard #2	Late 1974 (?)	n/a
Mendocino Husbandman #1	Nov/Dec (?) 1974	n/a
Pioneer #14	Early 1975 (?)	n/a
Patter	January 1975	Elanor January 1975
Patter	February 1975	FAPA February 1975
Mendocino Husbandman #2	Early 1975	n/a
Patter	April 1975	Elanor Apr/May 1975
Patter	May 1975	FAPA May 1975
"Paul Doerr's Supplement"	May 1975	REHUPA #15
Mendocino Husbandman #3	May 1975	n/a
Patter	July 1975	Elanor July 1975
Patter	May 1976	FAPA May 76/N'APA June 76
The Shangrila Pioneer	1976	*Ego Trip #2*(?)
Sanctuary News #3	1981-2 (?)	n/a
Filkin	August 1985	APA-Filk August 1985

APPENDIX B

letters, classifieds, misc.

Title/Explanation	Date
Weird Tales (new member on W.T. club list) (**193 E State St, Sharon, PA**)	1943-9
Weird Tales (on W.T. club list) (**203 E State St, Sharon, PA**)	1944-9
Sharon High School Year Book, Sharon Pennsylvania	1945
Acolyte #11 (letter re: abominable snowmen)	1945-6
Weird Tales (letter re: abominable snowmen)	1945-9
Doubt (letter re: abominable snowmen)	1946-1
Flying Roll Gamma I (letter/research re: abominable snowmen)	1946
National Fantasy Fan (1st. time on NatFantFanFed roster, dis/reappear thru decades)	1947-10
Fantasy Aspects #2 (note that Doerr has sent letter, F.A. offers no reply)	1947-11
Operation Fantast Supplmnt. (Doerr postcard re: trade US SF mags for UK SF mags)	1948-1
Fantasy Book Vol 1 No 2 (Letter complimenting iss. #1, asks ppl to write re: NFFF)	1948-2
1948 Sharon City Directory. Doerr listed as "mill worker."	1948
Marriage license. (Occupation: mill worker, August 20)	1949-8
Marriage certificate. (September 10)	1949-9
1950 US Census. Occup. "asst. chemist," live w/wife @ **481 US-62, Hickory, PA**.	1950-4
The Record-Argus (Doerr/wife buy property at **2107 Carolyn, Farrell, Penn**, Apr 27)	1950-4
The Aquarium (letter about freezing goldfish alive and bringing them back to life)	1951-6
The Record-Argus (Doerr/wife sell property on Carolyn, Aug 15)	1952-8
American Bee Journal (question about honey super storage)	1952-10
1952 Sharon City Directory. (Doerr listed at "laby worker." **689 Prindle, Shar.**)	1952
The Record-Argus (Doerr/wife sell (another?) property on Carolyn, Apr 3)	1953-4
1955 Sharon City Directory. (Listed as clerk at Century Market.)	1955
Inside #17 (classified seeking books including old *Marvel* pulps)	1956-6
Other Worlds (classified looking for HPL + ERB books & backissue SF/F magazines)	1956-11
The Record-Argus (Doerr/wife buy property Rt 18 South Pymatuning, PA, May 29)	1957-5
Cry of the Nameless (asks if they stole his subscription money, trade fanzines/books)	1957-11
1957 Sharon City Directory. (Millworker at Sawhill Tubes, **22 Davis, Sharpsville.**)	1957
Magazine Fantasy & SF (classified selling books & looking for Lovecraft books)	1958-4
QST (classified for Instructograph/tapes) (**P. O. Box 62 , Wheatland , PA.**)	1958-5
Skin Diver (classified looking for books & magazines, trade tropical fish magazines)	1958-5
Skin Diver (letter asking for specifications about compressors to refill tanks)	1958-6
Skin Diver (classified trying to sell/trade magazines)	1959-2
Skin Diver (letter asking for people in local area who like skin diving)	1959-4
Skin Diver (letter asks if *S.D.* is brave enough to print letters trashing advertisers)	1959-11
QST (classified looking for Instructograph and tapes)	1960-3
Skin Diver (letter asking re: paint & announcement of Doerr starting diving group)	1960-6
Skin Diver (letter says he sails to Florida this year and California next)	1960-7

Title/Explanation	Date
Skin Diver (letter asking for tips on how to start a career in oceanography)	1961-9
Skin Diver (letter asks anyone interested in sailing next year to FL then maybe CA)	1962-2
Aquarium Journal (classified looking to trade *A.J.* back issues for guns)	1963-3
Skin Diver (letter asking how to get back issues of magazines in French and Spanish)	1962-5
Skin Diver (letter explaining trip. FL, Canal, then CA. Claims will take a year.)	1962-6
Skin Diver (Doerr's two clubs listed Mercer County Divers' Association + Sea Dogs)	1963-1
Aquarium Journal (looking for info on snails limpets clams)	1963-6
Solano County Deed/Recorder. (Buy house **201 Great Jones St, Fairfield,** 24 Oct)	1963-10
Skin Diver (classified looking for powerheads for Addict Gun) **(Box 295, Fairfield)**	1963-11
San Rafael Daily Independent Journal (classified looking for boat to live on, Nov 20)	1963-11
Skin Diver (letter asking about 16mm movie cameras for underwater photos)	1964-4
Skin Diver (letter looking to trade 35mm slides) **(Box 1444, Vallejo)**	1964-11
Skin Diver (Doerr article about "Dam Diving" in Pennsylvania)	1964-12
Industrial Research (*I.R.* articles re: moon remind Doerr of childhood in Am.Roc.S.)	1965-4
GUNS (Letter looking for info on Shooters Club of America)	1965-4
Irish Digest (letter looking for friends to go mountain climbing and kayaking)	1965-11
Gems & Minerals (classified trying to trade quartz for coins, guns, artifacts, stamps)	1966-4
Gems & Minerals (trade quartz for Geiger counter, uv light, scintillator)	1966-5
Eureka Humboldt Times (classified looking for land, June 10)	1966-6
Gems & Minerals (classified looking for land, swap crystals)	1966-6
Electronic Design (Doerr denounces anti-Neo-Nazi editorialist)	1966-6
Gems & Minerals (classified trying to trade CA minerals for plants, seeds, etc)	1966-7
Solano County Deed/Recorder. (Doerr/wife sell first Fairfield house, 21 Oct.)	1966-10
Muzzle Blasts (classified, trade skin diving equip and books for muzzle guns)	1966-11
Gems & Minerals (classified to trade quartz for muzzle loaders, buckskin, kayaks)	1966-11
Electronic Design (Denounces anti-Neo-Nazi editorialist who denounced Doerr)	1966-11
Solano County Deed/Recorder. (Doerr/wife buy **225 E Utah St.**, 19 April.)	1967-4
Oceanology International (letter about underwater photography)	1967-7
Berkeley Barb (classified looking for woman to live in cabin w/no amenities)	1967-10
Berkeley Barb (classified for flintlocks, buckskins (patterns), and dogs. Nov 10 to 16.)	1967-11
Berkeley Barb (classified looking for brass microscope. Dec 15 to 21.)	1967-12
National Fantasy Fan (Doerr back on roster)	1967-12
Natural Gardening Magazine (letter asking what small scented plants grow indoors)	1967
The News-Herald (Doerr/wife sell property in Pymatuning, PA, Feb 16.)	1968-2
Salt Water Aquarium (2 letters looking to kill piranhas for So. Amer. Govnmts(??))	1968-5
National Fantasy Fan (writes asking about ERB + clubs)	1968-5
Rod & Custom (letter looking for manual for 1955 International Metro Van)	1968-5

Modern Photography (letter about SLR close up photography)	1968-6
Oceanology International (listing for Misc. Inc selling electronics etc)	1968-6
No-Eyed Monster (letter, unknown contents)	1968-6
Sirrush (letter about wanting to read *Gor* books, also mentions *Berkeley Barb*)	1968-7
National Fantasy Fan (wants info on APAs and reaching comic people)	1968-8
Muzzle Blasts (letter asking for people around Vallejo to start a Wilderness Meet)	1968-8
Hoom #2 (N'APA, responds *Pathan #1*, first person to beg Doerr for better mimeo)	1968-9
Berkeley Barb (classified looking for "Captain's Hat", Nov 1 - 9.)	1968-11
Magazine Fantasy & SF (classified selling *Pathan + Pioneer*)	1968-11
National Fantasy Fan (classified advertising *Pioneer*)	1968-11
Sonoma West Times and News (letter to establishing campsite non-profit, Apr 24)	1969-4
National Fantasy Fan (classified for *Alaska Sportsman* back issues)	1969-4
Tightbeam (letter about casting his own metal, disliking *Star Trek*)	1969-5
Berkeley Barb (classified seeking girls for boat travel. Aug 8 - 14.)	1969-9
Tournaments Illuminated (letter from Paul of Sun River about baskethilts)	1970-1
Berkeley Barb (classified looking for books on Ancient Greece & occult, Jan 23 - 29)	1970-1
Tightbeam (letter about 1 cent postage, anti poverty, APA, etc)	1970-3
National Fantasy Fan (wants WWIII books, Heinlein's address for "Jap. friend")	1970-6
Daily Times Salisbury Maryland (letter about UFO lights, July 13)	1970-7
SF Examiner/Chronicle (classified trying to sell land, Aug 6 to 12)	1970-8
BUFORA (sends "bulletin" about going to headless valley)	1970-9
Flying Saucer News (letter about Forteana including creation of giant chickens)	1970-9
The Seed (classified commune, Oct 10)	1970-10
it aint me babe (classified commune, Oct 30)	1970-10
National Fantasy Fan (writes asking advice about publishing fanzines)	1970-10
Off Our Backs (classified commune, Nov 8)	1970-11
The Fixer (classified commune, Nov 11)	1970-11
Green Dragon (note that *Hobbitalia* #1 available for free to anyone who sends stamp)	1970-12
Saucers, Space & Science #59 (classified looking for people with Fortean interests)	1970
Topside #34 (advertisement/classified for "new letterzine" *Unknown*)	1970-Sum
Berkeley Barb (classified looking partners for land buy, June 4 to 10.)	1971-6
The Page, Berkeley SCA (note re: Paul of Sunriver wanting to help SCA get land)	1971-6
Muzzle Blasts (three classifieds, 1 rifles. 1 for land partners. 1 microscope/rifle trade)	1971-8
Moebius Trip (letter about cats, land, and avoid attacks by being Meanest Bastard)	1971-8
Checkpoint (UK fanzine offers *Hob.* #1 for sale at 5p. A blinding deal, innit, mate?)	1971-9
The Page, Berkeley SCA (letter about fencing and wanting to buy Viking Axe)	1971-10

Title/Explanation	Date
Sanders (note that Doerr is trying to turn *Hobbitalia* into a Hobbit-themed APA)	1971-10
San Francisco Chronicle (classified looking for cheap 25' cabin sailboat, Nov 11)	1971-11
Alternatives Newsletter vol 2 no 2 (classified for starting commune)	1971
Tournaments Illuminated (letter from Paul of Sun River about beer)	1972-Win
Green Dragon (Received *Hob.* #2, which is misidentified as "PALDOR" due to cover)	1972-2
Tightbeam (complaint re: low quality of *Patter*, calls it "Spatter," discussion ensues	1972-3
California Entity #C0649850 (non-profit Metaphysical Life Sciences)	1972-4
San Francisco Examiner (letter to Guy Wright re: savages / guns, Apr 10)	1972-4
Aspidistra (letter from someone taking seriously Doerr's idea of "hobbit villages")	1972-6
Explorer's Journal (article "A New Cave is Found." Photo of Doerr beneath the earth.)	1972-6
Muzzle Blasts (classified looking to trade walk-in camper van for rifles)	1972-7
Akwesasne Notes (letter saying he wants to be adopted by tribe)	1972-8
Muzzle Blasts (classified offering finder's fee for land opportunities)	1972-8
Muzzle Blasts (book review of *Universal American Indian Sign Language*)	1972-10
Boating (letter about the nature of public/private property on public waterways)	1972-11
San Francisco Examiner (letter re removal of Supreme Court justices, Jan 24)	1973-1
Motor Boat & Sailing (letter about boat nonsense)	1973-1
The Page, Berkeley SCA (ad seeking bagpipes)	1973-4
Anomaly (clipping via "Vallejo correspondent" re: mystery aircraft, certainly Doerr)	1973-6
Tournaments Illuminated (article "Gemstones" by Paul of Sun River)	1973-Fall
Subterranean Worlds Of Planet Earth (article "Hollow Earth? Underground Races?")	1973
Berkeley Barb (classified looking for truck, May 24 - 30)	1974-5
Tournaments Illuminated (article "Bread" by Paul of Sun River)	1974-Fall
National Fantasy Fan (classified books sword/sorcery/boats)	1974-12
Against the Wall (letter about energy crisis and our economic masters)	1974?
It Comes in the Mail #14 (Doerr sends *Pioneer* #13 and #14)	1975-2
Rudder (classified trying to sell custom sailboat)	1975-2
It Comes in the Mail #16 (Sends WANT LIST, 6 May 1975)	1975-5
It Comes in the Mail #17 (Sends *Mendocino Husbandman* #3, 29 May 1975)	1975-5
SF Examiner/Chronicle (classified land Covelo, Aug 11)	1975-8
66th Ann. Report of North. Nut Growers Assoc. (Doerr member 1974 to 1975)	1975-8
Mother Earth News (letter about building low cost radio network) **(Fairfield address)**	1976-3/4
Appropriate Technology report (Subsistence farming group listed, doesn't exist)	1977-3
Southern Libertarian Messenger (Doerr quote from unknwn iss. *Trove* re: postal mail)	1977-7
Rainbook (perennial farming)	1977-11
Berkeley Barb (classified looking to trade land in Oregon/Covelo, Dec 2 - 8)	1977-12

Title/Explanation	Date
Santa Cruz Sentinel (classified looking to buy land, Dec 14 - 20)	1977-12
Spotlight (classfd looking to unload land in Oregon & Mendocino County, Feb 20)	1978-2
Santa Cruz Sentinel (classified boat, Apr 27)	1978-4
Fanzine Directory 2 (Doerr published *The Shangrila Pioneer* in 1976)	1978-8
California Register of Brands (Doerr registers Tuchuk brand from *Gor* novels)	1980-1
Shavertron (classified looking for books about witchcraft, satanism, sacrifice)	1980-1
Muzzle Blasts (classified looking to trade electronics for rifle)	1980-8
Soldier of Fortune (classified looking to buy assault rifles or trade his Ruger Mini-14)	1980-9
Which Way/Witch Way (column about survival subsistence)	1980-10
California Entity #C1079004 (non-profit Divine Sanctuary)	1981-5
Pagana (classified offering women to come live on his mountain land in Covelo)	1981-8
Soldier of Fortune (classified offering mercenary employment)	1981-9
Magickal Unicorn Messenger (article on "Sanctuary Living", Part 1)	1981-11
Magickal Unicorn Messenger (article on "Sanctuary Living", Part 2)	1982-2
SF Examiner (classified trying to sell boat, 28 Feb)	1982-2
Mount Shasta: Home of the Ancients (story about finding ruby near Mt. Shasta)	1982
Magickal Unicorn Messenger (article on "Sanctuary Living", Part 3)	1982-5
Message Post (brief note about utility of handcrank kitchen grinders)	1982-5
Soldier of Fortune (classified offering mail drop service)	1982-5
The Communicator (letter looking for female prisoners to live in Covelo)	1982-5
The Catalog of UFO Periodicals by Tom Lind (claims *Unknown* started in 1960)	1982-7
Jewelry Making Gems and Minerals (classified re: mail forwarding service & *Pioneer*)	1982-8
Pagana (offer to do mail forward, mentions dropping mailbox, sounds sad)	1982-10
Southern Libertarian Messenger (Doerr quote about loss of liberty via ignorance)	1983-1
Runestone (article on "Family & Tribe")	1983-1
Runestone (offer for discount *Pioneer*) **(Box 1064, Suisun)**	1983-3
Circle Network News (class. offers mail forwarding, *Homesteading*, and *Sanct. News*)	1983-Spr
Pagana (advertising Doerr's Documents, tips on herbs, survivalism, homesteading)	1983-8
Circle Network News (class. offers mail forwarding, *Homesteading*, and *Sanct. News*)	1983-Sum
Message Post (note about the inaccuracy of most survivalist writing)	1983-9
Circle Network News (class. offers mail forwarding, *Homesteading*, and *Sanct. News*)	1983-Fall
Runestone (wants to publish book on warriors and create system of dance/fighting)	1983-Fall
Ocean Freedom Notes (admits he never used boat and is selling it)	1984-2
Message Post (note about how various electronics are junk)	1984-6
Green Revolution (letter defining Vonu signed The Old Pioneer)	1984-Su?
Runestone (letter re: if Wooden/Woden was human, might all old gods be as well?)	1984-Fall

Science Fiction Review (wants microfiche bureau of National Fantasy Fan Federation)	1984-11
Farming Uncle (add for *Pioneer*)	1984-Wn
Which Way/Witch Way (column about survival subsistence)	1984
Southern Libertarian Messenger (note that Doerr is selling *Pioneer* back issues)	1985-1
Texas SF Inquirer (*Pioneer* #304 same as *Space Pioneer* #1, content re: space colonies)	1985-1
Science Fiction Review (announcement of *SCIFANT*)	1985-2
California Entity #C1271033 (nonprofit Investigator)	1985-3
Muzzle Blasts (classified looking for contributors to new magazine)	1985-4
Farming Uncle (letter about fall out shelters, Heinlein, space travel)	1985-Spr
Tightbeam (two letters, 1 about overpopulation, 1 on microfiche)	1985-6
Message Post (wears hunter's belt full of gear, including compass, all the time)	1985-6
Gleanings in Bee Culture (classified soliciting submissions for *Beekeeper's Life*)	1985-7
Circle Network News (classified offering to print other people's publications)	1985-Sum
Message Post (brief note about how many people live nomadic lives)	1985-9
Green Revolution (letter about women being abused, *Gor* in reverse)	1985-Fall
Circle Network News (two classifieds, 1 asks filkers to send cassettes)	1985-Fall
The Druid's Progress (letter about druidism, relationship w/ nature, cabin, microfiche)	1985
Message Post (note about how to wash clothes by hand)	1986-4
Pioneering the Space Frontier (Doerr spoke at public forum)	1986-5
Message Post (note about flashlight reflectors (!) to increase potency of lamps)	1986-9
Tropical Fish Hobbyist (letter saying he's going to publish something called *SHARKS*)	1986-9
Tightbeam (letter about microfiche)	1986-9
Southern Libertarian Messenger (inexplicable, exposition free ad for Luna Ventures)	1986-9
John Zube's *Peace Plans* #650 (Doerr answers questionnaires about achieving peace)	1986-9
Message Post (note about Native American gardening techniques)	1987-6
Muzzle Blasts (classified advertising SKINNER, fiche magazine)	1987-7
Science Fiction Chronicle (classified advertising SciFant as fichezine)	1987-9
J. Z.'s *Peace Plans* #724 (Pre-mid-'85 1pg ltr re: help with microfiched publications)	1987-10
Message Post (note about plastic buckets for storage) **(Box 398, Suisun)**	1988-6
The Page, Berkeley SCA (letter about trying to start SCA fencing group)	1988-9
Message Post (note about establishing underground hostel as a business for someone)	1988-12
J. Z.'s *Peace Plans* #811 (J.Z. letter to Doerr, allows inferences re: Doerr's publishing)	1988-12
Regional, state, and local organizations, Vol 4 (organization Live Free, No. Cal region)	1988
Touchpoint: Network for the Nonmonogamous (listing for *Poly*, runs through 1991)	1989-1
Mad 3 Party #33 (multiple letters about cons and organizing)	1989-3
VIDEO (letter about Doerr using computer monitor to watch television)	1989-3
Message Post (brief note about plastic septic tanks being junk)	1989-6

Title/Explanation	Date
Green Egg (classif. trade Covelo for townhome, letter re: reincarn., torture, witchcr.)	1990-2
Truth Seeker (letter seeking *T.S.* article reprint for *Poly*)	1990-4
Message Post (note about using full spectrum lights)	1990-5
SF Examiner (classified seeking stolen Volkswagen engine, Oct 4)	1990-10
Scouting (article "Camp Tricks" about camping, suggests Doerr was in Marines)	1991-M/A
American Survivalist (ltr re: *A.S.* being good / liberal justice sucks / stolen VW van)	1991-9
Dwelling Portably (2 notes abt old clothes/blankets as pillows, says sews heavy cloth)	1992-4
First Fandom (letter about Dungeons & Dragons, RPG, Renaissance Faires)	1992-Fall
Questbusters (letter looking for RPG related disks/etc)	1992-11
First Fandom (huge letter re: *Captain Future* / model rockets / *Marvel* pulps)	1992-Win
California Entity #C1894873 (nonprofit Luna Ventures Inc.)	1994-7
Low-Cost Living Notes by Jim Stumm (Doerr ltr re: grain + using trash for insulation)	1994
California Entity #C1928585 (Day After Faire non-profit, apparently Ren. Faire.)	1995-2
Dwelling Portably (note about clothes/equipment to be undetected by "enemies")	1995-5
Muzzle Blasts (letter about starting group dedicated to colonial boats)	1996-6
Next Generation (listed, possibly, in subscriber advert)	1998-3
Dwelling Portably (note about ammunition boxes good for storing electrical gear)	2000-4
Bee Culture (letter about bats preying on bees)	2000-10
Spotlight (classified looking to buy land near the ocean) Oct 23.	2000-10
Cruising World (letter asking about how people gather food while living on a boat)	2000-12
Muzzle Blasts (letter looking for survivalist friends and land in Oregon)	2001-3
Rural Heritage (letter about the old days, looking for land)	2001-Sum
Dwelling Portably (note about bee keeping)	2001-9
Bee Culture (letter about making war on bee enemies)	2001-9
Backwoods Home Magazine (letter w/ same old stories, jaguar substituted for tigre)	2001-11
Rural Heritage (letter about apple seeds being poison)	2002-Sum
Country Conversation & Feedback (letter about radioactive sea salt)	2002-7
Country Conversation & Feedback (letter about cooking and looking for land)	2002-9
Countryside and Small Stock Journal (article on "Raising Chickens")	2003-3
Muzzle Blasts (classified advertising publication "EASY OLD TIME LIVING")	2003-3
Mother Earth News (letter about growing grain)	2003-4
Countryside and Small Stock Journal (letter about farm technique, swap Covelo land)	2003-5
Country Conversation & Feedback (letter about inexpensive homes)	2004-5
Countryside and Small Stock Journal (note about wanting 5 acres of CA/OR land)	2004-5
Dwelling Portably (long summary about living on river from *DOE* #49)	2005-4
Muzzle Blasts (almost full page letter about going hunting in childhood)	2005-9
County of Solano Death Certificate. 2 August 2007.	2007-8

Vonulife/Vonulinc

	Issue/Date
Full page ltr (this & most subseq. *V.L.* ltrs are too long for summary)	Nov 1971, VLife#4
Pioneer #8 reprint re: smials & letter re: fake identity & Tolkien's Cirth	Jan. 1972, VLife #5
Nearly full page letter, demonstrates knowledge of cryptography	March 1972, VLife #6
Article "The Soddy" / classified looking for land	March 1972, VLife #6
"The Beehive House" / offers trade campervan for "worthless land"	May 1972, VLife #7
Two letters on one page	May 1972, VLife #7
Two letters on one page	July 1972, VLife #8
One half page letter	Sept 1972, VLife #9
Note of providing mail forwarding service	Nov 1972, Vlinc #10
Half page letter, mentions .22LR ammo in rifle, normal paranoia	Jan 1973, Vlinc #11
Article "A Small Boat for Live Aboard" in *Vonulife 73* supersized issue	March 1973
Roughly 5000-word letter mentions sending letters to *SF Examiner* without address / unattributed article about water guzzler	May 1973, Vlinc #12
Half hand-written, half typed letter about building nomad wagon	Jan 1974, Vlinc #15
Two short letters	May 1974, Vlinc #16
Short letter	Nov 1974, Vlinc #17

Green Egg

	Issue/Date
Looking for experimental sex colonies in "Harrad model"	#38 (May 7, 1971)
2 letters philosophical re: god and man, also wants communal land buy	#40 (July 1, 1971)
"Naked Truth," 3 pgs re: nudism, human skin self-regulating in -0°	#41 (August 4, 1971)
Two very long letters about every ol' thing under the Sun	#42 (Sept. 27, 1971)
Two letters, one about color theory & Zodiac belt	#45 (Feb. 3, 1972)
Three (!) letters about sacrifice, religion, almost everything	#46 (March 21, 1972)
"Man and Apocalypse" dystopia article that ends up being about grain	#47 (May 11, 1972)
Two book reviews, classified trying to start magaz. distribution service	#48 (June 30, 1972)
Letter re: evils Cath. Ch., boat-living & some bonus anti-Semitism	#49 (August 11, 1972)
1 letter w/ rape discussion, 1 ltr Doerr trying to start SF branch CAW	#50 (October 5, 1972)
Letter from Doerr & letter from other reader complaining about Doerr	#51 (Nov. 17, 1972)
Letter discussing the nature of Arab terrorists	#52 (January 1973)
Short letter follow-up on color theory	#54 (May 1973)
Long letter about everything, Doerr stakes out pro-choice position	#59 (Dec. 21, 1973)

	Issue/Date
Letter re: nonprofit corp, investigates Satanism, Doerr OK w/ "homos"	#60 (Feb. 1, 1974)
Letter re: church & state, farming, psychic attack & counterattack	#63 (June 21, 1974)
Letter, general responses to previous content	#64 (August 1, 1974)
Scandal at Spring Farm (no Doerr)	#65 (Sept. 21, 1974)
Letter with murder confession, asks not to print	#66 (Nov. 1, 1974)
Letter makes clear land in Covelo acquired & they can print his letters	#67 (Dec. 21, 1974)
Letter general responses to *G.E. 67*	#69 (March 21, 1975)
Recommends *Gor*	#70 (May 1, 1975)
Responds to G.E. #77, land, admonished by edit for poor handwriting	#77 (June 21, 1976)

American Pigeon Journal

	Issue/Date
Proposes "Beginner's Column," suggests pigeons useful for food + fun	1978-9
Column re: feed, housing, problems with pesticides, ask for help	1978-10
Column re: building best feeders	1978-11
Column re: turning street pigeons & others into food via their young	1978-12
Column re: building one's own pigeon trap	1979-3
Column re: pigeon nutrition and feed quality	1979-4
Column re: many topics & adding pigeon utility by eating their young	1979-8
Column re: chemicals and whether pigeons extend human life	1979-9
Column re: pigeon miscellany	1979-11
Column re: picking utilitarian breeds for food after nuclear war	1980-3
Column re: mail logistics in sending birds & eggs / Letter re: breeders	1980-10
Column re: sick squads, mountain land, & more egg mailing logistics	1981-1
Column re: more mailing, claims that he worked in a post office!	1981-4
Column re: miscellany + his ideal qualities for breeds in nuclear war	1981-6
Letter suggesting improvements to triangular nests	1982-10

Living Free

	Issue/Date
EGO TRIP (Contributor, on mailing list, letters in Kobek's possession)	1976–1978
Odd Man Out (ltr. re: farming, in favor of war to reduce numbers)	May 1978/OMO #2
Letter about govt coercion sent in response to *OMO #4*	March 1979/LF #1
2 Tarl Cabot ltrs. Mountain wives, Zodiac-themed cannibalism	July 1979/LF #3
Short note from Cabot about planting potatoes in a "tire tower"	Oct 1979/LF #4
Short note from Cabot suggesting joke answers to census questions	Dec 1979/LF #5

Cabot letter about seeds, islands and microfiche	February 1980/LF #6
Cabot asks for women, fertilizer, eating slugs, energy devices	April 1980/LF #7
Cabot letter about bees and weapons	Nov 1980/LF #9
Question from Cabot about resurrecting dead batteries	Dec 1980/LF #10
Final Cabot letter about bees, vehicles, batteries / question abt fridge	June 1981/LF #13
Letter from "paul d." / Subsistence & Survival column as Paul Doerr	Aug 1981/LF #14
First letter under his full name, mentions *Sanctuary News* #1	January 1982/LF #16
Letter about raising pigeons	April 1982/LF #17
Small classified for publication *The New Vonulife*	Oct 1983/LF #23
Letter with wide disparate comments	Aug 1984/LF #26
Vast & disparate comments on LF #26, including re: anti-Semitism	Oct 1984 /LF #27
Has a dozen microfiche copies of *Pioneer* #256 to #300, multiple ltrs.	June 1985/LF #30
Lng. ltr about living off the land, ends with inquiry about filk	June 1986/LF #34
Lng. ltr. re: usual topics, owns Eagle IV cmptr w/ modem and five megabyte HD, mentions filk/filkzine, asks for libertarian filk	June 1986/LF #36
Letter asking what happened to polygamy	January 1988/LF #42
General complaints, wants women to work on his mountain	Sept 1988/LF #45
Letter about foreigners invading the US and bringing disease	February 1989/LF #47
Letter inviting women on to his mountain & bitching about homeless	April 1989/LF #49
Ltr re: immigrants and disease. Someone calls Doerr out for creepiness	June 1989/LF #50
Letter about theories re: space exploration	July 1987/LF #51
Ltr looking for women, another letter bitching about government	March 1990/LF #55
Wants to execute leaders on first dereliction of duty	July 1990/LF #57
Wants a computer AI program to decide when to kill leaders	Nov 1990/LF #59
Re-emerges after 11 years, advert for *DOE* and classified about land	January 2001/LF #118
Doesn't watch TV's *Survivor*, fantasizes about "1900s house"	April 2001/LF #119
Cabin living, luna settlements	July 2001/LF #120
More cabin living, more luna settlements, the nature of history	Dec 2001/LF #122
Space, wants to torture his way up the drug hierarchy	May 2002/LF #124
Contribs. short story about surviving nuclear holocaust via mnt life	Dec 2002/LF #125
Letter about farm living	June 2003/LF #126
Very long letter about all the usual topics, bit nuts sounding	January 2004/#127
Sequel to short story, more nuclear holocaust mountain survivalism	Oct 2004/LF #129
Letter about planting nuts	Jan 2006/LF #132
Letter about terrorism, pandemics, announces health problems and can no longer go to Covelo, promises more publishing but elegiac farewell	Sept 2006/LF #134

APPENDIX C

An Internally Verifiable Possible Solution to Z13 & Z32 Produced by Multi-Stage Replicable Blind Data Test

An expanded and more visually comprehensible version at: http://jarettkobek.com/Z32.pdf

ABSTRACT

Two ciphers sent by the Zodiac Killer, known as "Z13" and "Z32," are generally considered unsolvable. This paper proposes a solution generated by a blind multi-stage data test of Z13, incorporating an interface with pre-existing search technologies. This test begins with a theoretical base of 371,651,680 procedurally generated potential outcomes and, through multiple stages, winnows the number to three. One outcome resolves not only Z13 but also Z32. Both resolutions are internally verifiable through decryption patterns and surrounding material, significantly discounting the possibility of random noise.

1 Introduction

In 1968 and 1969, a series of attacks and murders took place in the San Francisco Bay Area. Given the rising violence of the era, the killings would have been unremarkable but for the fact that their perpetrator adopted the *nom de guerre* "Zodiac" and began a correspondence with the press. On

31 July 1969, Zodiac mailed his first three letters to three different newspapers. Each included one-third of a homophonic substitution cipher, which has since earned the designation "Z408," after the number of characters in its ciphertext. It was decrypted within a week. Several months later, on 9 November 1969, Zodiac mailed another cipher, known as "Z340." This would not be solved until December 2020, when it was revealed to be a hybrid transposition and homophonic substitution cipher. (Oranchak, 2020)

On 20 April 1970, Zodiac mailed a thirteen character cipher known as "Z13" in a letter that included a curious illustration of a bomb.

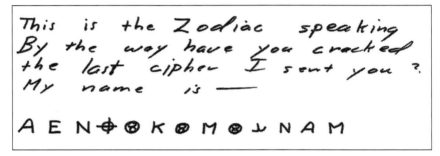

Figure 1. Z13 in Context.

On 26 June 1970, Zodiac mailed a thirty-two character cipher known as "Z32."

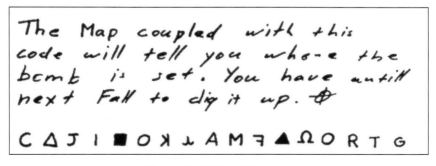

Figure 2. Z32 in Context.

Z32 was accompanied by a map of the San Francisco Bay Area, upon which Zodiac had drawn a modified version of the crosshairs symbol used as a signature on his correspondences.

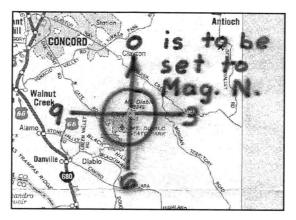

Figure 3. Map accompanying Z32..

Upon even the most rudimentary cryptanalysis, issues of solvability are immediately apparent. Z13 is far too short for easily drawn conclusions, and Z32's lack of repeating characters removes hope of frequency analysis.

2 Visual Analysis of Z13

Z13 demonstrates qualities that can be deduced from simple visual analysis. Reversing the character order and placing the result beneath the original cipher text, a pattern of duplication emerges that strongly suggests a palindromic nature: The ciphertext contains a unusual character in its

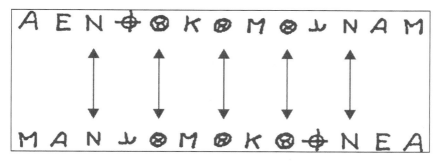

Figure 4. Z13 Reversed and compared.

10th position. On first glance, this appears to be an upside-down T. Yet in the Z340 and Z408, Zodiac employs an upside-down T as a substitution character. In both cases, the top bar is straight, rather than curved. The next reasonable conclusion might be an upside-down Y, but, again, previous ciphers include Y characters with appearances different than that of the Z13 character. A far more likely candidate is an upside-down Greek Upsilon, which, when righted, is depicted thus: Υ.

This character's connection to the Greek alphabet is supported not only by the name "Zodiac" but also the killer's previous ciphertexts which include Δ, Λ, π, τ, Φ, and arguably a variant Θ. Z32's ciphertext contains Ω.

3 Historical Context of Composition

Generally lost in discussion of Zodiac's communications is the reality that the letters and ciphers emerged in an evolving media context. Perhaps the Z340 plaintext is the best example: rather than reveal the killer's identity (as theorized for decades), it begins by responding to the recent appearance of a faux-Zodiac on a local television programme. (Oranchak, 2020)

Z13 was mailed on 20 April 1970. Early that morning, the front page of the *San Francisco Chronicle* ran an article entitled: "Bizarre 'Zodiac' Murder." The text recounts a Zodiac copycat murder, in which the assailant used the victim's blood to write SATAN SAVES ZODIAC and an Egyptian Ankh (identified in the article as a "bloody cross") on an apartment wall. (Anonymous, 1970) The Z13 envelope bears an AM postmark dated 20 April 1970, indicating that it was received and processed by postal authorities prior to noon on the day of this article's publication.

Figure 5. Postmark detail of 20 April 1970 envelope.

As the letter was Zodiac's first correspondence in nearly four months, we can assume that the news provoked the letter. This allows for at most—assuming that the murder made the previous night's televised news—a thirteen hour window for a cipher to be encrypted, a letter to be composed, deposited in a mail box or at a post office, and retrieved by the postal service.

In other words, Z13 was a rushed job.

4 Character and Palindrome Generation

If Z13's plaintext is a palindrome, then it provides a skeleton structure for a blind test. Its first six characters will mirror the concluding six, while the 7th and central character will be independent of other characters. This suggests a path forward: procedurally generated strings that can be compared against one another for potential matches, with an independent process of procedural generation on the 7th character.

The presence of the upside-down Υ suggests that there might be a rotational nature to any potential solution. A maximalist approach allows for eight possible positions of string generation, produced through vertical flipping, horizontal flipping, and full 180° rotation.

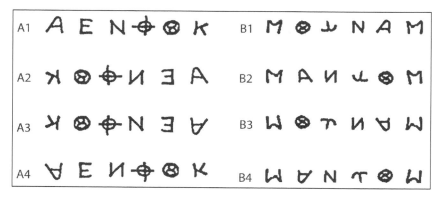

Figure 6. Rotational Positions

If Z13 was a rush job, then its most likely source for characters are Zodiac's pre-existing keys. In the creation of character sets, the most expansive possible approach is taken. For example, the letter N in our eight positions is assigned the following characters: N, Φ, Λ, O, E, D, Y, Δ. This includes the letter itself, all of its Greek and Roman alphabetical substitutions in the Z408 and Z340, and all plaintext resolutions in Z340 and Z408 for which N substitutes. Only symbolic characters in previous keys are excluded. In the case of non-alphabetic characters in rotational positions, like the backwards K of A2 and A3, which substitutes for I in both previous ciphers, only plaintext resolutions are generated. Unknown characters like the apparent upside-down Υ, the characters resembling pooltable eightballs, and upside-down As and Ns are assigned a 32 character set that includes all 26 English alphabetical letters and all Greek characters used in previous Zodiac keys, including Θ, which arguably serves as a substitution for H in the Z408. Strings are generated by a series of Perl scripts producing the following

A	⅃ 6 ▲ S	N	O φ Λ D
B	v	O	ᑫ T X ꓫ
C	Ǝ	P	⋔
D	◆ �	Q	
E	+ ⵕ W N Z ⊙ E	R	⊥ Я \
F	ꓶ Q	S	F K ▲ ⊡
6	R	T	● L H I
H	M ◆	U	y
I	U ꓘ Δ P	V	⊃
J		W	A
K	∕	X	τ
L	B ◩ ◼	Y	□
M	ⵕ	Z	

Figure 7. Z408 Key.

results: 64,512 strings for A1, 3,584 for A2, 4,608 for A3, 1,179,648 for A4, 516,096 for B1, 516,096 for B2, 9,437,184 for B3, 2,395,926 for B4.[1]

---

1   All referenced scripts are available via: https://github.com/jkpali/z

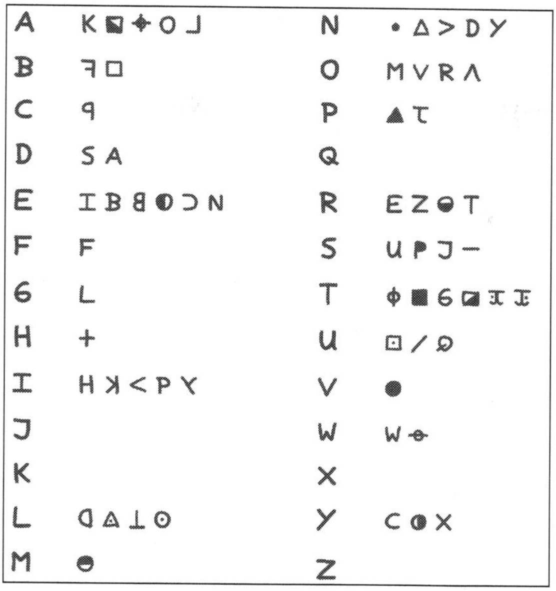

Figure 8. Z340 Key

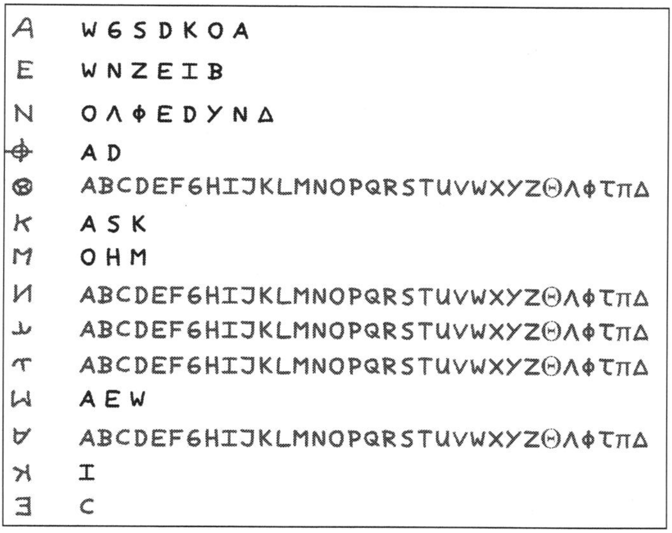

Letter	Symbols		Letter	Symbols
A	K ■ ✦ O ⌐		N	• Δ > D Y
B	⅂ □		O	M V ⋀ ⋀
C	q		P	▲ τ
D	S A		Q	
E	I B 8 O ⊃ N		R	E Z ● T
F	F		S	U ◗ ⅃ −
G	L		T	φ ■ 6 ▣ ェ ェ
H	+		U	□ ⁄ ⍥
I	H ⋊ < P Y		V	●
J			W	W ⊕
K			X	
L	◖ ⌂ ⊥ ⊙		Y	⊂ ● X
M	●		Z	

Figure 8. Z340 Key.

Char	Set
A	W 6 S D K O A
E	W N Z E I B
N	O ⋀ φ E D Y N Δ
✛	A D
⊗	ABCDEF6HIJKLMNOPQRSTUVWXYZΘΛφτπΔ
K	A S K
M	O H M
И	ABCDEF6HIJKLMNOPQRSTUVWXYZΘΛφτπΔ
⊥	ABCDEF6HIJKLMNOPQRSTUVWXYZΘΛφτπΔ
T	ABCDEF6HIJKLMNOPQRSTUVWXYZΘΛφτπΔ
W	A E W
Ɐᗡ	ABCDEF6HIJKLMNOPQRSTUVWXYZΘΛφτπΔ
⋊	I
Ǝ	C

Figure 9. Character Sets.

A quick comparison reveals that all strings in A1 are encompassed by A4, 43,101 duplicates between B1 and B2, and B3 encompassing all strings of B4. Removing these duplicates leaves us with 1,187,840 strings on the A side and 10,426,275 on the B. As any one of these might be transformed into palindromes generated with the same 32 character set on Z13's 7th position, we can infer a potential 371,651,680 solutions to Z13.

This number can be winnowed. A2 and A3 both begin with a backwards K. As noted above, this character produces only the letter I. None of the four positions on the B side begin with the letter I. Similarly, both B1 and B2 begin and end with the letter M, which produces the letters M, O, and H. No string generated by the A positions matches either B1 or B2. All four positions, and their resulting strings, are excluded.

If we assume that Z13 is palindromic, then B3's failure to mirror A4 and A1 means that it can be discounted. While B4 and A4 come close to one another, they produce a discrepancy: the N in B4 occupies but the same position as the N in A4, but the N in the latter is reversed. By contrast, a comparison between A1 and B4 produces a duplication on both the letter N and the Z13 character that resembles a pooltable eightball, making A1 and A4 the most likely candidates. A comparison of strings in A1 and B4 reveals a total of 6,144 matches. The initial 11M+ strings are reduced to just over six thousand, with the number of palindromes now at 196,608.

To generate the palindromes, a Perl script gathers each of the 6,144 matching strings, places the six characters at the beginning of a new string, generates each of the 32 potential characters on the central 7th position, and places the reversed original string after the 7th character. (This reversal is a necessity when one remembers that the strings of B4 are produced through a rotational flip on Z13.)

5 Search

While 196,608 is a greatly reduced number, it still precludes manual verification, arguing for corpus comparison. Here, the inclusion of Greek characters causes a series of problems. The issue of multiple language comparison need not be enumerated. A more significant concern arises when one considers that although the characters of the English letter A and the

Greek Alpha (A) are visually identical in most typefaces, both are represented by different Unicode characters.

The ubiquity of search engines in modern life allows us to parse the greatest collection of corpora in human history: all language on the public facing Internet. A further benefit is that search engine technology employs extremely fuzzy searching. Searching on a Unicode English A will also return a Greek Alpha. And vice versa. This fuzzy searching further attempts to correct for spelling errors and typos. For example: if one searches on "Bard Ptit," any decent search engine returns results on the actor Brad Pitt.

While the gold standard of Google Search lacks a publicly accessible API, an interface is available for the perpetual also-ran of Microsoft Bing. As such, a Python3 script is written to search on each of the 196,608 palindromes and return the number of results for each string in a .CSV format. For instance, a search on AIΦDIAJAIDΦIA returns 712000000 results. The script outputs this as: "AIΦDIAJAIDΦIA, 712000000."

When the script is run on the 196,608 palindromes, Bing returns positive hits on 7,963. A cursory examination suggests that Bing Search might be the superior technology for this approach. For instance, the string with the highest number of results, WWΔDOALAODΔWW, produces roughly 15,800,000,000 results. Bing identifies WWΔDOALAODΔWW as a variant spelling of "download" and returns results on the latter word. By contrast, a manual Google search of WWΔDOALAODΔWW returns zero results.

Bing Search allows users to employ "+" as an operator, explained thusly: "Finds webpages that contain all the terms that are preceded by the + symbol. Also allows you to include terms that are usually ignored."[2] A manual Bing search of "WWΔDOALAODΔWW +" produces zero results. The Python script is modified to search the 7,963 remaining palindromes followed by the plus sign. When run, it produces positive results on 66 palindromes, all of which begin and end with the letter A.

A manual Google search reveals that 63 of these terms return either no results or a melange of social media accounts, spam links, URL texts, and strings derived from non-human processes, leaving three potential candidates: ANODRACARDONA, with five results, ANNAPANAPANNA, with

---

2   https://help.bing.microsoft.com/\#apex/18/en/10002/-1

eight, and ABΛANAΘANAΛBA, with roughly 7,500. It is of some note that none of these solutions emerge from the English language.

ANODRACARDONA is the name of a dance performed during a 2015 festival Cardona, Spain.[3] The palindrome is the Catalonian town's name reversed and concatenated. Given its genesis date, this result can be readily discarded. ANNAPANAPANNA is "Anna pana panna," a phrase that appears in the 1969 Polish translation of James Joyce's *Ulysses*. ABΛANAΘANAΛBA is a Gnostic palindrome in Ancient Greek that transliterates as "Ablanathanalba" and translates, poorly, to "Thou Art Our Father." (King, 1887)

6 The Dissatisfaction of Z13

Can these two palindromes produce results in Z13? Beginning with ANNAPANAPANNA, we discover a resolution that requires multiple assumptions. (Figure 10.) In three of five instances of direct decryption, Zodiac's previous keys are used backwards. On these character resolutions, substitutions in the original keys become the substituted, and plaintext characters become ciphertext. The next assumption is that, in Z13's ciphertext, the letter N must be the plaintext not only for itself but also the central 7th character, while the other two instances of the "eightball" must stand for the letter P. Furthermore, the distribution of resolution is scattered across vertical and horizontal positions.

One point suggesting that we are near the proper path: the two instances of decryption matching original use in Z340 are the crosshairs symbol and the letter K. By 20 April 1970, the crosshairs had become known as the Zodiac symbol. Taken together, this might suggest an initialized signature of Z.K. in the decryption pattern itself.

When Z13 is decrypted to ABΛANAΘANAΛBA, we see a vastly superior, if still flawed, solution. (Figure 11.)

While not without its own problems, this pattern is more comprehensible, in essence an alternating ON/OFF scheme culminating with the final resolution of K and W to the letter A. In this scheme, the bottom string,

---

3 http://www.cardonaintegral.com/es/post/llega-anodracardona-la-danza-de-la-a
   cion-global-ciudadana

Figure 10. ANNAPANAPANNA in Z13.

comprised of Z13's final six characters each resolve using the Z408 key, while the top string, comprised of the first six characters, resolve using Z340.[4]

As mentioned earlier, the Z13 letter included not only the cipher but also a crude illustration of a bomb. Zodiac describes this device as a series of two photoelectric switches that respond to the Sun in alternating patterns.

---

4   On the surface, this scheme appears complicated by the presence of N in the top string on the 3rd position, which can resolve via Z408 to Λ. Given that the other five character resolutions adhere to the Z340/Z408 split, I suspect this N is intended to function like the A at the beginning of the same string—an indicator of the correct answer in the same position on the mirroring line.

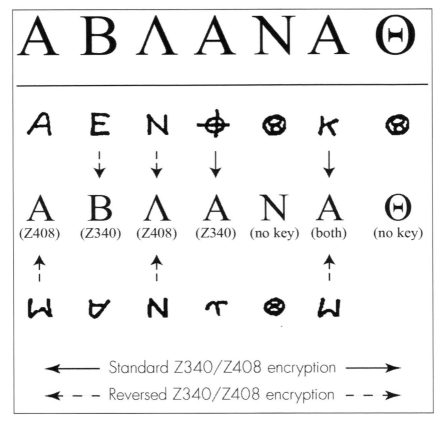

Figure 11. ABΛANAΘANAΛBA in Z13.

"When sun beam is broken A closes circuit / When sun beam is broken B opens circuit." (Figure 12.)

While this is not the clearest piece of writing, it can be assumed that both switches must be active for the bomb to explode. The decryption of ABΛANAΘANAΛBA can be represented like this: A,B,A,B,*,A/B. This is, exactly, how the theoretical bomb works, and may explain Zodiac's follow-up correspondence of 28 April 1970. A *San Francisco Chronicle* article dated 22 April 1970 reported on the Z13 letter, reproducing the cipher but failing to mention the bomb. (Avery, 1970) The 28 April correspondence includes this line: "If you don't want me to have this blast, you must do two things. 1 Tell every one about the bus bomb with all the details..." If the

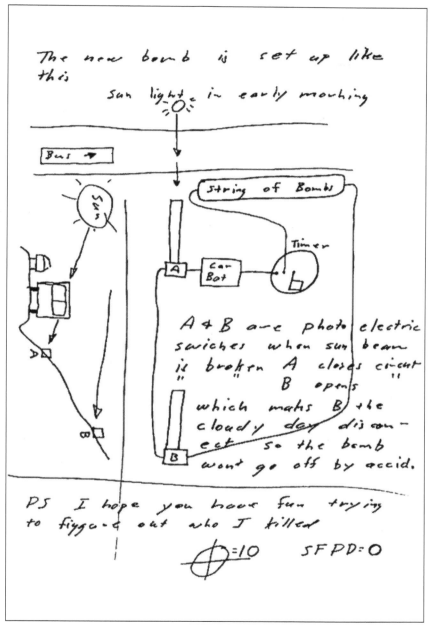

Figure 12. Z13 bomb illustration.

illustration is a clue to the cipher's resolution, this demand makes a great deal of sense, and suggests a logic to the assumptions that first emerged with ANNAPANAPANNA. (It seems of some importance that Zodiac's A/B photoelectric switches mirror the first and final two character sets in ABΛANAΘANAΛBA.)

The flaws in the ABΛANAΘANAΛBA decryption revolve around the "eightball" characters. For the palindrome to work, its central character must stand for Θ while the other two instances of the same character must stand for the letter N. A visual examination of the eightballs supports the idea that they might be Θs, but it is impossible to ascertain how they could resolve into Ns. If Z13 was a rush job, then this might be the fruits of that effort: a cipher that does not work, that can never be fully decrypted.

Helpfully, Zodiac himself appears to have noticed the issue and provided a corrective.

7 The Corrective of Z32

We return to Z32. For reference throughout the remainder of this paper, its vertical positions have been notated in Figure 13.

Figure 13. Z32 notated.

The top row V8 character is another upside-down Υ. If the ABΛANAΘANAΛBA Z13 solution is correct, then we may assume that the Greek letter's presence in Z32 indicates the same function. Visual analysis of Z32 and Z13 demonstrates two other repetitions: the letters AM in top row V9 and V10 match the final two characters of Z13, and the pattern E, [symbol], Zodiac symbol across bottom row V10, V11 and V12 match the same pattern on the 2nd, 3rd, and 4th characters of Z13.

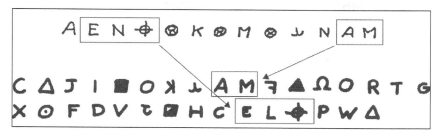

Figure 14. Z13/Z32 character comparison.

Here we must make a leap of logic, the results of which will either work or produce failure: these repetitions indicate a Z32 solution incorporating Z13's ciphertext. To evaluate this assumption, we must first attempt to find proper alignment. The most logical initial step is placing Z13 atop Z32, matching positions on the AM characters. Alas, this creates a problem: in this placement, the full Z13 runs three characters past V1.

As noted earlier, Z32 lacks statistically significant character repetition. However, it does employ resolution repetition across its vertical positions. In Z340, the C and X in V1 resolve to the letter Y. J and F in V3 resolve to F in, respectively, Z408 and Z340. The black triangle and Zodiac symbol of V12 resolve to the letter A in, respectively, Z408 and Z340. As the letter A is the first character of Z13, this suggests a placement for the first six characters of Z13. Separated from the rest of Z13, when placed over V12, they extend for Z32's remaining five characters, as seen in Figure 15.

A new problem emerges— if the AM overlap is the correct placement, we must assume that the E, [character], Zodiac symbol pattern on the bottom line is intended to match Z13. But how is this achieved? Again, we return to matching resolutions. If, starting with the circle character in V2, we move the bottom line over three positions, the circle now now occupies bottom V5, where its Z340 resolution to the letter L matches that of the topline V2 black square's Z408 resolution, as illustrated in Figure 16.

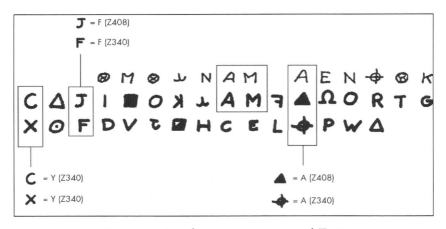

Figure 15. Resolution repetitions and Z13.

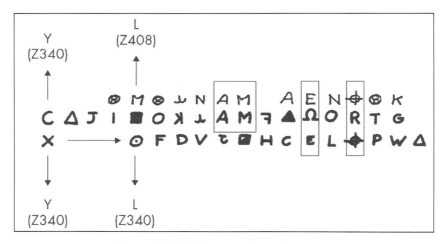

Figure 16. Z32 bottom line adjustment.

Armed with knowledge of ϒ's apparent function in Z13, we perform a 180° rotation on Z13 characters 7 through 13 and all Z32 characters below, producing the result in Figure 17.

Another issue arises, namely the I that previously occupied topline V4, now provisionally placed beneath V11. If this rotational scheme were absolute, said character should occupy the position of H in V11. Clearly, it can not. We again return to resolution duplication. Moving the bottom

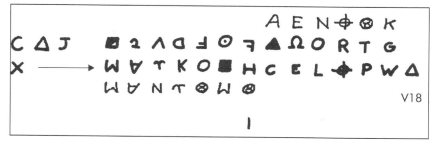

Figure 17. Z32 and Z13 rotated.

line creates a dangling position at this line's end, which we now term V18. The sole character occupying V18 is Δ, resolving to the letter I in Z408. This suggests that the proper location for the now displaced I of V4 is above the Δ in V18.

Again remembering Z13, we take the rotated characters and place them beneath the characters corresponding with Z13's first six characters, creating a six tiered system as illustrated in Figure 18.

Figure 18. A six tiered system.

We return to the map in Figure 3. Its vertical line contains the note that O is to be set to Mag N, and ends with the numeral 6. Figure 17 illustrates a six tiered system in which the first Z32 O is "set" to both Z13 Ns. Furthermore, the horizontal lines of the crosshairs, beginning with 9 and ending with 3, appears to be a hint as to the bottom line placement. In Z340, the sole substitution for C is the numeral 9, and we have moved the bottom line over 3 characters.

Examining the six tiered system, we discover that it not only double resolves the four tiers of Z32 to ABΛANAΘANAΛBA, while, rather remarkably, resolving Z13 to the same palindrome. (Figure 19.)

Figure 19. A six tiered system resolved.

With two exceptions, all vertical D positions provide cross-tier double resolution within the Z32 ciphertext. On D1, the black triangle resolves to A in Z408, while W backwards resolves to A in Z408. On D3, Λ substitutes for O in Z340, while Λ substitutes for N in Z340. On D4, both the Zodiac symbol and the letter K resolve to A in Z408. On D5, T resolves to O in Z408, while O resolves to N in Z408.[5] On D7, I backwards resolves to H in Z340, while H resolves to a symbol closely resembling θ, the lowercase variant of Θ, in Z408.

The first exception occurs on D2. Here, the E is the operative character, backwards resolving to B in Z340. (This is identical to the character's function in Z13.) Fascinatingly, on this position, cross-tier mirroring occurs on extraneous characters: Ω and an upside-down A. This is, of course, heavy Christian symbolism: the Alpha and the Omega, the beginning and the end, making perverse sense in the context of a palindrome that translates to "Thou Art Our Father."[6] The other exception occurs on D6, where the double verification occurs entirely in Z32 rows corresponding to the first six Z13 characters. G resolves to A in Z408, while W backwards resolves to A in Z408. This decryption mirrors that of D1 and has a simple explanation. The other Z32 characters in D6 are the L resolutions used to establish placement of Z32's bottom line, making impossible the standard resolution of other positions.

Z13 characters are present in each D position. When compared with Figure 11, Figure 19 improves upon the ABΛANAΘANAΛBA resolution in Z13. Four of the operative ciphertext characters in Z32 duplicate the ciphertext characters of Z13, while the rotational scheme performed on Z32 transforms the V previously in V5 into a plaintext Λ, which substitutes across both previous keys not only for its matching Z32 character but also both Z13 positional characters. D5 and D7 solve the problem of the "eightballs." All of this argues for Z32 as something of a "do-ever" that can be read as Zodiac recognizing Z13's fatal flaws.

---

5   This might be another instance of O being "set" to N.

6   Here, too, it's worth mention that the translation makes sense in the historical context of Z13's construction. One can imagine "Thou Our Art Father" as a response to news of a "bloody cross" and "Satan Saves Zodiac."

Unused characters in the four tiers of Z32 appear to be padding, an idea reinforced by the 180° rotation producing three characters with no appearance in previous keys.

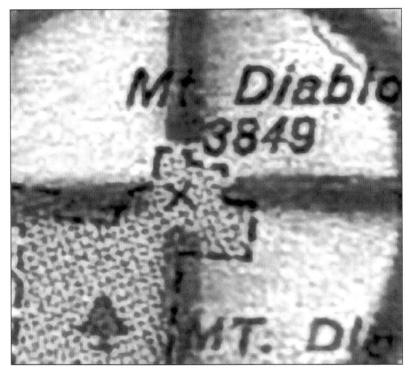

Figure 20. Map detail.

But what of the remaining characters? These are: C and X on V1, Δ on V2, and a J on V3. If we believe that the Bay Area map indicates 9 as a substitute for C, this character can be discarded. Leaving us with X, Δ, and J. As seen earlier, Δ substitutes for I in Z408. In Z340, J substitutes for S. Close examination of Figure 3 reveals that at, in the center of the crosshairs, there is a small X, allowing us to propose a full Z32 solution:

X IS ABΛANAΘ[ANAΛBA]

5 Conclusion

This resolution demonstrates its own interior logic and establishes what I would describe as a triangle of verifiability.

We may imagine any one of these ideas—ABΛANAΘANAΛBA in the data test, Z13, or Z32—as little more than a point on a piece of paper. Erase the point through challenge and we are left with a blank piece of paper. If two points are on the paper—the data test and Z13 solution—one can draw a line between them. But if one of the points is challenged—Z13 being the easiest candidate—then we return to our original position of a single point. Which itself may then be challenged.

All three points on our theoretical piece of paper form a triangle. Knock out one—again Z13, being easiest—and one must explain why both the data test and Z32 point to the conclusion of the removed point, and why Z32 employs the same 180° rotation on the same ϒ figure as Z13. I suggest that this triple system, which rests upon internalized verifications within the ciphers themselves, establishes not only a near definitive solution but also an extremely high level of confirmation.

One question that emerges: are Z13 and Z32 ciphers? I would argue that a better classifying label is complex visual puzzles that incorporate cryptography, and that this is what gives them a *sui generis* quality that eludes efforts of traditional cryptanalysis.

References

Anonymous. 1970. Bizarre 'Zodiac' Murder.
San Francisco Chronicle, Apr. 20.

Paul Avery. 1970. Zodiac Sends New Letter–Claims Ten.
San Francisco Chronicle, Apr. 22.

Charles William King. 1887. *The Gnostics and Their Remains, Ancient and Mediæval*. David Nutt, London, England. Second Edition.

David Oranchak. 2020. Let's crack zodiac - episode 5 - the 340 is solved! https://www.youtube.com/watch?v=-1oQLPRE21o, Last Accessed: 2021-10-23.

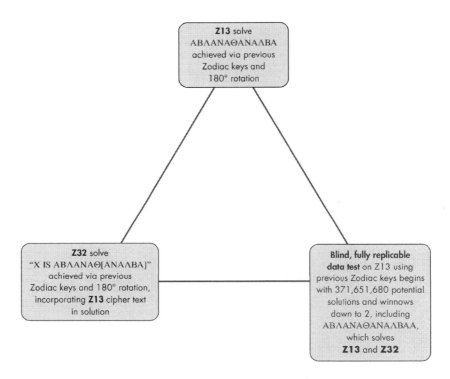

Figure 21. The Triangle of Verifiability.

APPENDIX D

paranoiac bits 'n' bobs

1.

Having established, to his own mind, a reasonable Z13/Z32 solution, Kobek looked at other Zodiac communications. To see if the killer had hinted towards this solution. The 28 April 1970 mailing was covered in the academic paper—Zodiac demands that the *Chronicle* print the bus bomb illustration accompanying Z13. Excluded from the original reporting. If the drawing were a visual key for the puzzle, then the demand made sense: how could the thing be solved if half its relevant information wasn't circulated?

The next best thing that Kobek came up with was the 5 October 1970 mailing, colloquially known as the "punch card." It was a cut-and-paste job, Zodiac cutting words out of local newspapers and pasting them upon an index card. Art brut with an extra dose of brutality. Zodiac also punched thirteen holes through the card.

Its rear side looked like this:

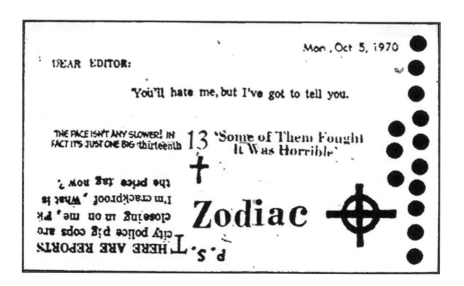

The police, the press, and Zodiac researchers assumed that the card's fixation on the number 13—placed at the center and represented by the number of holes—referenced the number of victims.

But. If the ABΛANAΘANAΛBA solution were correct, then the card was a working demonstration of the method.

The 13 was between two blocks of texts, roughly of equal width. And below the left block, Zodiac pasted another block, rotated 180°. This was, of course, exactly how one achieved the ABΛANAΘANAΛBA solution.

Pure paranoiac territory.

What the hell? What's the worst that can happen?

There's an illustration on page 206 *Amulets and Talismans*. Reproduction of a Gnostic inscription. Three pages before Budge offers the dubious translation of "Thou Art Our Father."

It looks like this:

Budge describes the illustration thusly: "1. Anubis, holding a sceptre and standing on an open left hand, the symbol of justice. The inscription behind him is the palindrome 'Ablanathan' of doubtful meaning. 2. The goddess of Truth (the Egyptian Maāt) standing on a figure of an internal organ of Isis. The inscription behind her means 'the Sun Everlasting' or the Sun of the World."

Kobek couldn't help but notice that the thirteen characters in the Sun Everlasting inscription, the one beside Maāt, had an almost identical positioning to the punch card's thirteen holes.

2.

For a variety of reasons, Kobek could not reproduce a sample of Doerr's handwriting from the 1968 to 1975 period.

Not in this book.

In 1981, Doerr formed a non-profit corporation called Divine Sanctuary. (California Entity #C1079004.)

In early 1987, Doerr dissolved the non-profit. Doerr hand wrote the documents of dissolution.

They were public domain, available online, no one's property.

And of dubious use.

Doerr's handwriting changed with time. If one knew what to look for, it remained recognizable, but the letter forms had altered, the strokes more uncertain with age.

1987 was almost twenty years from Zodiac.

And Doerr was 60 years old.

The utility was questionable.

But the lowercase Ds were interesting.

If one cared for that sort of thing.

For the sake of completeness:

CERTIFICATE OF DISSOLUTION   D238186 .1079004

Paul Doerr, certifies that:
He is the sole director now in office of
Divine Sanctuary D-1079004 DS8, a California
corporation

The corporation has been completely wound
up.

The corporation never incurred any known
debts or liabilities.

The corporation never acquired any
known assets.

The corporation is dissolved.

We further declare under penalty of
perjury under the laws of the state of
California that the matters set forth
in this certificate are true and correct
of our own knowledge.

Paul Doerr
director

0 2   0 1   8 7

Divine Sanctuary
D-1079004 DS8

225 E Utah
Fairfield, Co 94533

CERTIFICATE OF ELECTION TO WIND UP AND DISSOLVE   **D238185**   1079004

Paul Doerr, certifies that,

He is the sole officer remaining of Divine Sanctuary, a California corporation.

The corporation has elected to wind up and dissolve.

The corporation has no members, the election was made by the board of directors.

We further declare under penalty of perjury under the laws of the State of California that the matters set forth under this certificate are true and correct of our own knowledge.

Paul Doerr
pres, secr, etc
225 E Utah
Fairfield Ca 94533
02 01 87
Divine Sanctuary
D-1079004 058

APPENDIX E

QR codes

The car.

The cabin.

Palindrome scripts.

Z13/Z32.

Printed in Great Britain
by Amazon

86710125R10174